THE CRUCIFORM LEADER

ALAIN EMERSON

FOREWORD BY
MARK SAYERS

Muddy
Pearl

Published in 2025 by
Muddy Pearl, Isle of Mull, Scotland.
www.muddypearl.com
books@muddypearl.com

British Library Cataloguing in Publication Data.

A catalogue record for this book is available from the British Library.

ISBN 978-1-914553-29-5

ISBN Epub/Mobi 978-1-914553-30-1

Typeset in Minion by Revo Creative Ltd, Lancaster
Cover design by Faceout Studio, Jeff Miller.

Printed in Great Britain by Bell & Bain Ltd, Glasgow.

This book calls us back to first principles – leadership is just advanced discipleship. And the consistent message across the New Testament is that disciples follow the way of the cross through the power of the resurrection. The problem is that the cross is as foolish today as it was 2000 years ago. Thus, Alain gives us a prophetic call that cruciform leadership is the path to experience the power of God. The church needs to hear this word.

BEN C BLACKWELL
PRINCIPAL, WESTMINSTER THEOLOGICAL CENTRE

Our culture is experiencing a crisis of leadership just when we need it most. We elect braggards and bullies, put narcissists on pedestals then kick away the legs, nurse wounds of coercion – even (especially?) in the church – and in our pain resent and reject the very notion of leadership itself. In this timely book, a seasoned pastor depicts another kind of leadership, marked by the cross. Learning lessons from the greatest leader of all time, this is a message of healing and hope for those who aspire to lead with the counter-cultural humility and defiant kindness of Jesus.

PETE GRIEG
24-7 PRAYER

From beginning to end this book is Spirit-filled, cross-draped, pet-theory-denying, cosmically-alert, and Christ-shaped – and it is personal in the best sense of the word. The book is an apostolic, pneumatic, and christological pastoral theology. Church leaders have too often run to the latest book on leadership instead of, as Alain Emerson reminds us, turning back to the example of Jesus and the words of the apostles. We are at a turning point in the church worldwide, a turning point that (we pray) will lead to a new vision for what a pastor is. This book needs to be in the discussion of that turning point.

SCOT MCKNIGHT
VISITING PROFESSOR, WESTMINSTER THEOLOGICAL CENTRE

This book is prophetic – not in the sense of deserving a 'Christian' adjective to connote its specialness, but in the sense of humbly covering both corrective and constructive bases and capturing a 'now' word from the Lord to his people. To his leaders. In these pages, you will find not just an invitation to a particular form of ministry, but fresh invitations to encounter with the Lord himself. May we each heed this invitation to become more holy, humble and hungry.

DAMILOLA MAKINDE
TEAM MEMBER, KXC & EVANGELICAL ALLIANCE

The Cruciform Leader is a clarion call for Christlike leadership in the Church. With honesty, graciousness and simplicity Alain makes this call. The book leaves you with a hunger for God and a desire to serve Him and His Kingdom like Christ did. I would strongly recommend this book for any leader who wants to have the kind of impact Christ had in his or her assignment.

AGU IRUKWU
SENIOR PASTOR, JESUS HOUSE FOR ALL NATIONS

FOREWORD

In the 12 months before the Covid-19 pandemic hit, I felt a tremendous sense that the platforms of influence and postures of leadership that had long existed both within society and the church would be rocked. I was under no illusions about the damage and disruption this would cause. And so the reckoning arrived. To describe it in detail would require an entire book. Yet it ranged from moral failings, abuses of power and social upheaval to a loss of trust in institutions and leaders. We are still living in the implications of this reckoning. The danger is that in reaction, we retreat and recoil from leading. The potential pitfalls can seem too great. From this perspective there appears to be little upside to stepping into a calling of leadership. We can become cynical, rightly seeing what has gone wrong but doing so from a distance, offering little in the way of renewal, referring and reshaping our imagination of leadership.

Yet, there is another way. As I listened to the Lord, I began to recognise the movement of his hand in history. Yes there was a reckoning, but there was also a revealing. A new cohort of leaders was being called into leadership. Others, already leading, were being called to lead in a new way. This way of leadership would not be shaped by culture, which offers various models of leadership, many of which are running aground. Instead, it would be moulded by the living and leading that emerges from someone who understands Jesus' work on the cross. Such leaders would be hungry, holy and humble.

Such leaders would be hungry for God's presence. His holiness will shape those who live in his presence. Such proximity to God's presence inevitably leads us to understand our place in God's created order and to live with true humility – something missing in so many contemporary models of leadership.

As the pandemic broke across the world, breaking our sense of normality and putting immense pressure upon leaders, I saw many hungry, holy and humble leaders being shaped in the crucible of crisis. I will never forget the call I made from my house during lockdown in Melbourne, Australia, across the world to a gathering of Irish Christian leaders. As I shared this vision of a rediscovery of hungry, holy and humble leaders, I could sense the Spirit's presence. The book you are reading is Alain taking this idea and running with it, fleshing it out, and indeed, we need it fleshed out. It has been said everything rises and falls on leadership; therefore, if readers can take the wisdom of this book and apply it to their own leadership, becoming cruciform leaders, partnering with God, new creation and new possibilities break out in our world.

Mark Sayers
Senior Pastor, Red Church
Melbourne, Australia

ACKNOWLEDGEMENTS

This book would not have come about without the incredible patience, dedication and skill of my publishers Muddy Pearl and their team of editors, Katharine Grimes, Fi Boon and Pamela Shaw. In particular, I would like to thank Stephanie Heald for her belief in this book and her encouragement as I was writing it.

Many other people have influenced how this book has made it into the world. My friendship and shared love for New Testament ecclesiology with Roger Ellis has been a significant and ongoing source of wisdom and insight. I'm grateful to the staff and students of Westminster Theological Centre for granting me an opportunity to teach and develop the core content of this book. Friends around the world, particularly those who are part of the beautiful global 24-7 Prayer family, have inspired me immensely through their embodied examples of cruciform leadership – in season and out of season – and have helped form so many of the thoughts in this book. Thank you to Mark Sayers for writing the Foreword and for the anointed words along the way which have resonated deeply.

My local church, Emmanuel Church – everything I know about leadership has been learned by serving you and being loved by you. Thank you for your patience in all the times I have been less cruciform! And to the elders of Emmanuel Lurgan and Emmanuel Portadown, I count serving Jesus and his church alongside you the highest honour.

I could not have completed this book without the unflinching prayerful support, dedication and unconditional love of my parents, Alan and Geraldine, and my wider family circle. What an incredible tribe I have been blessed with.

My kids, Annie, Erin and Finn, loving you three is my greatest joy. Thank you for all the times you have released me to write this book. Let's go away together again soon!

And to Rachel, my incredible wife and the one my soul loves. Thank you for making me laugh, for knowing when to encourage me to keep going and when to take a break. I love all the ways you prevent me from becoming too intense. Thank you for embracing the cruciform way in ways others will never know so I might get to write about it. 'Your Father, who sees what is done in secret, will reward you' (Matthew 6:4).

CONTENTS

CALLING FORTH THE HUNGRY, THE HOLY AND THE HUMBLE

It was the final week of 2019. A whole new decade was beckoning. 2020 felt significant. 2020 even sounds significant. Closing the curtains on one year would simultaneously kick open the door to the next ten years. As a church leader this was a seismic moment of opportunity, one I had to take advantage of. Fifteen years of experience had taught me how to maximise the first 'Lord's Day' of every January. I had a well-established and pretty polished routine of presenting a compelling vision to our church family at the dawn of every new year. 'Vision Sunday' we like to call it.

The first Sunday of a new decade provided an even greater sense of opportunity that simply had to be seized. This was the chance to unveil the new '2030 vision' – a captivating presentation of how we would plan to change the world for Jesus over the next ten years. The pressure was on, but I had always thrived on that type of pressure.

Except this time.

There had been a lot of 'noise' in the surrounding culture throughout 2019. Debates in the public square and online around contentious issues of morality, race and ethics were getting louder and angrier. Shocking statistics concerning mental health and anxiety confirmed that we had reached a crisis point. The radical secularism which had been sweeping across the Western world over the past thirty years had become firmly established. Data was being released about the phenomenal wave of 'dechurching' that was taking place, particularly in the USA and the UK. Further to all of this, in my own country, Northern Ireland, where the sectarian spirit simmers under the surface of most public discourse, things were tense.

It felt like we needed a rallying cry. A clear and compelling vision that could counter the angst and negativity. Surely the turn of a new decade was a moment to stir up fresh holy ambition in the church.

I have a tendency to feel overly responsible for almost everything in life, so I was even more earnest than normal in my attempts to get this unique moment right. I adopted my usual routine over those final days of 2019 – seeking God in the holiday period between Christmas and the New Year; journalling earnestly and preparing myself for a few days of fasting in early January. All of this was in anticipation of a heavenly 'download' that I expected God to give me – a spine-tingling revelation for the next decade and a call to respond that I would present to our church.

The result of this intense seeking?

Almost nothing.

No big vision, no extraordinary prophetic words or images, no high-level strategic goals. No exciting blueprint about how we could change the world for Jesus in the incoming ten years.

Except …

A simple picture, a passage of Scripture and a gentle whisper.

The picture? *A tree.*

The Scripture? *Some verses from Psalm 1.*

The whisper? *'Be like a tree, son … hold your nerve … go deep … in this season you will take ground by standing your ground … stay faithful.*

I still have these words written in my journal.

And so, on the first Sunday of 2020, as we stepped into a brand new decade, I delivered my worst vision talk ever. Or maybe my best?

I told our growing and expanding church family, Emmanuel Church, '*to be like a tree*'.

Almost apologetically, I confessed to our church that our leadership team didn't really have a vision for the next decade. Except the words of Psalm 1.

> *Blessed is the one*
> *who does not walk in step with the*
> *wicked*

or stand in the way that sinners take
or sit in the company of mockers,
but whose delight is in the law of the
LORD,
and who meditates on his law day and
night.
That person is like a tree planted by
streams of water,
which yields its fruit in season
and whose leaf does not wither –
whatever they do prospers.

PSALM 1:1–3

I can't describe to you how difficult it was to dial down my inner activist to deliver this talk; to choose not to manipulate my sermon into something more aspirational. Beautiful and poetic as Psalm 1 is, surely it wasn't the right passage to launch into a new decade with. I mean, it's wonderful as a devotional but *'be like a tree'* isn't exactly the compelling headline required for mobilising the church of Jesus Christ into a new decade, right? Did we not need something with more strategic intent, something that carried more prophetic urgency, something more cutting edge?

Despite constantly questioning myself, I knew I had to be obedient.

'Be like a tree,' I told our church family. *'Let's hold our nerve as we enter 2020. Let's not be anxious. In this season we will take ground by standing our ground. Let's go deep.'*

Fast forward three months and the turbulence we were experiencing in our own little part of the world at the end of 2019 was dwarfed by a new worldwide level of disruption.

Covid-19.

Everything changed. As things do in global pandemics. We couldn't really do anything. We couldn't go anywhere. Everyone was scared, and people do and say strange things when they are scared. Everyone was 'pivoting' and everything was 'unprecedented'.

The pressure I had felt about presenting an aspirational vision at the start of 2020 completely dissipated, only to be replaced with much more intense and immediate pressure. Leadership in this season had nothing to do with inspiring people to achieve great things for Jesus over the next decade. It was simply about trying to help people get to the end of the day, alive.

Strangely, I felt that I had been partly prepared for such an 'unprecedented' season. I had been meditating on Psalm 1 ever since I shared it with our church family in January, three months before Covid came to our home town. I began to realise those divinely inspired words had carved a deeper reservoir of peace into my soul.

'Be like that tree, son, hold your nerve.'

But I needed to keep returning to these words often over the coming months as the implications of the pandemic further unfolded. As I adapted to the process of 'doing church' in this new normal – preaching online, leading Zoom prayer times, trying to do Covid-safe pastoral visits, leading our staff team remotely – I didn't always like what I was seeing in myself. Insecurity, competitiveness, striving – all of this was coming to the surface.

God was doing something deeper in me. Those whispers from the Father at the start of 2020 had been the perfect preamble to what he would teach me in the coming months. The hidden underground parts of my life were being invited to wind their way to fresh streams of living water again.

'Be like that tree, son …'

Prior to Covid-19, we had planned to launch a new event in May 2020 – an exciting new festival where lots of partnering churches would join together to seek God for a fresh awakening of the Spirit in Ireland. Covid meant we had to cancel everything. On the date of the planned festival, we hosted an online Zoom webinar instead. My friend Mark Sayers, pastor of Red Church Australia and author of a number of wonderful books, agreed to join us online. Mark helped us think about the unique ways God could use this extraordinary 'crisis' we were living through to challenge the church, especially the church in the West. In particular, he encouraged us to pay attention to the self-promoting shadows God was bringing into the light during this time of enforced solitude; shadows that had lurked behind the bright lights of the platforms of our ministries; shadows we could now see more clearly because we had no platforms to stand upon.

Many of those listening to Mark had grieved for the well-known and internationally respected Christian leaders whose private lives had been exposed publicly in recent years. Acknowledging our need to authentically lament the current crisis Covid had precipitated and to learn from the heartbreaking stories of fallen leaders, Mark then provoked us towards a more hopeful and redemptive reflection.

What if God might also be using this wilderness period, this time of testing, to raise up a new cohort of leaders around the world? What if there was a generation of men and women, hidden to the world but passionately seen and known by God, who were being prepared to lead the church in the days ahead with the courage and conviction required to change the narrative of our times? Mark described this new breed of leader he believed was being mobilised for such a time as this as *'the hungry, the holy and the humble'*. It was a simple sentence, but it was pregnant with prophetic potency. One of my friends listening online, overcome with emotion, literally fell off his chair as a tangible experience of the fear of the Lord drove him to his knees. Mark's words reminded me of the prophet Hanani's rebuke to King Asa recorded in the second book of Chronicles, 'For the eyes of the LORD range throughout the earth to strengthen those whose hearts are fully committed to him' (2 Chronicles 16:9). In 2020 God was still looking for hungry, holy and humble ones and I could almost see them, as if rising out of an open atlas, as Mark spoke to us.

Since that online meeting in 2020, devastatingly, many more well-known leaders have fallen. We are without doubt at a crisis point in the Western church when it comes to the area of leadership. The church has never been more scandalised. To help prove the point, Jon Tyson reflects how these days people attending your church are less interested in your worship style, your small group structures or even your theological distinctives. Rather, the questions people really want answers to are: 'Who is your leadership team accountable to?' 'What is the governance structure of this church?'* Of course these questions are important in their own right, but Tyson argues the sad consequence of the widespread leadership fallout we have experienced in recent years means we face a depressing new reality: many leaders are now being forced to prioritise staying out of the newspapers rather than courageously advancing the kingdom in the power of the Spirit.

Almost every week another leader's dirty washing is aired in public. What has been exposed is heartbreaking. Bullying. Abuse. Sexual immorality. Narcissism. Misogyny. Stealing. The body count of leaders falling is stacking up. Worse, the body count of individuals hurt by these leaders is exponentially higher.

People have been damaged.

Badly. Really badly.

Today as I write these words, I've become aware of yet another 'fall from grace' from another respected Christian leader.

Something needs to change. The time has come to disavow some of the elements of Christian leadership culture in the Western church.

On top of the integrity crisis surrounding leadership, we are managing decline in the church at a seriously depressing rate.

* Jon Tyson, 'Rediscovering Church: Restoring Leadership Credibility to a Scandalized Church', *Church of the City Podcast*, 17 July 2023.

Many denominations are haemorrhaging people at levels we have not known before. In the UK, church attendance has been steadily declining for the past forty years. Research led by the Policy Institute at Kings College London[*] has shown that, internationally, the UK public are now among the least likely to believe in God. Just under half the UK population (49%) said they believed in God in 2022, down from three quarters (75%) in 1981. The same research also reveals that the percentage of the UK population who say that belief in God is not important in their life has almost doubled in the last four decades. As many had ruefully predicted, America has followed these trends in the UK approximately twenty years later. According to Jim Davis, Michael Graham and Ryan P Burge, in their important recent book, *The Great Dechurching*, America has entered into its most significant religious shift in US history. The headline is forty million people in America have left the church in the last twenty-five years! To add to the dramatic effect, 'more people have left the church in the last twenty-five years than all the new people who became Christians from the First Great Awakening, Second Great Awakening, and Billy Graham crusades combined.'[**]

These are staggering statistics. Especially when we reflect that over the same time span on a human capability level we have witnessed the best and biggest versions of church that human beings have ever built. We have more resources, more technology, more intellectual know-how and more strategic vision than there has ever been, yet it is all proving insufficient to meet the need of the hour we are living in. It seems our well researched growth strategies and charismatic leaders are not enough to truly penetrate the zeitgeist of today.

[*] WVS team at the Policy Institute, Kings College London, 'God, Heaven and Hell, and Life After Death: Data Reveals UK's Low Religious Belief Compared with Other Nations', *UK in the World Values Survey*, 19 May 2022, uk-values.org (accessed 7 March 2025).
[**] Jim Davis, Michael Graham and Ryan P Burge, *The Great Dechurching: Who's Leaving, Why Are They Going, and What Will It Take to Bring Them Back?* (Zondervan, 2023), p5.

What do we need?

In short, we need a move of God.

And we need a new breed of leaders to lead the way. Hungry, holy, humble ones who will seek the manifest presence of God above all human methods, ministries and models.

Where are the hungry, the holy and the humble?

Vision is required in this next season, but it is the source of vision that the leaders of this hour need to critically discern. Yes, we need leaders with vision, but we need holiness more. Yes, we need leaders of competence, but we need hunger more. Yes, we need leaders who are confident, but we need humility more. The answer to the current leadership crisis we are facing is not no leadership, but cruciform leaders. This should be the defining characteristic of all leadership in the kingdom of God. As Scot McKnight says, 'The character of a king shapes the character of that king's kingdom, and the character of our King is cruciform'.*

The word 'cruciform' in most dictionaries is defined as 'having the shape of the cross'. Perhaps the best biblical definition of the cruciform life is given in Paul's letter to the church at Philippi when he exhorts these early Jesus-followers to embody the same mind as Christ, going on to quote what is confirmed by many scholars as one of the first hymns of the early church:

> *who, being in very nature God,*
> *did not consider equality with God*
> *something to be used to his*
> *own advantage;*

* Scot McKnight, 'You might be a kingdom-mission church if …' in *Gospel, Kingdom and Leadership: Voices from the Missional Movement – Volume 2 Chapter 4, North American Baptist Conference*, July 2019, nabconference.org (accessed 7 March 2025).

rather, he made himself nothing
by taking the very nature of a
servant,
being made in human likeness.
And being found in appearance as a
man,
he humbled himself
by becoming obedient to death –
even death on a cross!
Therefore God exalted him to the
highest place
and gave him the name that is above
every name,
that at the name of Jesus every knee
should bow,
in heaven and on earth and under
the earth,
and every tongue acknowledge that
Jesus Christ is Lord,
to the glory of God the Father.

PHILIPPIANS 2:6–11

The appeal at the heart of this book is for leaders of the church to return to these words of Philippians 2:6–11 in a spirit of humility and repentance. For these words speak not only of the death of Christ in his crucifixion but the life of Christ in his way of '*cruciformity*'. Theologian and author Chris Green is a helpful guide here as we further unpack the meaning and the shape of cruciform leadership. Green uses the physical structure of the cross to describe the kind of life which actually reflects true biblical holiness. The vertical beam of the cross, Green says, speaks of the otherness of God, whose ways and thoughts are far beyond ours. Cruciform leaders therefore are those who identify with Christ's death on the cross and as a result find themselves being transformed into his very likeness. The horizontal beam speaks to us about the otherness of our brothers and sisters, both those inside and outside of the church. Cruciform leaders learn to appreciate the strangeness of our fellow human beings in the same sacrificial ways Jesus showed us.* The cruciform way is therefore an ongoing participation with Christ in a life of joyful sacrifice which makes room for others to come into the glorious knowledge of the Father's love and the recreation of all things. Loving God and loving our neighbour – this is the cruciform way, and the world is crying out for leaders formed in this cross-shaped way.

What if we stopped co-opting the words from the latest celebrity leadership guru and obsessing about the biggest online 'influencers'? Or, what if, at least, we made sure this wasn't our primary form of inspiration? What if we returned to the Spirit-inspired words of Jesus, quite simply the greatest leader who ever lived?

As leaders of the church today I really believe we are being invited to submit ourselves to a process of relearning what we know about leadership at the feet of that luminous Nazarene. The church fathers were quick to point out that the blessed man of Psalm 1 points to The Man, Jesus Christ. "'Blessed is the man that hath not gone away in the counsel of the ungodly" (verse 1). This is to be understood of our Lord Jesus Christ, the Lord Man', stated St Augustine.** What if such a reorientation of our leadership in the way of Jesus is what the whole world is crying out for? Going back to the way of Jesus which was so climactically demonstrated on another tree at Calvary. Going down on our knees in repentance at the foot of the cross.

*Chris EW Green, *Sanctifying Interpretation: Vocation, Holiness and Scripture, Second Edition* (CPT Press, 2020).
** Augustine of Hippo, 'Expositions on the Book of Psalms' (1888) in P Schaff ed. and AC Coxe tr. *Saint Augustine: Expositions on the Book of Psalms - Volume 8* (Christian Literature Company), p1.

And what if we reflected on the example of the first Apostles,[*] who, after an intense three-year immersion and apprenticeship in the way of Jesus, literally led a movement which changed the world and is still continuing to this day. Why would we stop looking to them for inspiration? We could argue the first Apostles were the original 'influencers' of society. Up until this point in history, the world had never witnessed the radical effect of such powerfully embodied servant-leadership. Their words and their lives continue to shine as a beacon of hope to us in these bewildering times. For, as we step further into the uncertainty of our postmodern, radically secularised, Western world, many of the complexities, pathologies and changing realities we are facing are pointing us back to the context of the first churches.

Surely, those who planted the first churches in such a godless and idolatrous culture, buffeted by imperial might and persecution, yet able to say with confident humility, 'follow my example, as I follow the example of Christ' (see 1 Corinthians 11:1) have something to teach us? These imperfect men and women, flawed at almost every conceivable level, became the pioneers of a new type of humanity[**] simply because they actually led like Jesus.

In the chapters ahead we will seek to rediscover this cruciform way of Jesus and his Apostles, taking time to describe different characteristics of these servant leaders whose lives literally changed the world. In doing so my aim is to provide leaders today with what can be described above as lived theology – real, embodied examples of leaders who led like Jesus. They are still our best example of the cruciform way.

[*] For clarity, I will capitalise 'Apostle' when referring to one of the original Twelve and Paul, but not when referring to other sent-out ones of the early church.

[**] This phrase 'pioneers of a new humanity' was inspired by a quote from JB Phillips in *Letters To Young Churches: A Translation of the New Testament Epistles* (The Macmillan Company, 1956).

I do not believe the solutions to our problems today, whether within the church or the wider society, will be solved by 'cancelling' failed leaders or overreacting to those failures with our own politically correct virtue signaling. We may feel we have good reasons to be skeptical of leadership in this current cultural moment but we should be careful that we do not become cynical. For God can use the smouldering ashes of this intense refining moment for the church to remake crowns of beauty,* placing these upon the hungry, holy and humble servants he has been quietly preparing for this moment in history. My friend Pete Greig, leader of the 24-7 Prayer movement, often says, almost every move of God throughout church history has been preceded by some kind of crisis. What if the dark shadow of the recent leadership crisis that rests over the Western church could begin to disappear as leaders repent of their ways, turn again to Jesus and a new cohort of consecrated leaders is raised up for this hour?

I noted above how Davis, Graham and Burge have brought a stark wake-up call to the church, regarding the shocking trend of dechurching in the USA, but their analysis doesn't end there. They also have discerned the hopeful opportunities that exist on the other side of crisis.

> The Great Dechurching is reversible and doesn't have to have the final word for faith communities in our country … The Great Dechurching could well be the American church's most crucial moment and greatest opportunity. As church leaders, we consider it the privilege of a lifetime to serve in this moment.**

One recent piece of information which backs up this claim is that research has shown in the last year the sale of Bibles has jumped by 22% in the US, despite overall book sales in the country only

---

* See Isaiah 61:3.
** Jim Davis, Michael Graham and Ryan P Burge, *The Great Dechurching: Who's Leaving, Why Are They Going, and What Will It Take to Bring Them Back?* (Zondervan, 2023), p239.

rising by less than 1%.* On top of this, more and more stories of God moving powerfully on university campuses all over the USA are filtering through our media channels.**

And there is further evidence to back up this redemptive thread of opportunity. In the post-Christian culture of the UK, despite what many may think, God is moving. The statistics of decline and unbelief I outlined above should sober us, but they also require a more nuanced commentary. For, while the headlines often focus on what can appear like the terminal decline of the Western church, the truth is, growth is taking place somewhat 'under the radar'. Mirroring the increase in the Bible sales in the USA, research compiled by the SPCK Group in the UK has shown an 87% increase in Bible sales between 2019 and 2024, largely attributed to a sense of spiritual renewal among Gen Z.***

The 24-7 Prayer movement, of which I am a part, is witnessing more churches than ever hosting night-and-day prayer rooms around the UK. My friend and Senior Pastor of *Jesus House*, London, Agu Irukwu, has been instrumental over the past decade in gathering up to 40,000 people from across denominations and ethnicities to pray through the night in London's ExCel arena. Alpha, born out of Holy Trinity Brompton in London, has proven to be an extraordinary evangelism tool over the past thirty years, reaching thirty-two million people around the world, and in 2023 it had 200,000 participants in the UK alone. Reports are filtering through that in Wales hundreds of healing miracles have taken place over the past ten years. A fresh wave of church planting has also emerged in many streams of the church, with new life-giving

* Milla Ling-Davies, 'US Bible surge led by first-time buyers', *Evangelicals Now*, 26 December 2024, e-n.org (accessed 7 March 2025).
** Erin Conner, 'God is Moving in Secular Places', *Christian Union*, 4 March 2025, christianunion.org (accessed 20 March 2025).
*** Kaya Burgess, 'Spiritual Gen Z drive increase in Bible sales', *The Times*, 14 March 2025, thetimes.com (accessed 20 March 2025).

churches planted into the soil of major city centres, rural villages and council estates across England, Ireland, Scotland and Wales. A research project called *New Churches in the North East*[*] conducted in 2014–2015 by the Centre of Church Growth Research, based in Cranmer Hall, part of St John's College at Durham University, found that since 1980, 125 new churches have been planted in this region of England alone. Research undertaken in United Reformed Church[**] and Anglican Church circles has shown while there is undoubted decline in church attendance a high percentage of their churches continue to have a disproportionate impact on their local communities. Even smaller, often struggling churches continue to faithfully love their neighbours, feed the hungry and welcome the stranger. Maybe most encouraging of all are the stories of thousands of Gen Z and Gen Alpha young people, representing the breadth of the denominational spectrum sensing God calling them to a deep level of consecration and passionate pursuit of his presence. In Finland over the last eight years church attendance among young men between 15–29 has more than doubled.[***] In France at Easter 2024, a record 12,000 people were baptised across the country, 36% of which were aged between 18–25![****]

I could go on and on. The point is, Jesus is still building his church.

A tangible, real-time expression of this hope-born-out-of-crisis which took place during the months I have been writing this book, was the spiritual renewal that took place at Asbury University,

[*] 'New Churches in the North East', *Centre for the Study of Modern Christianity*, 2015, csmc.webspace.durham.ac.uk (accessed 7 March 2025).
[**] 'Church at a Crossroads: 6 Lessons from our United Reformed Church Research', *Theos*, 4 July 2023, theosthinktank.co.uk (accessed 7 March 2025).
[***] Santeri Marjokorpi, 'Against the Odds, Researchers Find an Increase in Religiosity Among Young Finnish Men', *Evangelical Focus*, 18 January 2024, evangelical-focus.com (accessed 7 March 2025).
[****] Caroline de Sury, 'Record 12,000 People were Baptized in France on Easter', *America – The Jesuit Review*, 4 April 2024, americamagazine.org (accessed 7 March 2025).

Wilmore, Kentucky in 2023. After a normal midday chapel service – a routine part of the seminary's weekly schedule – a number of students, under the conviction of the Holy Spirit, spontaneously made their way back to the chapel and began repenting of their sins. Their obedience occasioned a wonderful outpouring of God's love and power on the university and within hours the dumbfounded young leaders found themselves facilitating a gathering of continual worship which lasted for twenty-one days. It is estimated that this move of the Holy Spirit brought approximately 70,000 visitors to Wilmore during those three weeks. A specific call to repentance and consecration among the students marked this particular renewal and it resulted in multiple salvations, a deep work of healing in the many anxious minds, and a supernatural sense of peace in the Holy Spirit. Among all these wonderful results one of the striking characteristics of this move of God was its simplicity. The outpouring at Asbury will be known for how distinct it was from the platform and performance driven forms of church services we have become accustomed to in the Western church! It has been reported that the short talk given at the initial chapel service was, at face value, mediocre, and the musical standard of the worship during the revival, average. Not to mention they didn't even have PowerPoint! Rather, this wonderful outpouring of the Spirit was marked by hungry, holy and humble students, the names of which most reading this book still probably don't know. Asbury builds on the testimonies throughout history of God's revival power moving in out-of-the-way places. Whether it be the pagan island of my country Ireland where God captured the heart of a young slave boy named Patrick; the back streets of LA through the yielded life of William Seymour, the one-eyed son of a slave; or the Hebrides through the passionate and persevering prayers of two octogenarians. The common denominator in each of these revivals had little to do with the place and everything to do with the characteristics of hearts which God by his Spirit was drawn to. Holiness. Hunger. Humility.

Asbury gives us hope. But it also provides us with a challenge. The young students who stewarded the renewal there remind us that leaders of Jesus' church require less haughtiness and more holiness, less hubris and more humility, less hype and more hunger.

I could never have imagined what 2020 would have brought forth as I stood, seemingly 'visionless' at the turn of a new decade. But no impressive vision would have prepared me (or those I lead) for what was ahead anyway. All I needed were some simple words latent with ancient inspired wisdom, *'be like that tree, son, hold your nerve, let the roots go deep.'* I have since come to recognise that around 2,000 years ago the Apostle Paul gave his young apprentice Timothy similar advice for the turbulent days of leadership which would lie ahead for him, 'be prepared in season and out of season … keep your head in all situations, endure hardship' (2 Timothy 4:2, 5). Paul knew if Timothy established a life of deep-rootedness in the presence of Jesus, that this persevering stability would ultimately produce fruit of eternal quality which would feed others in times of disorientating instability.

Approximately 500 years after Paul wrote this leadership advice to Timothy, a young, ordained priest called Ciaran from my nation of Ireland had a vision of a tree growing high in the middle of his land. Ciaran was the son of a carpenter and as a boy worked as a cattle-herder. At some point in his early years, he was seized with a passion for Jesus and devoted himself to the monastic life. Columba of Iona would say of Ciaran, 'He was a lamp, blazing with the light of wisdom.'* Ciaran committed himself to study and spiritual formation under the tutelage of the great Irish saints, Finnan of Clonard and Edna of Inishmore. It was during Ciaran's time on Inishmore, one of three islands in western Ireland known as the

* Bridget Haggerty, 'St. Kieran of Clonmacnoise', *Irish Culture and Customs*, 27 September 2024, irishcultureandcustoms.com (accessed 7 March 2025).

Aran Islands, that he had his life-changing vision. The tree Ciaran saw in the middle of the 'Emerald Isle' was protecting the whole of Ireland, the sweet fruit it produced surrounded the whole country and Ciaran could see birds coming to take fruit to other lands. Having shared this vision with his mentor, Edna wisely recognised the tree was Ciaran himself. Ciaran had been called to plant his life in the soil of his own land and in doing so bring the blessing of God to Ireland and the nations. Edna therefore sent Ciaran to the middle of Ireland to establish a monastery and in AD 544 Ciaran finally settled in the strategic location of Clonmacnoise. Ciaran's monastery would be situated centrally in Ireland, at the place where the major east-west land route meets the River Shannon which runs from north to south. Tragically, Ciaran died at the tender age of thirty-three, only nine months after the monastery was established, but his vision of the miraculous tree came to pass nonetheless. In the years that followed Ciaran's death, Clonmacnoise flourished. The monastic settlement at the centre of Ireland became one of Ireland's most famous places, establishing itself as a major hub of religion, learning, craftsmanship and trade. Dignitaries and scholars from all over Europe visited it and many monks were trained, equipped and sent out to the nations to proclaim the gospel.

Fast forward another 1,000 years approximately when the great reformer Martin Luther was asked what he would do if he knew the world was ending. He famously answered, 'I would plant a tree.' For Luther, the planting of a tree was an act of defiant hope, the establishment of life-giving, fruit-yielding creation in the soil of a world full of decay. Hope, like the trees, that will outlive us.

It seems the words of Psalm 1 which I unexpectedly heard the Spirit whisper to me at the start of 2020 are ironically the kind of words which actually do change the world. In a church culture that has been poisoned by the cult of celebrity yet left disillusioned by the conduct of the leaders the people once looked up to, what if the great saints like the Apostle Paul, St Ciaran and Martin Luther recognised that the most visionary thing a leader can do in this hour is to concentrate on becoming people who are planted beside the streams of living water? Maybe then the church will be able to point once again with confidence to her steady, godly and consistent leaders. Men and women who have drunk deep from the river of God's presence and produced fruit that looks like the character of Jesus.

Calling forth the hungry, the holy and the humble.

Calling forth the cruciform leader.

CHAPTER 1

CHRIST, THE CROSS, CALLING AND THE CHURCH:
A BIBLICAL PARADIGM FOR CRUCIFORM LEADERSHIP

'The success of the church lies in the hands of its leaders.' This phrase, or a variation on the same theme, is one that most of us will have come across many times, at Christian conferences or in leadership books. Because throughout the last fifty years the evangelical church growth movement has focused on the subject of leadership.

This emphasis on developing leaders has led to many churches co-opting leadership principles and practices from the world of business, psychology, therapy and education. In many ways the church has benefitted from their practical insights, an important reminder that the wisdom of God is not confined to the pews of the church:

> *Out in the open wisdom calls aloud,*
> *she raises her voice in the public*
> *square;*

PROVERBS 1:20

The work of writers like Patrick Lencioni, Margaret Wheatley and Jim Collins, with their hard-earned wisdom drawn from their respective spheres of influence, has impacted my own life and leadership very much for the better. They have helped me to think more strategically, to lead meetings more efficiently, to understand the complex beauty of organisational behaviour and to embed culture that is aligned with clear vision and values more effectively. Tools like the Enneagram and Myers-Briggs, in the hands of wise spiritual directors and therapists, have increased my self-awareness as a leader, helping me become more emotionally healthy as a team player. I have been enriched by the outstanding work of engaging researchers like Brené Brown on subjects like vulnerability, courage and shame, and my communication and teaching styles have been sharpened by the creative inspiration of educationalists like Sir Ken Robinson.

It has become clear this kind of help was needed. For too long emerging church leaders had been graduating from seminary, Bible school and theological college with little or no specific leadership training and limited understanding of personal development. They had not been trained in the requirements of church administration, the building and leading of teams or the articulation of vision and strategy. Further, the lack of self-awareness of many leaders was embarrassingly exposed. Seeking the expertise from these other sectors of society, therefore, was well-intentioned and has proved beneficial.

But somewhere along the way I believe the pendulum has swung too far, and in doing so many churches have lost their scriptural moorings, selling out on their core text – the Bible – as the primary inspiration for Christian leadership. Today it is not unusual for churches to hire search firms to headhunt potential new pastors, who then apply leadership diagnostic tools and personality tests to prospective candidates not unlike those employed in the secular world of big business. Again, this is not necessarily wrong. Often such rigorous testing can be a helpful part of the recruitment process. The problem I believe has more to do with the reasons churches and Christian organisations prioritise such processes. The goal seems to be about discovering a standout leader with proven qualities needed to grow that church or organisation. Unfortunately, the requirements of leadership laid out in the New Testament – genuine Christlike character, proven experience in disciple-making and evidence of spiritual gifting – are pushed down the priority list.

With characteristic discernment, Martyn Lloyd-Jones picked up on this worrying trend in the second half of the twentieth century, and reminded the church of her deepest need – the Spirit and power of God:

> We must become utterly and absolutely convinced of our need. We must cease to have so much confidence in ourselves, and in all our methods and organisations, and in all our slickness. We have got to realise that we must be filled with God's Spirit ... What we need is not more knowledge, more understanding, more apologetics, more reconciliation of philosophy and science and religion and all modern techniques – no, we need a power that can enter into the souls of men and break them and smash them and humble them and then make them anew. And that is the power of the living God.[*]

CHRIST

My own observation is that in the evangelical stable of the Western church, of which I am part, we fervently acknowledge Jesus as Saviour and Lord. Yet it seems he is not always the telos of our leadership development. When it comes to the question 'how can I be a better, more effective leader?' many seem to want to find answers from trending podcasts profiling the latest high-performing celebrity, rather than to immerse themselves in the Gospels. Jesus does not always seem to be our North Star when it comes to how we grow in effective leadership. Reflecting on this, Scot McKnight says:

> One of the problems in finding a pastor is that most churches have a

[*] Martyn Lloyd-Jones, *Revival* (Crossway 1987), p19.

secular definition of leadership. Why? Go into any pastor's study and you'll find books and books on leadership. Because when churches talk about leadership, these are the books the congregation will quote. But would Jack Welch make a good pastor? Would Jeff Bezos make a good pastor? I don't think so … If churches keep looking for the wrong person, they will keep finding the wrong person. In the Scriptures, leaders are chosen by how close they are to God. Abraham had dinner with God. Moses regularly disappeared into the mountain to talk directly to God.[*]

This does not seem to be a new problem. In 1938, as the world stood on the precipice of World War II and national leaders flexed their geo-political muscles in response to Adolf Hitler's rampant Nazism, the German pastor and theologian Dietrich Bonhoeffer recognised the idolatrous cult of *Führer* ('leader') sweeping through his own nation. Aghast, Bonhoeffer detected how this dangerous ideology had even infected large swathes of the German church and so his response – a staunch anti-Nazism – led him to help establish an underground seminary in Germany called *Finkenwalde* where he trained and discipled emerging Confessing Church pastors. It was Bonhoeffer's experience of this community that formed the basis of *Life Together*, a profoundly challenging manifesto for the church, unapologetically calling God's people back to their countercultural 'cruciform' origins. For Bonhoeffer these origins began exclusively in Christ and therefore he courageously reminded the emerging leaders under his watch to be diligent not to allow themselves to be seduced by the dominant leaders of their culture but fix their eyes on Jesus Christ alone.

The church does not need brilliant personalities but faithful servants of Jesus and the brethren. Not in the former but in the latter is the lack. The church will place its confidence only in the simple servant

* Scot McKnight, 'The Secularization of Pastoral Leadership' *Scot's Newsletter*, 12 January 2024, scotmcknight.substack.com (accessed 7 March 2025).

of the Word of Jesus Christ because it knows that then it will be guided, not according to human wisdom and human conceit, but by the Word of the Good Shepherd.*

The first Apostles of Jesus Christ, for all their imperfections, no doubt inspired Dietrich Bonhoeffer as 'faithful servants of Jesus'. Why is it that we have somehow forgotten the incredible reality the New Testament gives witness to? The Apostles, ordinary men and women like you and me, actually walked in the way of Jesus and in doing so helped change the course of history. My experience is that while the church esteems Paul, Peter, John and the other Apostles for their inspired theology, many seem to bypass them as examples of church leadership.

GK Chesterton is attributed with the saying, 'Every high civilisation decays by forgetting obvious things.' Chesterton's insightful statement could easily be applied to Christianity and the Western church. We have forgotten 'the obvious things' the first Apostles established the earliest churches upon – the life and teachings of their rabbi and leader, Jesus Christ. Again, this is not just a recent problem. Much further back than Bonhoeffer and Chesterton's time, before the last of the original Twelve had died, it appears some of the earliest churches had already begun to stray from their most basic foundations. Near the end of the first century AD, the Apostle John, who outlived the other disciples, passed on this rebuke to the church in Ephesus: 'Yet I hold this against you: you have forsaken the love you had at first. Consider how far you have fallen! Repent and do the things you did at first' (Revelation 2:4–5).

The vision of and for the church was quite simply, Jesus Christ. Nothing more. Nothing less. Nothing else. Or, as Pete Greig, leader of the 24-7 Prayer movement, says, 'The vision is JESUS –

---

* Dietrich Bonhoeffer, *Life Together: The Classic Exploration of Faith in Community* (Harper & Row, 1954), p109.

obsessively, dangerously, undeniably Jesus.'* It is time the church of Jesus Christ returned to Jesus Christ.

THE CROSS

For the Apostles, these first things were of utmost importance and uncomplicated. The gospel – the 'good news' that God had come to us in the flesh, Jesus the Son, in order that he might destroy the works of darkness, forgive and liberate people from the power of sin and bring about the reign of the kingdom of heaven through the sacrifice of his own life – was the cornerstone that the first churches were established upon and around. The Apostle Paul would acknowledge that this message was 'foolishness' to the world (1 Corinthians 1:18). How could a God who would die save the whole world? At face value it didn't make any sense. Yet in Jesus the full expression of God's wisdom had come into the world. Jesus' death and resurrection had revealed, by the Spirit, a glorious new reality: the power of God's self-giving love, displayed through Jesus' willingness to lay down his life, was stronger than all the powers of darkness. Death itself could not contain such holy love. Jesus' disciples, the first-hand witnesses of the resurrected Lord, were baptised with the Holy Spirit as Jesus had promised. They were the first messengers (or Apostles: 'sent-out ones'), who would herald this majestic new truth coming into the world – 'the darkness is passing and the true light is already shining' (1 John 2:8). More than just proclaim this truth, the Apostles sought to embody it, as Jesus had commanded them – 'Whoever wants to be my disciple must deny themselves and take up their cross and follow me' (Matthew 16:24).

We will discover in the pages to come just how radically Jesus' disciples would fulfil this command through their own 'cruciform' lives, yet, from the outset, it is critical for us to grasp how convinced

* See 24-7 Prayer movement vision on 24-7prayer.com (accessed 12 March 2025).

these first Apostles were of the distinct, matchless, and 'once-and-for-all' nature of the sacrifice of Jesus. Paul could say boldly, 'we preach Christ crucified' (1 Corinthians 1:23) because he, along with the other Apostles, knew it was only the perfect atoning sacrifice of Jesus' death that had achieved salvation for the whole world in a way no other sacrifice ever could. Only one man who has ever lived had the authority in his final breaths to declare before every principality and power, 'It is finished' (John 19:30). Therefore, the Apostles knew that each one of them could only take up his own cross because Jesus had taken up *the* cross. While they dedicated their lives to emulating the sacrificial life of Jesus, they were completely persuaded that the power to do so flowed exclusively from the sacrifice of their great rabbi, the Anointed One, who had been lifted up on the cross of Calvary – the most decisive act in all of history. As Lesslie Newbigin put it, 'What is to be done, is to be done by him alone. Nevertheless they are to be his partners in it – afterward.'*

So, when the Apostle John called the church in Ephesus back to 'the first things', he was calling them to repent from the ways they had become enamoured with their own sense of greatness and to return to an unswerving, wholehearted dependency on Jesus and the cross. For all the many outward signs of the Ephesians' stability and maturity as an impressive, established church, they had tragically allowed their fascination and affection for their Servant King and his finished work on the cross to wane. Instead, a subtle arrogance had crept into their hearts and taken root.

I believe this is the primary cause of the problems the Western church is facing today: pride. More than anything else we need to repent of the ways our hearts have been seduced by other loves and self-centred agendas, asking the Spirit of God to open the eyes of our hearts to the unparalleled beauty of Jesus and incomparable power of the cross.

* Lesslie Newbigin, *The Open Secret: An Introduction to the Theology of Mission* (Eerdmans, 1995), p46.

The leaders of the church today should therefore take fresh inspiration from the cruciform leadership and exhortations of the apostles of old. Let me be clear. These men and women were far from perfect, and we should stay clear of over-romanticising their lives. Thankfully, the Bible does not fall into this trap. Wheat and tares, this side of eternity, will always grow together. That being said, the inspired story of the early church and her leaders through the pages of the New Testament has so much to teach us. It reveals what is possible when ordinary men and women are seized by an unflinching confidence in the gospel and a consuming captivation with Jesus. I am convinced the women and men of today's church, who embody this cruciform way, true shepherds who call the people of God back to the ways of Jesus Christ, will be those who carry the real spiritual authority in the church today – whether they have recognised titles or not.

CALLED

Flowing from the Apostles' confidence in Christ and his cross was the deep conviction they had been 'called' by God. God had spoken to them, revealing his will for their lives. They knew they had been specifically set apart for this task, their lives destined for this purpose. Listen to Paul's introduction to the church at Corinth: 'Paul, called to be an apostle of Christ Jesus by the will of God,' a claim he repeated a number of times in his letters.[*]

A clear sense of God's calling – and confirmation of that calling – is something every church leader should be able to point to. Stepping up into church leadership without this would be presumptuous, however talented or gifted that person might be.[**]

* 1 Corinthians 1:1; See also Romans 1:1; Ephesians 3:7–8; Galatians 1:11–16.
** In Chapter 4 we will explore specific biblical examples of the consequences of such presumption.

The stakes are too high for a leader of God's people to spend their lives wondering if they are doing the right job or not. There are plenty of days when the going is tough, the rewards non-existent, the loneliness all-consuming, and the temptation to quit extremely alluring. On these days, church leaders need to be able to draw from that deep and unshakeable conviction that God has called them to lay their lives down for Jesus and his bride. Doing anything less than this would therefore be an act of outright disobedience. Of course, every follower of Jesus is called by God. Each of us are loved by God and called by God. But, as Jonny Gumbel in his book *Called* explains, followers of Jesus have both a general calling and a specific calling.

> We are all called to belong to Jesus. We are all called to be holy … There are many things which all of us are called to do, like being kind and compassionate, sharing what we have with those in need and making disciples of all nations. But God has a specific calling for each of us … For Paul it was to be an apostle, for Mary it was to bear the Son of God and for Peter it was to be a 'fisher of human people'.[*]

As we will unpack in the chapters ahead, the glorious result of Jesus' death and resurrection is that we have all been called to play our unique part in God's mission to reconcile the world to himself. In this sense we are all priests (1 Peter 2:9), called to connect the beauty and healing which flows from heaven's throne to the brokenness of the world around us. We are all called to 'work the works of God, to do what Jesus did, to be who Jesus is.'[**] And yet the New Testament makes it clear that some will receive a specific calling that will look like a life set apart by God to love and serve his church. In other words, some of us are called to a priestly vocation of church leadership, whether that be bishop, pastor, deacon, teacher, minister,

[*] Jonny Gumbel, *Called: God's Purpose for Your Life and How it Changes Absolutely Everything* (Muddy Pearl, 2024), p2.
[**] Chris EW Green, *Sanctifying Interpretation: Vocation, Holiness and Scripture, Second Edition* (CPT Press, 2020), p20.

evangelist or intercessor. We come to know this through a mixture of our own journey of faith, as God reveals his will for our lives, and the wisdom of leaders who help us discern the call of God upon our lives.

Perhaps a brief personal reflection will help to make the point. As a seventeen-year-old, ambushed by the love of God and surrendered to the purposes of God for my life whatever that would mean, I gradually became aware of a desire growing within me to be involved in leadership in the church in some capacity. How, what and when this would happen was all up for grabs and not immediately clear. It took me a few years to fully figure it out – including a gap year and a business degree at university – but as I continued to invite the Spirit to lead me it became increasingly apparent that, ultimately, where my life was heading was towards some type of vocation wrapped up in service to the church. This was confirmed by spiritual parents, soul-companions and prophetic voices who also sensed this 'calling' upon my life. Taking further steps towards this through intentional discipleship, leadership development and theological study, I 'tested' out my sense of calling by serving practically, in any way I could, in my local church. As my church elders recognised God's purpose for my life and the evidence of the gift of leadership upon me, they laid their hands prayerfully on me and commissioned me into leadership in my local church. There is biblical precedence for this: the church elders and Paul did this with Paul's young apprentice, Timothy (see 1 Timothy 4:14; 2 Timothy 1:6). I've been serving my local church ever since. I've never felt called to do anything else.

Leading and serving the church of Jesus Christ is a calling from God. It's not more important than what anyone else is called to do for God. Many people are called by God to serve and advance the kingdom of God in different spheres of society and millions of Christians around the world are doing this faithfully every single day. In fact, as we will see in the chapters ahead, the church leader's role is to help members of Christ's body understand more fully the incredible purpose God has for their lives and equip them to outwork this more effectively where God has positioned them for his glory. Equally, if God has called you to lead and serve his church, then recognise the awesome and holy sense of purpose that rests upon your life. If God has called us to leadership in his church, we should aim to lead with dilligence and follow Jesus in the cruciform way. Our attitude to leadership should be just like the great nineteenth-century preacher Charles Spurgeon:

> I would not shun my Master's service, but I tremble in his presence. Who can be faultless when even Moses erred? It is a dreadful thing to be beloved of God. 'Who among us shall dwell with devouring fire? Who among us shall dwell with everlasting burnings? He that walketh righteously and speaketh uprightly' – he alone can face that sin-consuming flame of love. Brethren, I beseech you crave Moses' place, but tremble as you take it. Fear and tremble for all the good that God shall make to pass before you. When you are fullest of the fruits of the Spirit bow lowest before the throne, and serve the Lord with fear.[*]

Lead with diligence and follow Jesus in the cruciform way.

The content of the chapters ahead will unpack the different elements and characteristics of what I believe this type of leadership should look like. But before we begin to describe the characteristics of cruciform leadership, we need to end this chapter by making sure we are on the same page about what we believe about the church.

---

[*] CH Spurgeon, 'Lectures to my Students, Lecture XIV: The Holy Spirit in Connection with our Ministry', cblibrary.org (accessed 15 April 2025).

THE CHURCH

It should be clear by now that the conversation this book seeks to provoke does not stem from the question: 'Is leadership in the church important or not?' The Bible is overwhelmingly affirmative of the need for leadership among God's people. The real question we want to explore is: 'What kind of leader should the church leader be?'

To answer this question, we first of all need to back up one step and ask an even more fundamental question: 'What do we mean when we talk about the "success" of the church?'

- Number of people?
- Size of building?
- Level of finances?
- Influence online?
- The charisma and reach of the leader?
- Growth strategy?
- Quality of worship experience?
- Facilities for children and all-round family accommodation?

It's important to try to honestly answer this question – what do we mean when we talk about the 'success' of the church?

None of the measures of 'success' I have mentioned above are inherently wrong in themselves and much nuance is required to talk about this subject maturely. But the point I want to emphasise here is the fact that none of these measures above describe the core reason Jesus left his followers here on earth. Moreover, serious problems arise when we prioritise these metrics above the true vocation of the church. Martyn Lloyd-Jones once said, 'The great concern of the New Testament Epistles is not about the size of the Church, it is about the purity of the Church.'* Along the same lines, Scot McKnight writes, 'When "success" is measured by "numerical

* Martyn Lloyd-Jones, *The Christian Warfare: An Exposition of Ephesians 6:10–13* (Banner of Truth, 1976), pp108–120.

growth," we have abandoned what the gospel says flourishing is."*
And Eugene Peterson goes further still, raging against worldly
forms of success which he believes have infected the church:

> The biblical fact is that there are no successful churches. There
> are, instead, communities of sinners, gathered before God week
> after week in towns and villages all over the world. The Holy Spirit
> gathers them and does his work in them. In these communities of
> sinners, one of the sinners is called pastor and given a designated
> responsibility in the community. The pastor's responsibility is to
> keep the community attentive to God. It is this responsibility that is
> being abandoned in spades.**

Often this process of misjudged 'success' begins subtly, a quiet
self-promoting insurrection in the heart of a leader. Seduced by
the success of noise and numbers, the church's vision becomes a
projection of the leader's own ego and ambition.

> *Noise + numbers = narcissism.*

Sometimes this process is obvious to others but often it lurks
underneath the surface, disguising itself in a form of godliness but
ultimately devoid of gospel power. Like any enthusiastic hiker who
has veered one or two degrees off his or her original reference point
without realising, only to eventually find themselves a long way from
their destination, many church leaders have ended up taking their
churches to places miles away from their original starting point.
These perils of self-promotion and self-centeredness were what the
original Apostles fought so strenuously to protect the early churches
from.

Human praise. This is the perennial problem.

KJ Ramsey offers a powerful prophetic reflection about how

---

* Scot McKnight, *1 and 2 Timothy, Titus, and Philemon: Wisdom for Every Church
Leader* (Harper Christian Resources, 2023), p98.
** Eugene Peterson, *Working the Angles: The Shape of Pastoral Integrity* (Eerd-
mans, 1987), p26.

many contemporary churches have followed suit in this regard, 'spiritually abusive churches and leaders don't set out to be abusive, they set out to be amazing.'* The idol of 'amazing' in the West is damaging the church. But we were never called to be amazing. This was never our starting point. So, what was then? What are we called to first and foremost? How should a local church measure their success or effectiveness then? The answers to these questions revolve around some of Jesus' final words on earth:

> *Therefore, go and make disciples of all nations, baptising them in the name of the Father and of the Son and of the Holy Spirit, and teaching them to obey everything I have commanded you. And surely, I am with you always, to the very end of the age.*
>
> MATTHEW 28:19–20

In short, the level of success any local church should be measured by is their level of faithfulness towards the effective fulfillment of these words of Jesus.

This shouldn't seem like new wisdom or revelation. But the reality is, while one stream of the Western church has become so consumed with managing decline and the other so obsessed with building their own 'empires', both have drifted from this central reference point. The hearts of too many leaders have stopped burning with these final commissioning words of Jesus. At best we are working out of the wrong paradigm. At worst we are building churches out of completely wrong motives. We will get to wrong motives in later chapters. For now, though, let's dig a little deeper into the New Testament to realign our thinking on the vocation of the local church.

---

* KJ Ramsey, a trauma-informed licenced counsellor who has written extensively on suffering and, in particular, spiritual abuse, offers a powerful prophetic critique in this regard. Ramsey argues many spiritually abusive churches and leaders never set out to be abusive but they did set out to be amazing. See her website: www.kjramsey.com (accessed 12 March 2025).

AN APOSTOLIC MOVEMENT AND THE KINGDOM FAMILY

I am convinced a central part of becoming the kind of leaders Jesus called us to be starts with establishing a rigorous biblical framework to underpin our understanding of the purpose of the church on the earth.

The New Testament provides us with rich metaphors for the church: the Body of Christ, a living organism of which Christ is the head; the Bride of Christ; the one new humanity in Christ; a living temple; the family of God; the pillar of truth; a flock; the household of God. All these metaphors capture beautiful aspects of the Christian community in action and reflect the 'multifaceted wisdom of God' (Ephesians 3:10, NASB) which God sovereignly planned for his people on earth to display. Some of these biblical metaphors are only used on one or two occasions. Others are used more frequently, and more detail can be gleaned from them. However, if we focus on one metaphor exclusively and fail to hold it in balance with other descriptions, we soon end up with a lopsided perspective.

I want to acknowledge the beauty of each of these metaphors and regret that this book will not have scope to cover each of them adequately. Given that my focus here is on Christian leadership, I want to concentrate on two elements of New Testament ecclesiology that need to be rediscovered if we are once again to give priority to the development of Christlike leaders in the way I believe the Book of Acts and the New Testament epistles do. Alan Hirsch gets to the heart of what I want to explore:

> Many of the problems that the church now faces can actually be resolved simply by thinking differently about the church and its God-designed mission in the world. In other words, by changing our metaphors, or paradigms of church, we can change the game. The name I give to this 'different paradigm' of church is simply apostolic movement.

It's not new, in fact it's ancient, and it describes completely the fluidity and dynamism of the spiritual phenomenon we see evidenced in the pages of the New Testament itself. Some churches are now beginning to reframe themselves as movements, and they are unleashing the sheer power of New Testament ecclesiology as a result. This is the church as Jesus intended it to be – a gospel-empowered, unfettered people movement, perfectly designed for nothing less than the transformation of the world and the destruction of the forces of evil (Matthew 16:18).[*]

Let's take a moment to remind ourselves of the origins of the church, and in doing so pray the Holy Spirit helps us rediscover what Hirsch describes as 'the sheer power of New Testament ecclesiology'. Ten days after Jesus had commissioned the disciples and ascended to heaven, the promised Holy Spirit was poured out upon the disciples. The church was born and the world's greatest ever people movement was launched on the earth. The wind that rushed through the building and the tongues of fire that rested on the disciples in the upper room symbolised the new temple that was being founded on the earth, a temple not constructed by man, but a spiritual building made of living stones bound together by the Spirit of the living God. This was nothing less than a new humanity, a colony of heaven resident on earth. The fledgling Christian community we read about in Acts 2:42–47, built on the love of Jesus and the hope of his resurrection would now be the locus of God's presence on the earth – a kingdom family where heaven and earth interlocked and overlapped.

The book of Acts then goes on to tell the story of how devoted Jesus-followers, fuelled and empowered by the Holy Spirit, advanced the kingdom of God in new countries and cultures, establishing a whole new network of kingdom families in those places, founded on love for Jesus and a radical commitment to his ways. Jeff Reed brilliantly and succinctly summarises what the story the book of

* Alan Hirsch, *What is a Missional Community?* Verge Network, January 2011, vergenetwork.org (accessed 23 April 2025).

Acts is telling us:

> The key to understanding Acts seems to be in Luke's interest in this movement, orchestrated by the Holy Spirit, of the gospel from its Jerusalem-based, Judaism-orientated beginnings to its becoming a worldwide, Gentile-predominant phenomenon.[*]

A review of all of this allows us to identify two key overarching themes which shape the birth and the growth of the early church – kingdom family and apostolic movement. These two themes help us appreciate more intelligently the central elements of New Testament ecclesiology and as a result provide us with a canonical context for how best to understand the true call to Christian leadership in the church. I like to say it like this: the primary motif for the church is family and the primary function of the church is apostolic.

The church is called to hold both these dynamic realities together in a divinely orchestrated tension. The temptation for many churches is to hold tightly to one of these biblical themes at the expense of the other. For example, some churches will invest the majority of their resources in establishing a strong family-centered church built around pastoral and teaching gifts. Members will feel well cared for and enjoy good teaching, but less emphasis is placed upon intentional evangelism and there may be a lack of vision for the ways the church can demonstrate the life of the kingdom of God in the surrounding city. Other churches will focus on cultivating a more fluid missional community of believers where individual members are empowered to influence their everyday spheres of influence but with little attention given to the pastoral needs of the body or healthy relational dynamics among the family of believers.

If we want to properly understand the true purposes of the church in the world, we must grasp how the Holy Spirit is always releasing movement and building family among the community of

* Gordon D Fee and Douglas Stuart, *How to Read the Bible for All Its Worth* (Zondervan, 1982), p167.

Christ at the same time. The key here is in remembering it is the Holy Spirit, not the church's self-propagating 'missional strategies', who is the primary agent of the mission of the God in the world. As Lesslie Newbigin says: 'It is thus by an action of the sovereign Spirit of God that the church is launched on its mission. And it remains the mission of the Spirit. He is central.[*]

The church of Jesus Christ is therefore a family joined by the Spirit, sent out in the power of the Spirit, to overflow with the love of Jesus into all the broken parts of the world.

The New Testament theologian Michael Gorman unpacks this symbiotic relationship between apostolic movement and kingdom family by using different but equally helpful language. Gorman argues that the effect of the Holy Spirit's life in the church is both *centrifugal* (meaning, moving away from the centre) and *centripetal* (meaning, moving towards the centre). He contends, 'the continuous back and forth, the in and out, of this dynamic relationship, it seems to me, is the nature of the church.'[**]

The *centrifugal* effect of the Holy Spirit is demonstrated in the obvious outward impulse of the Pentecost event. The first Apostles were thrust out of the upper room in the power of the Spirit to proclaim and embody the gospel of Jesus. Pentecost revealed and enabled what God has always desired – image-bearers filled with God's own personal presence, stewarding this presence to the ends of the earth. Popular missiologist David Bosch in his seminal work *Transforming Mission* describes the centrifugal nature of the church powerfully:

> Mission is thereby seen as a movement from God to the world; the church is viewed as an instrument for that mission. There is church because there is mission, not vice versa. To participate in mission is

* Lesslie Newbigin, *The Open Secret: An Introduction to the Theology of Mission* (Eerdmans, 1995), p58.
** Michael J Gorman, *Becoming the Gospel: Paul, Participation and Mission* (Eerdmans, 2015), p20.

to participate in the movement of God's love toward people, since God is a fountain of sending love.*

The *centripetal* effect of the Holy Spirit is witnessed as the first converts of the new radical Jesus movement were bound together in the new kingdom family. By pledging allegiance to Jesus these believers were knit together in covenant community:

> *All the believers were one in heart and mind. No one claimed that any of their possessions was their own, but they shared everything they had.*

ACTS 4:32

The Apostle Paul would later describe the countercultural nature of this new oneness that characterised the early church in his letter to the Galatians:

> *There is neither Jew nor Gentile, neither slave nor free, nor is there male and female, for you are all one in Christ Jesus.*

GALATIANS 3:28

These are words the prominent Catholic theologian Hans Kung described as 'an ecclesiological formula [which] refers not primarily to an individual and mystical union with Christ, but to the state of being a part of the body of Christ'.** These communities, reflecting the nature of the triune God, established themselves all over the Mediterranean basin in the decades after Jesus' ascension. Their witness carried a powerfully magnetic missional force. Christopher Wright argues as these new kingdom families anchored themselves in God's presence through regular rhythms of worship and praise, 'there [was] a centripetal force, God's own gravitational pull, that draws

* David J Bosch, *Transforming Mission: Paradigm Shifts in the Theology of Mission* (Orbis Books, 1991), p400.
**Hans Kung, *The Church* (Burns and Oates, 1967), p229.

people into the sphere of his blessing."* The watching world was quite simply fascinated by the level of love and connection these kingdom families had for one another.

Michael Gorman helps us understand that as wide as the implications of the Great Commission were (taking the gospel to 'all nations'), it was deep (baptising new disciples of Jesus into their new Trinitarian identity and establishing them in the family of God as dearly beloved children). Centrifugal and centripetal. Wide and deep. Apostolic movement and kingdom family. This is the nature of the church and these two overarching themes of New Testament ecclesiology, reproduced throughout church history, provide the scriptural architecture we need to understand the cruciform nature of leadership in God's church.

SUMMARY

In summary we can affirm the fact that there is much the church can learn from leadership in other sectors of society, but we should be wary of an imbalance. We should also note that many parts of our wider Western culture are already beginning to reject forms of leadership in more secular places, anyway, as many scandals in these sectors have also become front page news. It seems the crisis of leadership extends far beyond the church. From the high profile disgraces surrounding the personal morality of global political leaders, to the misogyny and narcissism rife in Hollywood exposed through the #MeToo movement, to the shocking abuse of power within taxpayer institutions such as the British Post Office and the BBC laid bare in recent TV documentaries and podcasts, the structures and theories propping up leadership across every sphere of society today in our Western world are under serious scrutiny. Rightly so.

* Christopher Wright, *The Mission of God's People: A Biblical Theology of the Church's Mission* (Zondervan, 2010), p129.

Ultimately, I hope the introduction and first chapter of this book have made a strong case for why the church must stop outsourcing its leadership development. More pertinently I pray these words will encourage leaders in this current cultural moment to ruthlessly resist worldly forms of power that have crept into our churches and, even worse, into our own hearts. As we shall see in the next chapters, the leadership characteristics of the first Apostles were often diametrically opposed to the leadership principles in the wider culture. We can train our leaders to become competent speakers, strategic thinkers, culture-savvy analysts, impressive presenters or incisive administrators – all these are worthwhile supplementary additions to a Christian leader's development, but my contention is they do not primarily characterise what Jesus taught his closest followers. If the church is not raising leaders within the context of apostolic movement while incubating them in the deep loving relationships of the kingdom family then, quite frankly, we are raising them up for something other than the kingdom of God.

Martin Luther King mobilised those in the Civil Rights Movement with the saying, 'the means we use must be as pure as the ends we seek.'[*] Applying this to all forms of Christian leadership we should conclude 'the ends' are not larger platforms, getting to the top of the speaker roster, increasing our online influence, keeping up appearances or selling more books. The 'end' is obedience to Jesus, proclaiming the gospel and making disciples in all nations. The 'means' therefore is quite simple – living a life of 'cruciformity', for this is the essence of all genuine discipleship unto Jesus.

In many ways this book is therefore nothing new but an application of the inspiration of the New Testament and a conviction that the 'crux' of our problems today can be solved by returning to the 'crux' of history itself – the person of Jesus and the way of the

* Martin Luther King Jr, 'Letter from Birmingham Jail', African Studies Centre, University of Pennsylvania, 16 April 1963, africa.upenn.edu (accessed 2 April 2025).

cross. In the chapters ahead we will explore the different elements of cruciform leadership Jesus taught and embodied for his disciples: having a surrendered soul (Chapter 2); having a servant heart (Chapter 3); being tested as an apprentice (Chapter 4); becoming a spiritual parent (Chapter 5); being an equipper of saints (Chapter 6); being part of a community as a team player (Chapter 7) and adopting the spiritual disciplines of a focused follower (Chapters 8 and 9).

As we move through these chapters you will recognise the themes of apostolic movement and kingdom family woven through our learning. Each chapter will weave examples of Jesus' life with examples of how the Apostles actually demonstrated each of these characteristics in their own lives and leadership. As the chapters unfold you will notice how I pay particular attention to Paul's writings, partly because his writings make up the majority of the New Testament letters, but also because it is in Paul's work, especially his letters to Timothy, that we have a front-row seat to a lived theology of cruciform leadership development.

And, on the subject of 'lived theology', you will also notice at the end of each chapter that I have included an accompanying study guide which I have called 'Practising the Cruciform Way'. I believe the best learning is done in context, within some form of group setting where conversation and prayerful reflection can take place and I would encourage you to consider reading the book alongside others – i.e. fellow elders; a small group of emerging leaders; a classroom of students; a staff team; a kindred spirit. My hope is that each chapter will provoke plenty of fuel for discussion and prayer which can be explored further in this section. There are three different options for you in each chapter, so you can adopt a pick-and-mix approach as you judge best – you'll find a mixture of devotional-type reflections, thought-provoking questions and some suggested group exercises to aid your discussion. If you aren't able to get together with other leaders in person, then try doing so with a regular video call. And if that isn't possible, then keep a journal and write your reflections in there. The point is to apply this learning to your own life, in your own context, in the hope that we may all become more shaped in the cruciform way.

PRACTISING THE CRUCIFORM WAY

Consider the questions and readings below in discussion, reflection, journalling and prayer.

ONE:

Yet I hold this against you: you have forsaken the love you had at first. Consider how far you have fallen! Repent and do the things you did at first.

REVELATION 2:4–5

- Reflect on Jesus' rebuke to the church at Ephesus, one which by human standards was impressive and influential.
- Do these words resonate with you, too? In what ways are you challenged to return to Christ, his cross and the cruciform way as a leader in Christ's church?

TWO:

A clear sense of God's calling – and confirmation of that calling – is something every church leader should be able to point to. Stepping up into church leadership without this would be presumptuous, however talented or gifted that person might be.

Reflect on this quotation from the chapter.

- What does the word 'calling' mean to you?
- In your group, share the ways each one has felt 'called' to church leadership. Alternatively, prayerfully bring to mind the story of your calling to the ministry and write it in your journal.

THREE:

Therefore go and make disciples of all nations, baptising them in the name of the Father and of the Son and of the Holy Spirit, and teaching them to obey everything I have commanded you. And surely I am with you always, to the very end of the age.

MATTHEW 28:19–20

Reflect on these final commissioning words of Jesus to his disciples.

- Consider some of the ways the church in the West has moved away from this, her primary mission. How has she been seduced by other measures of 'success'?
- Where have you in your own church leadership let go of the Great Commission? How might you better prioritise it?

CHAPTER 2

A SURRENDERED SOUL

Whoever wants to save their life will lose it, but whoever loses their life for me will find it.

MATTHEW 16:25

'Leadership is not the point.' Please read that again. It may seem a strange statement considering this is a book studying the importance of leadership, but I truly believe this is a crucial corrective for many leaders who want to serve God and God's church.

What *is* the point then?

Well, let me make another statement I read a number of years ago which I believe explains the essence of the corrective I want to propose is needed:

'God isn't preparing you for leadership, he is using leadership to prepare you for himself.'

Tragically many leaders of today's Western church have lost a vision for Christlikeness. While biblically it's clear God wants to use leadership to draw others to himself and, as I have explained in the previous chapter, God calls men and women to the role of leadership in his church, many churches and individual Christian leaders have focused more on drawing attention to themselves. They have become more obsessed with their own leadership profile and sphere of influence than becoming like Jesus. This is completely at odds with the central principles of the New Testament teaching.

In the Gospels and the letters to the first churches, we find that leadership, while highly valued, was never emphasised at the expense of Christlikeness. For the first Apostles, the ambition 'to become a great leader' would have been viewed as a hollow and superficial substitute to the much more expansive and beautiful vision of actually becoming like Christ. Further, the idea that you could be a leader in the church but not really embody proven Christlike character would have been a horrid misnomer to the founding mothers and fathers of the church. True, Paul instructed Timothy that desiring leadership in the church was a noble aspiration (1 Timothy 3:1) but the qualifications of leadership which Paul then outlines in the verses which follow point not to impressive external leadership qualities but a life of Christlikeness.

The Apostles would have had no understanding of some of the current practices of leadership recruitment in many churches today such as headhunting dynamic CEO types, elevating polished communicators or discerning potential leaders based on how big their online platform is. For the Apostles, the essential criteria of leadership were evidence of the fruit and anointing of the Spirit on an individual's life, an obvious servant heart, a willingness to die to all forms of selfish ambition and a lifestyle which exemplified radical obedience to the ways of Jesus.

Somewhere along the way, it seems the criteria have shifted. The author Skye Jethani hints at where some of the problems we are facing currently lie. Jethani coined the phrase 'The Evangelical Industrial Complex' to describe the networking power of Christian media, publishers and ministry partners in the Western world today. Caught up in this powerful web of influence, many leaders of the church today rely on each other for promotion, book deals, conference invites and, ultimately, income. According to Jethani some estimate the total turnover within the evangelical market to be over seven billion dollars a year! While much of what is produced within this 'industrial complex' is worthy and hugely resourceful for the body of Christ, a large shadow looms.

Jethani is deliberately provocative:

> There is an evangelical industrial complex that helps create, and then relies upon, the existence of celebrity leaders. Have you ever wondered why you don't see pastors from small or medium sized churches on the main stage at big conferences? Or why most of the best-selling Christian authors are megachurch leaders?[*]

To demonstrate these perils of celebrity more acutely, reflect on some of the Christian leadership conferences you may have attended over the past decade. Often the books promoted are weighted heavily towards themes such as 'how to grow your church', 'top tips to become a more effective leader', or 'unleash your leadership potential'.

I want to be really clear. I don't have a problem with any of these books. Some of them are on my bookshelf and I am thankful for the learning that many of them have granted me. My concern is that, for many church leaders, these are the only books on leadership they are reading. And I believe this imbalance is doing damage. What I often don't see in these leadership environments are books such as Augustine's *Confessions*, or Brother Lawrence's *The Practice of the Presence of God*, or Teresa of Ávila's *The Interior Castle*, or Julian of Norwich's *Revelations of Divine Love*, or Henri Nouwen's *In the Name of Jesus: Reflections of Christian Leadership*, or Dallas Willard's *The Spirit of the Disciplines*, or Dietrich Bonhoeffer's *The Cost of Discipleship* – all spiritual classics which have been treasured by the church for centuries. What I find fascinating about each of these masterpieces is that none of the authors was

---

[*] Skye Jethani, 'The Evangelical Industrial Complex & the Rise of Celebrity Pastors (Pt 1)', *Christianity Today*, 20 February 2012, christianitytoday.com (accessed 7 March 2025).

interested in becoming the most impressive leader. Rather, they were consumed with a passion to be like Jesus and to conform to his words, 'Be perfect, therefore, as your heavenly Father is perfect' (Matthew 5:48). Unfortunately, today it appears worldly excellence has seduced many away from such authentically biblical spirituality. As Scot McKnight states:

> The tendency toward clever leadership skills is a problem these days. Far too many pastors are more in tune with the leadership ideas from business books than they are from the pastoral theology of people who pastor, like Paul and Timothy, like Phoebe and Priscilla, like Barbara Brown Taylor and Lesslie Newbigin. Leaning too much into business leadership manuals creates a business culture in a church instead of a Christlikeness culture and, as the rector of our church told me recently, it turns pastors into CEOs instead of pastors.[*]

The superficialities latent in this performance-based, often ego-driven leadership are now being brutally exposed. The 'idol of amazing' has proven to be a counterfeit religion. Yet the life of Christ displayed in the true spiritual giants I have referenced above continues to witness through the ages, standing in stark contrast to our current leadership predicament. The saints of old were focused on a life of virtue, not on gaining popularity. Each of them had surrendered their own need for fame, performance and approval so they might be consumed by a much greater vision – being formed into the image of the Son of God, the firstborn of humanity (see Romans 8:29). In the end they became some of the most influential leaders in history and ironically, they sold more books than most leaders today could ever dream of!

---

[*] Scot McKnight, *1 and 2 Timothy, Titus, and Philemon: Wisdom for Every Church Leader* (Harper Christian Resources, 2023), p98.

JESUS AND PETER

Imagine you are standing before Jesus right now. Do you think his first question would be addressing the level of your popularity or performance as a leader, the size of your church or the number of people listening to your sermons? Rather, like Jesus' post-resurrection encounter with Peter on the beach (John 21:15–25), imagine Jesus tenderly asking you something much more elemental but far more piercing.

'Do you love me?'

Henri Nouwen, reflecting on Peter's encounter with Jesus, says:

> The question is not: How many people take you seriously? How much are you going to accomplish? Can you show me some results? But: Are you in love with Jesus?*

How would you answer?

A gentle question, but one which exposes the pretentious imposter lurking in the shadows of all of our lives, calling into question every other love, allegiance, ambition or form of identity outside of Jesus.

Do you love me?

Remember the context of Peter's encounter with Jesus. This question came only a few weeks after Peter had denied him. We can assume Peter was still tormented by shame and wracked with feelings of failure. In denying Jesus three times, Peter had not just blown it, he had done the very thing he vowed he never would do, 'Even if all fall away on account of you, I never will' (Matthew 26:33). Doing the thing you thought you would never do – as each of us can testify – this is the worst type of failure. Yet notice how Jesus' question to

---

* Henri JM Nouwen, *In the Name of Jesus: Reflections on Christian Leadership* (Darton, Longman & Todd, 1989), p24.

Peter does not focus on his mistake. Nothing is even mentioned about Peter's former sins. Jesus is here not to increase Peter's shame but to dissolve it in all-consuming grace. Peter is about to experience radical forgiveness not by having his sins pointed out but by being given the chance – actually three chances – to say 'yes' to the unconditional love of God that covers a multitude of sins.

Moreover, Peter's restoration has nothing to do with his ability. In order to get Peter back in the game, Jesus does not stroke Peter's ego by affirming his undoubted leadership skills, despite his recent failure. He does not flatter Peter by listing his strengths to simply boost his confidence again. He does not give Peter the quick 'I'm sorry, let's move on' option to rescue him from the awkwardness of the moment. Rather, Jesus goes right to the heart of the matter with a question.

'Do you love me?'

This approach probes deeper than any of these superficial remedies. Frankly, Jesus does not want Peter's leadership in this moment. He wants Peter. He is inviting Peter to surrender to an even deeper revelation of Calvary love, where all of Peter – his strengths and his sins – are swallowed up in amazing grace.

Jesus has come for Peter.

As the question, *'Do you love me?'* came the second and third time, I imagine Peter beginning to realise what was happening. Beginning to recognise that a standard platitude was not what Jesus was looking for. Disarmed by Jesus' gentle probing, Peter was learning the fundamental truth at the heart of the gospel – despite our best attempts to prove we are worthy and heroic and capable, something has to be done for us that we cannot do for ourselves. Peter had been humbled. He had to face the reality that he couldn't even save his own soul, let alone Jesus' life. Counterintuitively though, accepting this truth meant Peter was more qualified than ever to be the first leader of the church – the rock on which Jesus would build his kingdom family. Peter's final response, 'Lord, you know all things; you know that I love you' (John 21:17), is the cry of a man broken of his pride, found out by the love of God and now utterly surrendered to Jesus.

Jesus' beautiful encounter with Peter on the Galilean shore reminds us that all Christian leadership starts in this place of radical surrender to God's gracious invitation of forgiveness and abundant life. At that moment we are broken open by the love of God in a sovereign act of God's grace. If it doesn't start here then quite frankly it's not Christian leadership, because truly following Jesus cannot take place outside of a surrendered heart. You can't be a Christian, never mind a Christian leader, without the cross. The triune God from whom everything and everyone is created is self-giving love. Jesus, the Son of God and the head of the church, demonstrated this in the most radical ways through his life and ultimately in his death. The leaders of Jesus' church are therefore called to do the same – to live fully surrendered to the love of God. Surrender is the place where all cruciform leaders are born.

Like Peter, Jesus has come for you. All of you. Remember, God isn't preparing you merely for leadership. That's playing way too small. God is using leadership to prepare you for a much more expansive vision for your life – to become like Jesus and, as a result, participate with Jesus in his mission for the world. When we submit ourselves to this crucible of love, the possibilities are endless. The rest of Peter's life bears witness to such – the preacher at Pentecost, the healer of a lame man, the leader of the first churches during those explosive days of exponential growth and the instrument through which the Spirit fell first upon the Gentiles. All of this was Peter's destiny. But he could only truly live into this sense of purpose when he fully relinquished to Jesus. As the seasoned leadership mentor Terry Walling says, Peter learned 'the prize of surrender is revelation … and our own personal renewal can be the catalyst to corporate change.'*

* This insight is gleaned from the *Rebuilders Podcast*, Red Church, Australia.

Ultimately, cruciform leaders are those, like Peter, who have heard the question of Jesus, *'Do you love me?'* and it has ruined them for any other love. They have chosen to relinquish control, strip themselves of all human pride and capability and in doing so receive the revelation that can only be found in the place of wholehearted surrender. David Benner in his little classic, *The Gift of Being Yourself*, describes powerfully the essence of such a glorious revelation:

> The self that begins the spiritual journey is the self of our own creation, the self we thought ourselves to be. This is the self that dies on the journey. The self that arrives is the self that was loved into existence by Divine Love. This is the person we were destined from eternity to become – the 'I' that is hidden in the 'I AM.'*

This quote deserves meditating upon for months! Only by reaching the place where we have nothing to give God but our true selves, including all our weakness, failures and sin, can we truly experience the life-transforming power of his love.

It is the paradoxical nature of the Christian life that, as Henri Nouwen concludes, sits at the heart of all Christian leadership: 'I am deeply convinced the Christian leader of the future is called to be completely irrelevant and to stand in this world with nothing to offer but his or her vulnerable self.'** Men and women who have courageously passed through this vulnerable crucible are the hungry, holy and humble ones who will be able to serve the church in the days ahead more selflessly, and love more deeply and more authentically.

* David G Benner, *The Gift of Being Yourself: The Sacred Call to Self-Discovery* (InterVarsity Press, 2015), p102.
** Henri JM Nouwen, *In the Name of Jesus: Reflections on Christian Leadership* (Darton, Longman & Todd, 1989), p17.

HARNESSING

It would be wrong to think Peter's journey into this place of surrender was the product of this sole encounter with Jesus. Peter had been immersed in a process of intentional discipleship with Jesus for three years. A careful reading of the gospel narratives reveals Jesus' patience with Peter, even granting him a measure of responsibility when it was obvious he still needed some serious development and formation. Throughout these years Jesus never lost sight of Peter's destiny despite Peter's mistakes, his overinflated ego and his obvious impulsiveness. While Jesus knew Peter would completely blow it, he could still see who Peter was becoming. I find Jesus' words to Peter before his denial incredibly moving:

> *But I have prayed for you, Simon, that your faith may not fail. And when you have turned back, strengthen your brothers.*

LUKE 22:32

Lean into these words to grasp what is happening here. Jesus knew the overwhelming sense of failure Peter would feel, so Jesus committed himself to praying Peter through his darkest days in order that Peter might become the person God had always created him to be. Hallelujah. Jesus never loses sight of our destiny, despite the fact that his loving gaze towards us knows the worst about us.

Like a wild horse full of potential, yet driven by 'self', Jesus will patiently endure the harnessing process even when we kick out at any kind of leadership that is exerted upon us. Wrapping himself around us in committed love, like an experienced horse rider, Jesus will 'break us' where we need to be broken, wrestling our sin and selfish ambition into a place of gentle submission. If we let Jesus take control of our lives, he will always prove how his love is stronger and more committed than the stubborn forces of our independence.

For naturally gifted leaders in particular, this process of harnessing is essential if we are to prevent ourselves from doing untold damage. I remember a particular season of intense harnessing as a young leader. From my late teens I intuitively sensed a call to church leadership upon my life. Numerous other seasoned leaders had recognised this and spoken it over me. I had been given a number of opportunities to lead at that age and for the most part I had shown myself fairly accomplished. It seemed natural to gather people and then take them somewhere. But this wasn't enough for me. There was an insatiable desire within me to want more leadership opportunities, a higher profile. I was part of a young and exciting church plant, and I wanted to do pretty much everything! I began to find myself frustrated with almost every area of church life where I wasn't leading! And with the people leading them. I thought I could lead the church better than the pastor (who happened to be my uncle); I thought I could preach better than those who were preaching; I was convinced I was the best person to provide the vision for how we move forward together better. *If only I had the chance to speak more, envision more, build our strategy more – the church would be in a much better place. In the process everyone would become aware of how good I really am!'* This was the narrative constantly spinning around my head. I couldn't stop it. On a Sunday night after a whole day around church these thoughts would consume me. I was keeping it together on the outside, but inside a wild unharnessed horse was frantically kicking out of control.

The thoughts and attitudes I had then disgust me now. It's embarrassing to write about it. But I am even more embarrassed to tell you they still come back from time to time. Let's keep it real. Perhaps elements of this self-obsession never fully go away, which is why as a younger leader it was so important for me to learn how to deal with them. I needed a cruciform schooling. I needed to learn how to undergo discipline from the Lord and to be harnessed by the Spirit. In this process, God would affirm my genuine love for Jesus and my heart's desire to serve him, but he would also expose the selfish ambition tangled up in my heart. 'Vainglory' is what some translations of the Bible call this. I needed the Lord to do something in me. There is no easy way to say it – so much more of me had to die.

So, every Sunday night for a period of weeks, I returned to my university halls of residence in Belfast where I was studying during that period of my life. I locked the door on my own little student dorm, closed the curtains, put on some worship music and lay face down on the floor. My Bible lay open at Galatians 2:20 beside me.

I have been crucified with Christ and I no longer live, but Christ lives in me. The life I now live in the body, I live by faith in the Son of God, who loved me and gave himself for me.

GALATIANS 2:20

There, week after week, as a nineteen-year-old who thought he was a much better leader than he actually was, I learned the art of dying to myself. I wrote Galatians 2:20 down in capital letters and stuck it up beside the mirror in my bedroom. Every morning before I went to class, I meditated on these words, memorising them internally so I could bring them back to my conscious awareness throughout the day. Over a period of months, the carnal side of my nature, which was desperate for the admiration of others, lusting for recognition and driven by performance, was crucified with Christ. The words of that radical Christ-follower Dietrich Bonhoeffer haunted me in that season: 'When Christ calls a man, he bids him come and die.'*

Twenty years later I am still trying to practise this 'dying to self' process most days of my life. My morning ritual of spending time with Jesus usually includes a prayer, something along the lines of *'Jesus today, I choose to die to my "self". I have been crucified with you Jesus, now live your life through me today in all your fullness.'*

I still pray this daily because, quite frankly, I need to! CS Lewis, who has always helped me understand myself better, described my predicament powerfully, 'Fallen man is not simply an imperfect

---

* Dietrich Bonhoeffer, *The Cost of Discipleship* (SCM Press, 2024), p99.

creature who needs improvement: he is a rebel who must lay down his arms.'*

The older I get and the more I experience the intense pressures of church leadership, the spiritual attacks of the evil one and the temptations of my own flesh, the harder it gets. After twenty-five years of leadership in the kingdom I need to pay attention to the motives of my heart more than ever. I've learned the truth of what Tim Keller once said: 'Ministry is either going to make you a far better Christian or a far worse Christian than you would have been otherwise,'** which is why I am so grateful to God for teaching me the art of dying to self – the cruciform way – all those years ago as a nineteen-year-old.

The current leadership crisis is revealing that leaders who short-circuit this harnessing process will undoubtedly do serious damage to themselves and many others. We dare not be unaware of the devil's schemes. He has done his homework on each of us. He knows our weaknesses, our past hurts and our family-of-origin wounds too well for us to get presumptuous or lackadaisical about the work of formation into Christlikeness each Christian leader simply must submit to.

RESURRECTION

The good news of the gospel is that the cruciform life is steeped in resurrection power. As Scot McKnight writes, 'The cross is the pattern of life while the resurrection is the power of that life.'*** When we joyfully surrender to the love of God through the harnessing process, we are not only liberated from the powerful lure of self but we make a 'public spectacle' of the enemy – rehearsing once again

* CS Lewis, *Mere Christianity* (Harper San Francisco, 2009), p56.
** Tim Keller, '3 Ways Ministry Can Make You Conceited', *The Gospel Coalition*, 5 July 2017, thegospelcoalition.org (accessed 7 March 2025).
*** Scot McKnight, 'Cruciformity *and* Resurrecti-formity? Or…', *Jesus Creed*, 22 October 2019, patheos.com (accessed 7 March 2025).

his defeat through the victory of the cross. As fresh realisation of the resurrection power of Jesus surges through our bodies we experience new creation in a dynamic way.

During the intensity of my 'dying-to-self' season as a young leader I can distinctly remember experiencing moments of transcendent joy rising up within me as the victorious nature of the power of the cross became a tangible reality in my life. I love how Bono, lead singer of U2, concluded his autobiography *Surrender*:

> Surrender might be the most powerful word in the world … Maybe I'm discovering surrender doesn't always have to follow defeat and may be all the fuller after victory.*

Experiencing this joy of surrender is the good news at the heart of the gospel and the source of all authentic Christian leadership. For sure, surrender is hard. As the old revivalist Leonard Ravenhill is reported to have said, 'We want to be clothed upon with power; God wants to strip us. We want power; He wants to expose our weakness.' There are days when the pull of our flesh is so strong or the heaviness of life pressing down on our souls is so intense that it feels like surrendering to the process of transformation into Christlikeness is the last thing we want to do. But when we get a fresh glimpse of what (who!) is on the other side of this process – a fresh glimpse of the beauty of our resurrected Lord – it makes it much harder to surrender begrudgingly. What's more, Jesus has gone before us in this process. The writer of Hebrews tells us he endured unimaginable torment and pain for us because he was anticipating the incomparably greater joy of our friendship. 'For the joy set before him he endured the cross' (Hebrews 12:2). Meditating on Jesus' joy-anticipating surrender calls us to fall down before him in wholehearted worship and empowers us to follow him along the cruciform path.

* Bono, *Surrender: 40 Songs, One Story* (Hutchinson Heinemann, 2022), p543.

THE CONTEMPLATIVE LEADER

With all of this in mind, I want to propose that the cruciform leader should learn to become a contemplative leader – one who learns the art of 'beholding' God. The art of dying I have described above can only truly happen as we grow in this type of knowledge of God – beholding the face of God. The Apostle Paul reminded the young church in Corinth, who had been corrupted by self-promoting, arrogant leaders, to meditate on the profound reality now possible for them through Jesus' death and resurrection.

> *And we all, who with unveiled faces contemplate the Lord's glory, are being transformed into his image with ever-increasing glory, which comes from the Lord, who is the Spirit.*
>
> 2 CORINTHIANS 3:18

By contemplation I am not talking about an esoteric ascent into free-floating mysticism, nor some limp form of candle-lighting spirituality. Rather, I am talking about the cultivation of a way of life that is continually captivated by the beauty of Jesus Christ. I am talking about the prayerful process of being transformed into the image of the luminous One who loves us like no one else can or ever will. I am talking about learning to become attentive to the Father's love in all things and at all times. Chris Green puts it like this:

> In contemplation, the Holy Spirit broods sweetly over my spirit, slowly and secretly freeing me from 'slavery to cravings and fantasies', making me permeable to Christ so that his character begins to alter mine, filling me with the goodness of his own Spirit – joy and peace, gentleness and self-control.*

Peter could only completely surrender to God as he contemplated the face of the resurrected Jesus on that Galilean shoreline, inviting

* Chris EW Green, *Surprised by God: How and Why What We Think about the Divine Matters* (Cascade Books, 2018), p5.

him to the all-consuming love of the Father. Surely the depth of this encounter with Jesus influenced what he would write to the churches under his care approximately thirty years later.

> *His divine power has given us everything we need for a godly life through our knowledge of him who called us by his own glory and goodness. Through these he has given us his very great and precious promises, so that through them you may participate in the divine nature, having escaped the corruption in the world caused by evil desires.*

2 PETER 1:3–4

These verses are some of the most important words ever written in the history of the world. Beholding the love of God, in the face of Jesus Christ, will lead us into the stunning reality of 'participation in the divine nature'. What! This inspired phrase will never not blow my mind.

As a young leader driven by all sorts of messiah-complexes and ashamed of my overpowering self-centredness I, like Peter, was set free when I looked into the eyes of Jesus. True contemplation has brought me further into the knowledge of God – a kind of knowing that flows from God's unconditional love and invites me deeper into this love. 'We love Him because He first loved us' (1 John 4:19, NKJV). Invited by the Spirit beyond the outward appearance of my life into the parts only observed by God, it is here, gazing upon the loving face of Jesus, I have received the tender mercies of Jesus. Gregory of Nyssa in his beautiful little book, *The Life of Moses*, describes how precious such prayer is to God:

> Scripture teaches us, I think, that the voice which is melodious and ascends to God's hearing is not the cry made with the organs of speech but the meditation sent up from a pure conscience.*

---

* Gregory of Nyssa, *The Life of Moses* (HarperCollins Spiritual Classics, 2006), p64.

This is the type of meditation all the great saints of church history took time to master, and in doing so their lives have been transformed into exemplars of humility, peace, virtue and unflinching confidence in God.

TAKE, BLESS, BREAK, GIVE

The most important way Jesus exhorted his followers to contemplate him after he returned to heaven was in the rudimentary form of a meal. Bread and wine. This meal (the Eucharist) is the sacrament that sits at the heart of the Christian tradition. In the bread and the wine, we are constantly reminded that our lives, never mind our leadership, are not built upon a programme of self-help but saving grace. In celebrating this meal together Jesus told us that in some spiritual way we are receiving him and his self-giving love afresh in our lives. Eugene Peterson gives texture to this ancient ritual by drawing on the wisdom of an Anglican monk called Gregory Dix who presented a paper in 1941 bringing prominence to a fourfold liturgical shape at the heart of the Eucharistic meal.* Dix outlined a pattern recorded in the Gospels apparent when Jesus shared meals with his followers. Mark in particular uses four verbs – take, bless (or thank), break and give – when describing Jesus' final Passover meal with his disciples.

> *While they were eating, Jesus took bread, and when he had given thanks, he broke it and gave it to his disciples, saying, 'Take it; this is my body.'*
>
> *Then he took a cup, and when he had given thanks, he gave it to them, and they all drank from it.*
>
> *'This is my blood of the covenant, which is poured out for many,' he said to them.*

MARK 14:22–24

* Eugene Peterson, *Christ Plays in Ten Thousand Places: A Conversation in Spiritual Theology* (Eerdmans, 2005), p208.

What's fascinating is that these four verbs occur in the same sequence in Mark's account of Jesus' feeding of the five thousand and the four thousand. John's record of the feeding of the five thousand and Luke's narration of Jesus' meal with the Emmaus pilgrims also follow the same verbal pattern. Furthermore, the Apostle Paul's admonishment to the church at Corinth concerning communion stands in line with this verbal tradition, 'the Lord Jesus, on the night he was betrayed, took bread, and when he had given thanks, he broke it'.*

Take. Bless. Broken. Given.

These four verbs, which provide liturgical shape to the communion meal, grant us a profoundly practical contemplative framework for the path the cruciform leader must walk. Peterson argues these four words 'get us in on everything Jesus is doing from the cross.'** As I briefly unpack each of them below, try to map each verb onto the process of Peter's apprenticeship to Christ described above in this chapter, as this provides a helpful summary of the truths we have already discovered.

1. JESUS TAKES US

We come as we are. Like Peter (and me!), when we are young, we think we are capable of giving Jesus something that can contribute to our salvation and his cause. But as life happens to us, we become aware of how little control we really have. Humbled by our own brokenness and sin, we come to realise, 'the only thing we contribute to our own salvation is the sin which makes it necessary.' Nevertheless, when all we can give Jesus is what's left after our failed attempts to make it on our own, he receives us unconditionally in love. 'He refuses nothing of what we are or what we have done.'*** He takes all of us.

* See Matthew 14:19; Matthew 15:36; Mark 6:41; Mark 8:6; Luke 9:16; Luke 24:30; John 6:11; 1 Corinthians 11:23–24.
** Eugene Peterson, *Christ Plays in Ten Thousand Places*, p212.
*** *Ibid.*

2. JESUS BLESSES US

When we give ourselves to Jesus, he presents us before the Father. Despite the fact there is nothing we can give Jesus that he actually needs, Jesus wants us. Astonishingly, he receives what we give him with heartfelt gratitude. Like the five loaves and two fish, which seem so inadequate in light of what is needed, Jesus blesses and sanctifies what we offer. We could never imagine Jesus saying – 'What? is that all you've got?' Rather, Jesus gathers what we give him into his own being and lifts us up before the loving gaze of the Father. Here, the potential for our lives has never been greater.

3. JESUS BREAKS US

While Jesus receives whatever we give him, what we give him isn't usually the true us. Jesus has work to do with us. Max Lucado articulates the depth of this simply for us, 'Jesus loves you as you are but he loves you too much to leave you that way.'* Many of us don't realise that when we come to Jesus he wants to set us free from every diminished form of love, and every imposter seeking to control our destiny. This is the crucible of surrender Peter had to endure and to which every cruciform leader must submit. The words of Thomas Keating never cease to hit the mark in this regard, 'the spiritual journey is not a career or a success story. It is a series of humiliations of the false self that becomes more and more profound.'** Leaders in particular must pay serious attention to this process of 'humiliation' because they are often more susceptible to deceitful self-projecting illusions than others. Eugene Peterson concurs with this warning to Christian leaders, 'I don't know of any other profession in which it is quite as easy to fake it as in ours.'***

Cruciform leaders are the ones who have come to understand that Jesus loves them too much to allow them to pretend they are

---

* Max Lucado, *Just Like Jesus* (Thomas Nelson, 2000), pxi.
** Thomas Keating, *The Human Condition: Contemplation and Transformation* (Paulist Press, 1999), p38.
*** Eugene Peterson, *Working the Angles: The Shape of Pastoral Integrity* (Eerdmans, 1987), pp5–6.

something they are not. Moreover, Jesus loves his church too much to allow those who represent him to stay self-sufficient, independent and partially surrendered. In allowing us to be broken, God in his grace is actually limiting the potential damage we could do to ourselves and others. 'For the Lord disciplines the one he loves' (Hebrews 12:6).

Sometimes this process of 'breaking' comes through direct correction from God's word or the truth-in-love spoken by a trusted friend or mentor. More often than not, however, this 'breaking' comes through the devastating tribulations of life. In this present age, where we endure the pain of smashed ideals, broken hearts and searing grief, the Wounded Healer meets us there. The beauty to be found in this brokenness is the realisation that Jesus' own unquantifiable level of suffering is the source of our healing. The early Christians saw in their instruction to 'break bread' an identification with the co-suffering God, the broken body of Jesus, a sacrifice through which would come the salvation of the world.

Entering into our darkness and never rushing us out of our grief or our questions, Jesus gently begins to lead us out of the place of suffering, redeeming even the bleakest of circumstances for his good purposes in the world. Surrendering this brokenness to him in childlike trust, the place of our deepest woundedness becomes the source of our greatest revelation. It is here we are set free from our independence and false identities and moulded into mature sons and daughters of love. Here we learn, in the words of Brennan Manning, how to, 'define [ourselves] radically as one beloved by God. This is the true self. Every other identity is illusion.'*

4. JESUS GIVES US

Jesus gives back what he has received, only now we are different. The breaking of our own self-sufficiency opens us up to the potential for new life, to serve the church and join in Jesus' priestly ministry

* Brennan Manning, *Abba's Child: The Cry of the Heart for Intimate Belonging* (Navpress, 2015), p40.

to bring healing to the world. Jesus gives us to others as his hands and feet. We may have had to wrestle God through the night like Jacob but, in the process, we will have come face-to-face with the 'Angel of the Lord'. As we persevere through the pain of the divine wrestle, we eventually realise it is here we were touching the face of God. On the other side of this everything is different. In submitting to the denial of self we have entered into the fullness of life. Remember 'cruciformity' is suffused with resurrection. Having been broken by Christ, we are now more qualified to participate with Christ in the salvation healing of the world. Only now far more effectively than we could have ever imagined. This is the hyper-abundance of the kingdom economy, when five loaves and two fish, after they have been taken, blessed and broken, are given back to feed thousands.

Take, Bless, Break, Give.

A PERSONAL REFLECTION

As a seventeen-year-old, wounded from relationships and searching for the transcendent in all the wrong places, I finally surrendered my life to Jesus. Jesus took it and I experienced the joy of forgiveness. Despite the work Jesus still needed to do, Jesus blessed my life before the Father, filled me with his Spirit and gave me a glimpse of the destiny of my life to serve his church. As I have already described, lots of breaking was needed during my university years. I came through that season and God gave me back to the world to serve him in some wonderful ways. But not many years later another season of brokenness came my way. In 2005, at twenty-five years old, I married the woman I had become convinced God had given me to grow old with. Lindsay Anderson was twenty-one and we fell in love. We wanted God and we wanted each other. In our wedding vows to one another we promised to give our lives to the service of God and his kingdom. One year later we found out Lindsay had a brain tumour. After nine months of treatment, she died. She was 23. I felt like I had died too. Every part of me hurt like hell. Broken beyond belief. The complex process of grief is the subject of another book and for those currently navigating the sheer horror of such acute loss can I please recommend my book *Luminous Dark* which describes my journey and pathway to healing in detail. But for the purposes of this book, I am simply sharing a little of my own personal tragedy to testify to the redemptive power of God's love.

Over a number of years God patiently and tenderly healed my heart. Nothing in me believes God 'planned' for Lindsay to die. Yet in God's sovereign mercy I came to believe God had allowed me to walk this path. This was not because God took any pleasure in seeing me endure such searing levels of grief but because he had heard the cry of my heart as a seventeen-year-old longing to know the reality of Philippians 3:10–11 – 'that I may know Him and the power of His resurrection, and the fellowship of His sufferings' (NKJV). As a teenager I had learned these verses off by heart quite simply because I had fallen in love with Jesus, but I had no clue about what praying these words might actually mean for my life. In a world broken by the effects of sin, God had allowed me to suffer with him, choosing me to be the man who would love Lindsay, literally to her last breath on this earth.

A number of months, or perhaps a year after she had died, the sheer intensity of grief lifted ever so slightly, and I tried to turn my heart towards the future. Contemplating whether my life still held any purpose and pondering what contribution I could still make for the kingdom of God, I sensed the Spirit draw me to these words of the Apostle Paul in 2 Corinthians:

Praise be to the God and Father of our Lord Jesus Christ, the Father of compassion and the God of all comfort, who comforts us in all our troubles, so that we can comfort those in any trouble with the comfort we ourselves receive from God. For just as we share abundantly in the sufferings of Christ, so also our comfort abounds through Christ. If we are distressed, it is for your comfort and salvation; if we are comforted, it is for your comfort, which produces in you patient endurance of the same sufferings we suffer.

2 CORINTHIANS 1:3–6

These words came to me with a powerful new sense of revelation. I began to realise how Paul had reframed his own understanding of suffering in a cruciform (vertical and horizontal) way. Not only were his tribulations an opportunity to receive the deep comfort of God for himself (the vertical connection) but this comfort would then overflow into the brokenness of the world around him (the horizontal connection). By choosing to participate in the suffering of Christ, Paul's life had become an instrument through which God's all-powerful comfort could plunge into the depths of his own brokenness and burst forth into the world around him.

The illumination I received from these words of Scripture became the renewed mission statement for my life. They've been imprinted on my heart ever since. This is how Jesus would *give* me back to the world. As I wrote in my book *Luminous Dark*:

> I had received an avalanche of the healing balm of God; I had encountered a depth of love and measure of his comfort I would not have known without this experience of loss. I now understood that this was for much more than my own desperate need of healing – in the redemptive economy of God this love would overflow for the consolation of broken people all around me.[*]

This is the life of the cruciform leader. A wholly surrendered disciple of Jesus. One who has been prepared not primarily to prove themselves as the greatest leader but one who has been prepared to be a vessel of the love and healing of Jesus. One whom Jesus has taken, blessed, broken and given. As acclaimed author and educator Parker Palmer has suggested, this is the kind of leadership our world needs. To serve with integrity and courage, we must keep our hearts 'open in those very moments when the heart is asked to hold more than it is able ... Identity and integrity have as much to do with our shadows and limits, our wounds and fears, as with our strengths and potentials.'[**]

[*] Alain Emerson, *Luminous Dark: Leaning into Pain, Holding on to God, Breaking Through to Light* (Muddy Pearl, 2017), p158.
[**] Parker J Palmer, *The Courage to Teach: Exploring the Inner Landscape of a Teacher's Life* (Jossey-Bass, 2007), pp12, 13.

PRACTISING THE CRUCIFORM WAY

*Consider the questions and readings below in discussion,
reflection, journalling and prayer.*

ONE:

Again Jesus said, 'Simon son of John, do you love me?'

JOHN 21:16

Revisit John 21:15–19 describing Jesus' post-resurrection encounter
with Peter on the beach and reflect on his recurring question shown
above.

- Take some time to prayerfully imagine Jesus standing in front
  of you asking you the question, *'[insert your name], do you
  love me?'* Ponder Jesus asking you this question three times,
  pausing in between each one. How do you respond?
- Journal what this provokes within you and discuss the
  emotions and reflections in your group.

TWO:

God isn't preparing you for leadership, he is using leadership to
prepare you for himself.

Take time to ponder this quotation from Chapter 2.

- Are there ways in which becoming a 'better' leader has
  become more important to you than becoming like Christ?

THREE:

Discuss any parts of your life that God may want to 'harness' in this
season.

- Where might you need to surrender to his will and ways all over again?
- What leaders are emerging in your community that you believe require a season of harnessing before they are fully released into leadership? How can you disciple them best in this season?

CHAPTER 3

A SERVANT HEART

*'You don't know what you are asking,' Jesus said to them. 'Can you
drink the cup I am going to drink?'*

MATTHEW 20:22

In 2001, Jim C Collins published his bestselling book *Good to Great*.
Since its release it has sold over four million copies and has received
widespread praise as one of the best business management books
ever written. Based on extensive research and data, Collins and his
team produced a masterclass analysis on how ordinary or 'good'
companies made the leap to become 'great' companies. Analysing
1,435 companies over a span of forty years Collins was able to
draw insightful conclusions about what set eleven outperforming
companies apart from the others, identifying some key strategies,
habits and practices which all the 'great' companies had adopted. I
do not have time to unpack all of Collins' fascinating insights here,
but one of his most significant findings emphasises a characteristic
of cruciform leadership we are going to explore in this chapter.
Collins' team of researchers discovered the success which the 'great'
companies enjoyed was, more often than not, directly connected
to a particular type of leader. The fact that a leader's character
could influence the success of their business was not in itself overly
surprising. But it was the style of leadership characterising those

who led the 'great' companies and therefore set them apart from the 'good' companies which startled the researchers. Collins summarises below what they discovered:

> The good-to-great leaders never wanted to become larger-than-life heroes. They never aspired to be put on a pedestal or become unreachable icons. They were seemingly ordinary people quietly producing extraordinary results.[*]

Collins goes on to describe the leaders of 'great' companies as Level 5 leaders, arguing that they transcended four other types of leadership – the Highly Capable Individual (Level 1); the Contributing Team Member (Level 2); the Competent Manager (Level 3); the Effective Leader (Level 4). Level 5 leaders embody all these first four levels of leadership but have a number of other distinguishing traits. Level 5 leaders, Collins' research revealed, possess a mixture of 'personal humility and professional will'. In other words, they are self-effacing individuals, deflecting praise to other team members when success comes and taking personal responsibility for failure when things go wrong. It was also noted that they were the hardest working people in the organisation and had little interest in their own profile and public image. How refreshing it is to hear of successful leaders demonstrating compelling modesty rather than elevating their own persona.

It's perhaps not surprising that *Good to Great* resonated with many of Collins' Christian readers, as his findings on leadership, especially the characteristics of Level 5 leaders, map easily onto a New Testament understanding of leadership. It's ironic to think it took a book from the business world to get Christian leaders thinking seriously again about servant-hearted leadership. From a secular context, Collins was helping reframe how people thought of greatness. Through extensive empirical proof, his team peeled back the layers of distorted secular assumptions and revealed that

---

[*] Jim Collins, *Good to Great: Why Some Companies Make the Leap and Others Don't* (HarperCollins, 2001), p28.

human beings really do respond well to hardworking and servant-hearted leaders. In short, Collins has shown that, despite human beings' propensity to get caught up in the superficial halo effect associated with our modern-day celebrity culture, deep down the world is crying out for leaders who lead like Jesus! In a sense Collins has revealed a kind of ontology of leadership wholly in keeping with biblical principles[*] – this is the kind of person most humans long to be led by. His research has applied to the economic systems of Western capitalism the illuminating truth which sits at the centre of the kingdom of God – true greatness comes through humility. I'm not sure how much the business world has listened to Collins since his book was published, but I wish more church leaders had done so.

CAN YOU DRINK THIS CUP?

In Matthew 20:20–28 we read about how the mother of James and John came with her sons and knelt before Jesus. When Jesus inquired what she wanted, this matriarch asked if her boys could sit at the right and left of Jesus' throne in his heavenly kingdom. A bold ask!

In one sense this mother's request was admirable. Her sons had recognised Jesus was the Messiah. There were worse thrones they could have wanted to sit by in those days. Was it not a noble desire, a godly ambition even, to want to reign with Jesus forever in this way? And was it not courageous to make such a request? Even if they did get their mum to do it for them.

Jesus' response however, exposed the naivety of the self-promoting shadow which lurked behind the request. 'You don't know what you are asking,' Jesus said.

---

[*] I am grateful to Scot McKnight for this thought in his article – Scot McKnight, 'Leadership Re-Imagined', *Jesus Creed*, 5 September 2014, patheos.com (accessed 7 March 2025).

James and John, along with their well-meaning mother, needed to have their idea of greatness reframed. They hadn't yet grasped how unlike any other king Jesus actually was. No king could ever compare to him, not in the whole of Israel's history, never mind the surrounding empires. The way Jesus would ascend to his throne was incomprehensible to the disciples at this point in their kingdom apprenticeship. The royal crown Jesus would receive would only come through an unimaginable level of suffering. Therefore, Jesus' gentle rebuke to the two brothers took the form of a question. 'Can you drink the cup I am going to drink?'

Peter was asked by Jesus, 'Do you love me?' James and John are asked, 'Can you drink the cup I am going to drink?' These are piercing, disarming questions; questions every cruciform leader must face. The brothers' reply was rash but earnest. '"We can," they replied' (Matthew 20:22). Like Peter's initial reply to Jesus' line of questioning on the Galilean shore, we can detect a tone of self-confidence in the brothers' reply. But this is that type of over-reaching confidence which belies insecurities bubbling beneath the surface.

In the long run both James and John will honour this 'yes' in their lives and in their deaths: James through a bloody persecution leading to death; John through a long life of suffering in faithful service to Jesus (Acts 12:2; Revelation 1:9). But in this moment the other disciples were indignant. Essentially James and John had tried to steal a march on the rest of the disciples, seeking to secure the best seats in the house! Imagine the ego-driven squabble breaking out among this group of testosterone-fuelled young men, all jostling for position and power. Jesus had to step in. It was time to flip the disciples' understanding of greatness on its head. Quietening the rabble, Jesus said:

You know that the rulers of the Gentiles lord it over them, and their high officials exercise authority over them. Not so with you. Instead, whoever wants to become great among you must be your servant, and whoever wants to be first must be your slave – just as the Son of Man did not come to be served, but to serve, and to give his life as a ransom for many.

Matthew 20:25–28

These words of Jesus collided with the disciples' understanding of power and greatness on every conceivable level. On one side the disciples were surrounded by, and subject to, the formidable military and administrative structures of the Roman Empire and the brutality with which imperial government was enforced. On the other side they were ruled by Israel's compromised religious leaders who manipulated the temple system to reward the wealthy at the expense of the poor. The way to be upwardly mobile and achieve admiration and status in first-century Judea was to leverage any wealth or influence you could get your hands on. Not much has changed. The world's path to greatness was the same then as it is now, so we should be able to understand the radical nature of Jesus' rebuke to his disciples, cutting right across cultural norms and assumptions. 'Whoever wants to become great among you must be your servant' would have been as uncomfortable a sentiment for any first-century leader to hear as it is to us today.

THE ROCK AND THE STUMBLING STONE

For the disciples, captivated as they were by Jesus' social bias to the poor and his countercultural vision for the world, they couldn't quite reconcile this Jesus with their pre-existing categories of Messianic kingship. They struggled to understand how their rabbi's teachings would ultimately lead to the dismantling of the mighty Roman Empire. Surely the long-awaited Messiah who was coming to liberate God's people from slavery needed to demonstrate leadership characteristics which were a bit more authoritarian? A bit more militant? Surely Israel's king would need to exercise his authority from above, not from below?

Matthew records a conversation between Jesus and his disciples which provides an example of just how difficult they were finding it to accept the way of Jesus. Ironically, the scene comes directly after Peter's courageous declaration of Jesus as Messiah: 'You are the Christ, the Son of the Living God' made in response to Jesus' probing question to his disciples, 'Who do you yourselves say I am?' Jesus affirms Peter's inspired answer and pronounces his future destiny, 'I tell you that you are Peter, and on this rock, I will build my church' (Matthew 16:13–19, NASB). But this illuminating moment concerning his true Messianic identity was also Jesus' cue to speak more openly about the difficult days which lay ahead. Let's read what happened next.

> *From that time on Jesus began to explain to his disciples that he must go to Jerusalem and suffer many things at the hands of the elders, the chief priests and the teachers of the law, and that he must be killed and on the third day be raised to life.*
>
> *Peter took him aside and began to rebuke him. 'Never, Lord!' he said. 'This shall never happen to you!'*
>
> *Jesus turned and said to Peter, 'Get behind me, Satan! You are a stumbling block to me; you do not have in mind the concerns of God, but merely human concerns.'*
>
> MATTHEW 16:21–23

This is a fascinating swing of events. Drawing on the prophetic threads of Isaiah, Jesus had begun to speak of his future as one in which he would endure suffering, even death, but ultimately resurrection. The disciples simply could not accept this. Peter, moments earlier, had rightly recognised Jesus as the Messiah but quickly followed it up with wrong notions about how Jesus would fulfil his Messiahship. Note the seriousness of Jesus' retort to Peter. Words to the effect of: *Get behind me, Satan! You are standing in my way. You are not thinking how God thinks. You are thinking how man thinks.*

Why so harsh?

Because the way Jesus would ultimately fulfil his mission and ascend to his throne was as important to him as his elevation to it. Chris Green, describing Peter's see-sawing responses says:

> Peter who had been called 'the rock' in the receiving of that revelation and the giving of that confession, is nonetheless a 'stumbling stone' for Christ because what he bears in his heart and mind in receiving that revelation and making that confession is *false*. Satanically false.[*]

Ouch!

Ultimately, Jesus would not let Peter, or the rest of the disciples, idolise him in these moments, because he knew it would only compromise their understanding of the true nature of a co-suffering, servant-hearted God. Despite the revelatory clarity which had come through Peter's declaration of Jesus' true Messianic identity, the disciples still had so much to learn. The following passage from St Athanasius' enduring classic, *On the Incarnation*, beautifully describes how Jesus refused to resort to worldly forms of showmanship in order to remain faithful to his divine assignment:

> The Lord did not come to make a display. He came to heal and to teach suffering men. For one who wanted to make a display the thing would have been just to appear and dazzle the beholders. But for Him who came to heal and to teach the way was not merely to dwell here, but to put Himself at the disposal of those who needed Him, and to be manifested according as they could bear it, not vitiating the value of the Divine appearing by exceeding their capacity to receive it.[**]

Jesus' rebuke to Peter is a rebuke to the church today, for, like Peter, often without realising it, we have appropriated divine revelation

---

[*] Chris EW Green, *Sanctifying Interpretation: Vocation, Holiness and Scripture, Second Edition* (CPT Press, 2020), p89.
[**] St Athanasius, *On the Incarnation* (St Vladimir's Seminary Press, 1977), p78.

and applied it to our own humanly constructed worldviews. Just as the children of Israel were not content with the leadership of their Great Deliverer, Yahweh, but hankered after a king like other nations (1 Samuel 8) we want to fashion Jesus into our version of a twenty-first century charismatic leader. Moreover, like the disciples at this stage of their spiritual development, our generation is addicted to revelatory moments yet unprepared to incarnate these inspirational soundbites into a life of sacrifice. Many pearls have been cast among swine in the Western church today as spiritual thrill-seekers bounce around churches, conferences and events, aping and idolising the latest flavour-of-the-month leader who will deliver their next fleeting shot of inspirational pleasure. There seems to be an intrinsic part of our fallen human state which aches for a mascot, someone who will represent us to validate our ideologies, and so we elevate these individuals to places in our minds that they were never supposed to occupy. And because this hero-worship is so dangerous, it drew an appropriately sharp response from Jesus.

Many years before, in some of his last words, Moses had warned the Israelites about the perils of human kings, and prophesied the day when Israel would desire such a type of leader. He cautioned about the type of behaviour they should (and should not) look for in a future king, including that he should, 'not consider himself better than his fellow Israelites' (Deuteronomy 17:14–20). If anyone had reason to consider themselves better than others, it was Jesus. But Jesus, the fulfilment of the Torah, knew this was not the type of leadership God wanted for his people. Today, too many church leaders have not followed in Jesus' footsteps. Like many of the kings which eventually came to the throne during the time of Israel's monarchy, these leaders have been seduced by the favour of man that often accompanies the favour of God. As a result, their hearts have tragically become divided. In sum, the people of God need to stop treating leaders like this. And leaders need to create cultures where this type of hype is not tolerated and actively discouraged.

UNCLE PHIL

One of the most significant conversations during my own development as an emerging leader was with my Uncle Phil. Phil was not only my uncle but the founder of our church. Bankrupted after a devastating business loss and trying to pay back his debts, Phil found a job as a coalman. Through these difficult days Phil's love for Jesus, ignited in him as a young boy, burned even brighter. Delivering coal to households in some of the poorest parts of our city, Phil found numerous opportunities to share the love of Christ with broken people. Unsure where and how to disciple these people, Phil, encouraged by his wife Jill, brought these people to his home where he began a gathered time of worship in his living room every Sunday. Raw, passionate and slightly crazy, this eclectic little community soon became known as Emmanuel Church. In the sovereignty of God, the birthing of this beautiful community coincided with my own personal faith awakening. I was seventeen years old, and Jesus had taken hold of my life after a typical teenage heartbreak experience.

Phil and I spent many nights chatting and praying, hungry for the presence of the Lord and a move of God's Spirit in our area. Phil could see my youthful zeal and made room for me to exercise my gifts in our small but burgeoning church community. As I alluded to in the previous chapter, I had a passionate desire to lead in the church in all the best and the worst possible ways. I remember earnestly saying to Phil one day: *'Phil what am I supposed to do with this desire to lead, it feels like it's consuming me, where and how can I lead more?'*

Phil, the quintessential pastor, is always encouraging. Always. Except for this time. He replied, with a shrug of the shoulders, *'I don't know what to tell you Al, because I never wanted to lead anything, I only ever wanted to serve God.'*

Ouch!

Phil hadn't intended to challenge me but what he said touched a nerve deep within. I realised in that moment, my desire to lead was driving me more than my desire to serve. As I reflected more on this, I came to realise Phil had become a great leader with considerable influence, not because he ticked all the boxes as to what our culture defines as strong leadership, but because he had been faithful to the servant-hearted way of Jesus with those God had entrusted to him. When God gave Phil a handful of people in his living room to love and disciple, he did it diligently and in the fear of the Lord. When it pleased God to give him even more, Phil just kept repeating the pattern with more servant-hearted obedience. In turn, God steadily increased the sphere of his leadership influence. Phil's 'success' was not built upon a suite of textbook leadership skills, although he possesses plenty of them, but upon his humble stewardship of what God had given him. Phil is a Level 5 leader. He has that magical mix of personal humility and steely determination which characterises great leaders, as Jim Collins' research confirmed. Phil's example stands in line with many of the 'unlikely heroes' of the biblical story, imperfect men and women who continued to give their 'yes' to God and his purposes in the world, whatever that required of them. In doing so God chose to raise them up to become some of the greatest leaders in all of history. Their lives, along with my Uncle Phil's example, pointed me to the ultimate example of servanthood.

THE FOOT-WASHING

Perhaps the most salient image of Jesus' servant nature is recorded by the Apostle John in Chapter 13 of his Gospel. The scene is the night before Jesus' crucifixion and a few hours before his betrayal. Imagine the disciples gathered in the upper room as Jesus poured out his heart to his closest friends in intimate and breathtaking vulnerability. Unlike the other gospel writers who focused their accounts of Jesus' final night on earth on the institution of the

Eucharist meal, John focuses on a different but no less powerful action which took place:

> *Jesus knew that the Father had put all things under his power, and that he had come from God and was returning to God; so he got up from the meal, took off his outer clothing, and wrapped a towel around his waist. After that, he poured water into a basin and began to wash his disciples' feet, drying them with the towel that was wrapped around him.*

JOHN 13:3–5

Despite the protests of the disciples, who knew the act of foot-washing was a task reserved for slaves, Jesus deliberately knelt before each of his friends, pouring water over their feet and drying them gently with a towel. This stunning act of humility disarmed the disciples. They were watching sovereignty incarnated in servanthood. No doubt this encounter was imprinted upon each of the disciples' hearts and minds for the rest of their lives. They had watched Jesus teach the crowds, feed thousands and heal multitudes. Now he was personally and deliberately washing each of their feet. As he knelt before the disciples, I imagine Jesus lifting his head to give an affectionate smile and offering a unique, quiet word of encouragement to each one. These young men had never felt so loved, so seen and so known.

In the light of all of this it's easy to understand why Jesus' life of servanthood is the primary way the early church remembered Jesus. Yes, those earliest Christian communities marvelled at his miracles and exorcisms, his healings and radical teachings. Yet it seems Jesus' embodiment of 'self-emptying' love was what fascinated them the most. Many of the earliest Christian writings document how the servant nature of Jesus was a central focus of the first church's times of worship. It is widely believed that the well-known words of Philippians 2, which I referenced in the introduction to this book, were actually the lyrics of one of the first hymns the early Christians would have sung together.

Who, being in very nature God,
did not consider equality with God
something to be used to his
own advantage;
rather, he made himself nothing
by taking the very nature of a
servant,
being made in human likeness.
And being found in appearance as a
man,
he humbled himself
by becoming obedient to death –
even death on a cross!
Therefore God exalted him to the
highest place
and gave him the name that is above
every name,
that at the name of Jesus every knee
should bow,
in heaven and on earth and under
the earth,
and every tongue acknowledge that
Jesus Christ is Lord,
to the glory of God the Father.

PHILIPPIANS 2:6–11

I love to imagine the early believers reflecting on the person of Jesus, their hearts enthralled by the truth that his life of sacrificial love, culminating in his brutal death on Calvary's cross, had gloriously revealed to the world the essence of servanthood at the heart of the triune God. I imagine them reflecting on how he had healed those who were seen as an inconvenience to others; how he had touched the untouchables; how he had allowed his days to be interrupted by the needs of those on the margins; how he had fed the hungry crowds;

how he had compassionately restored dignity to each image-bearer he interacted with; and how ultimately he would allow himself to be led like a little lamb to the slaughterhouse as he willingly laid down his life. Picture these fledging communities of Jesus followers, still surrounded by the dominant expressions of empire all around them, rejoicing in the truth that Jesus' life of continual outpouring had literally changed the world.

Reflecting on this passage of Scripture, Michael Gorman writes:

> Although Paul employs Philippians 2:5–8 in order to further internal unity at Philippi, it is stating the obvious to say that the first purpose of Christ's self-humbling, self-giving incarnation and death narrated in those verses was missional in a centrifugal sense: to save humanity.[*]

The lyrics of this inspired hymn take us right into the heart of what theologians refer to as God's *kenosis* nature. *Kenosis* is the Greek translation for the key word in this passage of Scripture, which in English is translated as 'emptied'. The meaning and implications of *kenosis* have been debated by theologians for centuries but 'self-emptying' is what most believe to be the truest meaning of this word. *Kenosis* is the idea that, without losing any of his divine essence, Jesus emptied himself of his divine privilege in order more fully to express who God is. As Brad Jersak explains:

> Far from giving up, hiding or hindering God's nature, we shall see that Christ's kenotic and cruciform life is the revelation par excellence of God's glory. Kenosis is not a surrender of the divine attributes; kenosis defined as self-giving or self-donation is the premier expression of God's nature – of God's love and grace – seen most clearly on the cross.[**]

* Michael J Gorman, *Becoming the Gospel: Paul, Participation and Mission* (Eerdmans, 2015), p39.
** Bradley Jersak, *A More Christlike God: A More Beautiful Gospel* (Plain Truth Ministries, 2015), p99.

In other words, Jesus' life of service reveals God does not reign by imperial power. Yes, God is Lord over all, but God reigns through *kenotic* love. God does not exercise his authority by lording it over people, God exercises his authority by laying down his life. Theologian and pastor Gregory Boyd expresses it brilliantly in words to this effect, 'When God wants to flex his omnipotent muscle, it looks like a cross.'[*]

It should come as no surprise then that the primary image the biblical authors are inspired to use in worship to celebrate the victorious Christ, who is ruling and reigning over the universe, is that of a lamb. A slain lamb (Revelation 5:6). The Passion of Christ had emphatically confirmed that this is the very nature of who God is. Jesus' life and death showed the world that God is not merely a kind of cosmic benevolent being. Rather, the divine energy at play in the inner life of the triune God is all-consuming selfless love. Always and forever, this is who God is. The slain Lamb who has conquered death and hell, the Holy One to whom the angelic beings give glory and honour: Jesus Christ our atoning sacrifice will serve us for all eternity.

> *For the Lamb at the centre of the throne*
> *   will be their shepherd;*
> *he will lead them to springs of living*
> *   water.*

REVELATION 7:17

God will shepherd us and serve us forever. Selah.[**]

---

[*] This is an adaption of what Gregory Boyd describes in Chapter 2 of his book, *The Myth of a Christian Nation: How the Quest for Political Power Is Destroying the Church* (Zondervan, 2007).
[**] This may seem hard to grasp, but see Luke 12:37.

DOWNWARD MOBILITY

It will come as no surprise then that while the New Testament esteems the role of leadership in church, it actually prefers to talk about servanthood. In fact, throughout the whole Bible the term 'leader' is only mentioned six times, but the word servant (in different forms)* is mentioned 900 times! The statistics alone make the point. Radical servanthood is at the heart of all cruciform leadership. Jesus told the disciples after he had finished washing their feet:

> *'Now that I, your Lord and Teacher, have washed your feet, you also should wash one another's feet. I have set you an example that you should do as I have done for you'*

JOHN 13:14–15

The message from Jesus was clear – in the kingdom of God, if servanthood is beneath you, leadership is beyond you. Nothing has changed. As James and John came to find out, if we want to be the kind of leader who looks like Jesus, we must start by slaying our ideals of greatness.

> He entered the world wearing swaddling clothes and exited it in the towel of a slave. Think of him whatever we may. Greatness looks different now.**

Too many leaders in the church today treat acts of service like a footnote to their leadership, regarding the more platform-centric duties as the main body of their work. But Jesus teaches us that leaders never outgrow the 'servant-stage' of leadership. Leadership is servanthood. Servanthood is leadership in the kingdom of God.

* The main Hebrew word for 'servant' in the Old Testament is *ebed* and the main Greek words for 'servant' or 'slave' in the New Testament are *doulos* and *diakonos*.
** John Ortberg, *Who Is This Man? The Unpredictable Impact of the Inescapable Jesus* (Zondervan, 2012), p86.

Jesus did not just fulfil a certain quota of servant-type chores as some kind of token gesture. Jesus was a servant. Therefore, as followers of Jesus we must ask the Spirit of God to transform our very nature into that of a servant, rather than thinking the odd occasional gesture of service will do the job. As Richard Foster points out, there is a difference between choosing to serve and choosing to be a servant.[*] The latter is the lifelong choice Henri Nouwen beautifully describes as downward mobility:

> The story of our salvation stands radically over and against the philosophy of upward mobility. The great paradox which Scripture reveals to us is that real and total freedom is only found through downward mobility. The Word of God came down to us and lived among us as a slave. The divine way is indeed the downward way.[**]

In time the Apostles did become wonderful examples of this downward way. Following in their rabbi's footsteps their lives inspire us to push against the grain of 'upward mobility' which characterised 'the spirit of the age' then as much as it still does now.

But how did they learn this? And how are we actually transformed from people who occasionally serve into actual Christlike servants? To answer this question, we need to return to John 13 for some clues in the treasure of detail found in verses 3–4.

THE INNER GARMENT

Jesus knew that the Father had put all things under his power, and that he had come from God and was returning to God; so he got up from the meal, took off his outer clothing, and wrapped a towel around his waist.

JOHN 13:3–4

* Richard Foster, *Celebration of Discipline* (John Murray Press, 2008).
** Henri JM Nouwen, *The Selfless Way of Christ: Downward Mobility and the Spiritual life* (Darton, Longman & Todd, 2007).

The brilliant Catholic theologian Roland Rolheiser, in his book *Sacred Fire*, argues that the details John includes here hold a kind of mystical significance. Rolheiser believes the fact that John tells us Jesus took off his outer garment and wrapped himself in the apron of service speaks to something beyond this physical action. Metaphorically John wants us to realise that as Jesus takes off his outer garment he was willingly and vulnerably allowing the disciples to see himself dressed only in his inner garment. Rolheiser believes the inner garment speaks to Jesus' most intimate self,[*] that part of him that knew 'he had come from God and was returning to God' (John 13:3). Rolheiser believes John wants us to realise that the source of Jesus' radical servanthood was his secure understanding of sonship. How else could Jesus fulfil this servile act so effortlessly, without any sense of pride, competitiveness or resentment? Simply because Jesus knew who he was. And Jesus knew whose he was. In taking off his 'inner garment' he had revealed his truest essence – a beloved son living in perfect loving communion with the Father.

Jesus' act of foot-washing emphasises a vital characteristic of cruciform leaders – the purest expression of servanthood flows from the fullest sense of sonship and daughterhood. Perfect love releases us to serve others indiscriminately and without fear or pride. Like Jesus, cruciform leaders are called to take off their 'outer garments' – to deny themselves, to choose to forgo personal dignity and privilege in order to reveal to those we serve an 'inner garment' of self-giving, vulnerable love. Rolheiser concludes:

> Our inner garment is the image and likeness of God inside us, and when we are in touch with this, we can find the strength to wash one another's feet across any divide.[**]

[*] Roland Rolheiser, *Sacred Fire: A Vision for a Deeper Human and Christian Maturity* (Random House, 2017), pp124–125.
[**] *Ibid.*

The problem we have is that, unlike Jesus, we are complex humans twisted by sin and therefore tempted to serve others in our outer garment rather than our inner one. This type of serving is what Richard Foster calls 'self-righteous service'* – on the surface, we may look like we are serving others but in reality, we are serving to be seen by others. We must first of all be stripped of pride, judgmentalism, superiority and selfishness before the 'inner garment' of our new identity in Christ can be fully expressed. Authority in the hands of a leader not broken by his or her own sense of fragility is dangerous.

I am embarrassed to tell you the number of times I have succumbed to self-righteous service because my yearning for the acclaim of others was so strong. But in God's long-suffering grace, I am slowly learning to take off my 'outer garment' and serve others in hiddenness and with anonymity. To help me in this, the Holy Spirit often reminds me of those wise and piercing words from Uncle Phil, *'I never wanted to lead anything Al, I just wanted to serve God and others.'*

This is the path of relinquishment which all cruciform leaders must take. A willingness to take off our 'outer garment', to relinquish our pretence and false self in the presence of the Lord so we can be healed in the Father's love. Then we will be able to confidently reveal our inner garment of 'belovedness' to those we serve, washing their feet with joy-infused love.

THE CORINTHIANISATION OF LEADERSHIP

Rolheiser's treatment of John 13 doesn't stop here, though. He goes on to explain why he believes John's Gospel focuses on Jesus' foot-washing as distinct from the other gospel authors, who chose to emphasise Jesus' final Passover meal with his disciples. Given John

* Richard Foster, *Celebration of Discipline*, Study Guide Edition (Hodder & Stoughton, 1999), p162.

outlived all the other disciples and most likely wrote his gospel approximately sixty years after Jesus, Rolheiser writes:

> by the time the Gospel of John was written, there were already, not unlike today, a variety of practices around the Eucharist and all kinds of disagreements about it. Hence, what is highlighted in John's Gospel about the Last Supper is not the institution of the Eucharist with bread and wine, but one of the major meanings of the Eucharist, namely, a reaching across distances that divide us, through the basin and the towel.[*]

Rolheiser's thesis stacks up when we reflect on the fact that in his first letter to the Corinthians, Paul clearly addresses tensions around the Lord's Supper within the church there. Considering this letter was written well before John's Gospel (at least thirty years)[**] we can surmise John's focus on Jesus' foot-washing would have been building on previous apostolic correctives to these churches around their stewardship of the Lord's Supper.

Let's remind ourselves about what was going on in the church in Corinth to help us understand the essence of this correction and the true spirit of the meal Paul and John were calling their first churches back to. Ironically, the Corinthian church possessed some pretty impressive characteristics – strong preaching and teaching gifts and a vitality in the area of spiritual gifts. Yet it had also developed a number of strikingly un-Christlike traits. Along with their overemphasis on glossolalia, arrogant leadership and lack of concern for the poor, it was their handling of the Eucharist which was deeply troubling to the Apostle Paul. Like many of the first churches, the believers in Corinth practised the Lord's Supper often by sharing a full meal together. Usually, the church would have met in the home of one of the wealthier members of the

---

[*] Ronald Rolheiser, *Sacred Fire*, p122.
[**] Most theologians agree Paul's letters to the Corinthians were written somewhere between AD 54–56 and John's Gospel AD 90–94.

congregation and each person would have brought their own food. It had been reported that the wealthier members were bringing disproportionate amounts of food for themselves compared to others in attendance. Their over-indulgence highlighted that the poorer members had little to eat or drink, which in turn meant they were often reduced to the role of spectators as the wealthier believers wined and dined. Into this context, Paul brought a strong rebuke to the Corinthians:

> *Or do you despise the church of God by humiliating those who have nothing? What shall I say to you? Shall I praise you? Certainly not in this matter!*

1 CORINTHIANS 11:22

For the Apostles the good news of the gospel worth celebrating and protecting was that Jesus had dismantled the pyramid of worldly leadership and that through the Holy Spirit a new countercultural family of equal sons and daughters was being formed. The inequality on show in the Corinthian church was the complete antithesis of the cruciform way and everything the Eucharist was supposed to represent. Further, what becomes clear from the rest of Paul's letters to Corinth is that this problem stemmed from a distinct lack of cruciform leadership. A worldly influence, not wholly dissimilar to our contemporary context, had infected the young church. David Starling calls this influence 'The Corinthianisation of Leadership'[*] and defines it as: 'the uncritical absorption and imitation of the mindset and power-structures that were prominent and influential in first-century Roman Corinth.'[**]

A little more context is important. Corinth was an influential and wealthy Greek city under the rule of the Romans. The Roman

[*] David Starling, *UnCorinthian Leadership: Thematic Reflections on 1 Corinthians* (Eugene: Cascade, 2014), p12.
[**] David Starling in Scot McKnight's book, *Pastor Paul, Nurturing a Culture of Christoformity in the Church* (Brazos Press, 2019), p153.

way of honour which focused heavily on patronage and status heavily influenced the cities within its empire. Both Greek and Roman models of leadership therefore had structural impacts on the associations which existed within Corinth. In his book, *Pastor Paul*, Scot McKnight explains how this influenced the daily way of life in Corinth:

> This path was competitive to the core, and once there, one marked one's status in what one wore, in one's occupation, in where one sat at public events and banquets, and how one got along in the legal system.[*]

In other words, the influential and wealthy in the house churches of Corinth had established a party system of allegiance, influenced by the dominant cultural traits of patronage and 'upward mobility' they were surrounded by. This gave rise to a number of personality cults which in turn meant a kind of factionalism began to control the Corinthian church: 'For when one says, "I follow Paul," and another, "I follow Apollos"' (1 Corinthians 3:4). Unfortunately, it appears that for a number of the believers in Corinth a person's status and influence still mattered more to them than their Christlikeness. Members of this church, driven by a competitive spirit and motivated by the leadership personalities they were associated with, damaged the health of this young church dramatically.

RESISTING THE CORINTHIANISATION OF LEADERSHIP

It is easy to apply the New Testament's account of the problems in Corinth to our contemporary context. Many of the issues we face today in the church are symptomatic of this diseased type of leadership. In acquiescing with the surrounding culture, the church

* Scot McKnight, *Pastor Paul*, p152.

has been seduced by the cult of celebrity and leaders have become motivated by popularity and status. McKnight writes, 'the pastor as celebrity, then, is the world at work in the pastor's heart and the congregation's soul.'* Too many leaders today are driven by the need to be seen and who to be seen with. We are quick to identify a narcissist these days, yet we can miss the shadowy narcissistic tendencies in our own hearts. The spirit of the age has infiltrated our churches, and we must learn how to drive it out. How do we do this in a culture obsessed with self? How do we reverse such a deeply worrying trend in our churches? Let's conclude this chapter by exploring the Apostle Paul's response to the Corinthian problem for an inspiring 'cruciform' answer to these questions.

It's important to understand Paul was not only dealing with the complex pastoral and theological issues arising out of the church in Corinth. To make matters worse, he also had to face extreme hostility as the believers there had completely turned against him. A number of visiting teachers had come to Corinth after Paul's first visit and completely eviscerated him. These 'super apostles', as Paul sarcastically called them, were self-aggrandising public speakers. On the face of it, they were impressive charismatic communicators, but in reality, they fronted only a veneer of spirituality. In truth, they were more interested in their own publicity and lining their own pockets – the kind of 'hired hands' Jesus had warned his disciples about years before. What was so damaging for the church in Corinth, though, was that these 'super apostles' sought to systematically dismantle Paul's influence and reputation among the believers there. They slandered the very core of his ministry, called his gifts into question, claimed he was of weak and contemptible speech, and even attacked his physical appearance and personal integrity (2 Corinthians 10:10). McKnight describes what Paul endured as '… nothing less than verbal crucifixion.'** This was first century cancel culture on steroids.

* Scot McKnight, *Pastor Paul*, p153.
** *Ibid.*

As we read through Paul's second letter to the Corinthians it is clear Paul was deeply wounded by what had gone on in his absence. Yet Paul's response was Christlike in every way, powerfully subverting the Corinthian leadership culture and, as such, providing us with an outstanding example of the transformative power of cruciform leadership. McKnight continues:

> The Apostle's strategy was to surrender to them, to turn leadership upside down, and to form a theology of leadership rooted in the life of Jesus, the cross and the resurrection-ascension.[*]

In a culture of boasting, Paul chose not to list his achievements. In a culture of self-promotion, Paul chose not to defend himself. In a culture of competitiveness, Paul chose not to win. In a culture where gifted communicators and philosophers accepted patronage from the wealthy and influential individuals, Paul, while stressing he had every right to receive renumeration for his efforts among the Corinthian church, chose not to take anything so he would not 'hinder the gospel of Christ' (1 Corinthians 9:12). On the contrary, Paul degraded his eloquence and his skills. He told the believers in Corinth that he had not shown up among them 'wise in man's eyes' but in weakness; not with impressive words but in the power of God (1 Corinthians 2:4). He reminded them it was this 'Jesus-way' of servant-heartedness and sacrificial love which had, in the wisdom of God, triumphed over the principalities and powers. Paul's formation in the way of Jesus enabled him to be completely vulnerable before the Corinthian church, using the 'stripping' he had endured personally as an opportunity to reveal his 'inner garment' to his sons and daughters in the Lord. Paul came to realise that Christ's strength could be more fully revealed through his weakness. Following in the footsteps of Jesus he chose to exercise an authority not from above but from below. And this was not just a one-off. Throughout the

* Scot McKnight, *Pastor Paul*, p156.

rest of the New Testament writings, we witness a man who had fully embraced the downward mobility at the heart of *kenotic* love. Paul risked his life on multiple occasions as he travelled to be with his children in the Lord, enduring all sorts of persecutions along the way. He worked with his own hands to provide for himself so as not to be a burden to the churches – something the false apostles would never have dreamed of doing. He gave himself to constant prayer for the churches to the extent that he groaned like a mother in childbirth for Christ to be formed in them. And when he came to live among them, he shared not just the gospel with them but his whole life.*

I imagine Paul would be aghast at many of the elements now entrenched in the leadership culture of the Western church today. He would loathe the competitive spirit among many leaders and their obsession to 'make it' on the speaking rosters at large Christian events or attract the most followers online. He would despise the branding of Christian ministries in a leader's own name and the self-promoting propaganda that we have normalised in the wider Evangelical Industrial Complex. He would flip the tables of the 'green rooms' we have created at our conferences where headline preachers are treated like celebrities. He would be horrified by the huge sums of money many speakers are paid because they are deemed charismatic communicators while at the same time demonstrating questionable moral integrity. He would be angered by the hierarchal structures of our churches which monopolise power around one dominant, controlling figure at the top. He would challenge the somehow contemporary distorted view that good leadership requires a safe distance from those we are called to lead.

I am convinced Paul would call us back to Jesus Christ, the way of the cross and a life of *kenosis*.

---

* See 1 Thessalonians 2:8.

THE CORINTHIAN WAY OR THE CRUCIFORM WAY

As we close this chapter, I want to suggest we are living in a critical moment in history when leaders of God's church have a decision to make – will we choose the cruciform way of leadership or the Corinthian way of leadership? Quite frankly, I don't believe the world needs any more famous speakers. But I'm convinced it needs more Christlike cruciform leaders.

Jim Collins helped us understand that even in the corporate world, two thousand years since Jesus lived, people respond best to 'Level 5' leaders. This is what the world is crying out for. Leaders who forget about their own greatness and choose the *kenotic* way of love, laying down their lives for others. Are we willing to repent, humble ourselves and slay our ideals of recognition and status? Are we willing to accept that leadership in the kingdom of God was never a call to be on the stage but a continual outpouring in a life of service?

'Can we drink this cup?'

PRACTISING THE CRUCIFORM WAY

Consider the questions and readings below in discussion, reflection, journalling and prayer.

ONE:

'You don't know what you are asking,' Jesus said to them. 'Can you drink the cup I am going to drink?'

MATTHEW 20:22

Revisit Matthew 20:20–28 describing the request that the mother of James and John made for her sons to sit on Jesus' throne with him, and reflect on Jesus' response in verse 22.

- Take some time to prayerfully imagine Jesus responding to *you* with these words, *'[Insert your name] can you drink the cup I am going to drink?'* Allow yourself time to reflect on what this question means for you.
- Journal what this provokes within you or discuss with your group.

TWO:

Jesus knew that the Father had put all things under his power, and that he had come from God and was returning to God; so he got up from the meal, took off his outer clothing, and wrapped a towel around his waist. After that, he poured water into a basin and began to wash his disciples' feet.

JOHN 13:3–5

Reflect on this passage describing Jesus washing his disciples' feet.

- How do Jesus' actions remind us that *'the purest expression of servanthood flows from the fullest sense of sonship and daughterhood*'? Write your thoughts in your journal, or discuss with your group.

- Recall how Rolheiser speaks of the 'inner garment' that Jesus reveals in making himself vulnerable and serving as foot-washer. How does this challenge our understanding of leadership today? Do you also have an inner garment?

THREE:

Who, being in very nature God, did not consider equality with God something to be grasped, but made himself nothing...

PHILIPPIANS 2:6–7 (NIV 1984)

Revisit Philippians 2:6–11, and reflect specifically on these verses considering Jesus' cruciform approach towards leadership.

- How does Jesus' life of *kenosis* challenge our leadership and understanding of 'greatness' today?

CHAPTER 4

A TESTED APPRENTICE

*Then Jesus was led by the Spirit into the wilderness to be tempted
by the devil.*

MATTHEW 4:1

The year was 1998. I was eighteen and preparing for my final school exams. The focus of my teachers and friends was on revision, planning for university and getting the best career advice possible at this critical threshold of life. I had summoned up just about enough enthusiasm to study for exams, but my real focus was on responding to the whisper of the Spirit – a gentle but firm instruction to consider something different to the generally expected next step of university. Instead, I sensed an invitation from God to give him the next year of my life, in the form of a gap year – a year which would involve leaving everything familiar to find God for myself. A 'homebird' raised in a close-knit family and friendship circle, this was a big deal for me. Yet through the Spirit of God, the same ancient words God had spoken to Abram echoed in my own heart, 'Go from your country, your people and your father's household to the land I will show you' (Genesis 12:1).

Growing up in a Christian family, I had spent my whole life thinking of myself as a Christian, but it was only the previous year when everything I knew in my head had crashed gloriously into my heart. Now, consumed by an insatiable desire to know Jesus more personally and passionately, the idea of taking a gap year felt like the natural next step of obedience. South Africa was the destination that drew me, and became the place where I would volunteer for the wonderful ministry of Youth for Christ.

Rather idealistically, I expected my gap year to be an intimate, contemplative journey into sweet communion with Jesus – I pictured myself walking along a beach as the Lord whispered profound insights into my soul, or sitting meditating by candlelight, annotating my Bible as I listened to ambient worship music. Instead, I found myself serving in a street-kids' shelter on the outskirts of Johannesburg, ten thousand miles from home, the only white person in an African-Indian township, sleeping in a tin-roofed outhouse, surviving on mealie pap and chicken feet. Blindsided by culture shock and unrelenting homesickness in the first few months, I also had to try somehow to process the harrowing levels of pain, abuse and brokenness the street kids had suffered.

It was intense.

Yet amid all this emotional and mental disorientation, there was something even more troubling I had to face – the crushing realisation of how little I actually knew God. An uncomfortable reality was unfolding before me – for eighteen years my knowledge of God had been intertwined with those who had helped form my identity – my parents, my wider family, my friends and my church. Now, stripped of the people and reference points that had shaped my life and my sense of meaning and belonging in the world, I was realising that the roots of God's life in mine were not as deeply formed as I had thought. My knowledge of God, for the most part, had only been by way of association. Uprooted and utterly bewildered, I was entering my first wilderness schooling, a testing I hadn't expected. I didn't realise it at the time, but this was the beginning of my apprenticeship into Christian leadership.

BEARING THE YOKE IN OUR YOUTH

One passage of Scripture that anchored me during that year was in Lamentations:

> *Because of the LORD's great love we are*
> *   not consumed,*
> * for his compassions never fail.*
> *They are new every morning;*
> * great is your faithfulness.*
> *I say to myself, 'The LORD is my portion;*
> * therefore I will wait for him.'*
> *The LORD is good to those whose hope*
> *   is in him,*
> * to the one who seeks him;*
> *it is good to wait quietly*
> * for the salvation of the LORD.*
> *It is good for a man to bear the yoke*
> * while he is young.*

LAMENTATIONS 3:22–27

These are well-known verses, and verses 22 and 23 in particular, celebrating God's never-ending faithfulness and compassion so poetically, are often quoted in our worship liturgies. What is important to recognise, however, is that this passage of Scripture is buried in the middle of a long narrative of bitter lament. Written during the time of Israel's exile, these verses lift the reader out of the language of loss, heartbreak and disorientation of the preceding chapters. The prophet* confirms that even in times of the very greatest testing, we can experience God's never-failing and daily-renewing mercy. During my own exile, thousands of miles from home, these verses began to slowly anchor my fragile soul in God's presence. I had to learn to 'wait quietly on the Lord', to receive a fresh deposit of his mercy each morning.

---

* Tradition holds that Lamentations was written by the prophet Jeremiah.

Yet it was the words of verse 27 that imprinted themselves upon my heart most profoundly: 'It is good for a man to bear the yoke while he is young.'

This may seem somewhat strange at first reading, but it resonated deeply with me in those bewildering days. I was young. I was naïve. I assumed because I had given up a year of my life to leave everything and serve God that it shouldn't be so hard! Surely, I didn't deserve a gap year which was so downright gruelling? I could be at home, like any normal nineteen-year-old, having fun with my friends who were heading to university. Or, at the very least I could be experiencing a slightly more glamorous gap year. Yet, here I was, enduring horrendous homesickness and a crisis of faith in the most intense of environments. All the ideals I had formed about how exhilarating this year would be for the development of my faith had been smashed.

Yet I knew I had to stick it out. And these words, 'It is good for a man to bear the yoke while he is young' would not leave me.

Every time I was preparing to throw the towel in, every time I was tempted to phone my mum and dad and ask them to get me a flight back home, these words would come back to me. I began to understand that I was being tested. More than that, I slowly began to realise why I was being tested. The reason I was experiencing the agony of 'the unknown' was so that in the end I could become truly known. The reason my other 'loves' and attachments were being exposed, thousands of miles from home, was so that I could experience a depth of love none of those could ever be a substitute for. I had to be tested in an environment where every source of security in my life had been removed in order to truly discover the One who would never leave me.

So, at night when all the kids were in the shelter sleeping, I would walk outside, look up into the starry African sky and simply whisper the words, *'Abba, Father.'* Those words, spoken from the depths of my spirit, released in me a new stream of intimate Father-knowing. I was nineteen and I was meeting with my Maker. The darkness of the night sky mirrored the deep loneliness I was experiencing in my soul. And yet, just as the stars lit up that sky, God pierced the darkness of my soul with shards of light, filling the emptiness with the fullness of his love. Night after night, in this hidden place far from home, the Spirit of God witnessed to the most primal part of my being, and I have never been the same again. I was being tested but I was learning to trust the process. I was being led into beloved sonship.

THE WILDERNESS

Reflecting back on this season of my life, I now realise that I shouldn't have been surprised how difficult this period would be. Throughout the Bible we discover how all the women and men who make up the great cloud of witnesses endured a testing season in their lives which prepared them for all that lay ahead. Abraham, Jacob, Moses, Ruth, Hannah, David, Esther, Peter. I think particularly of the Apostle Paul, after his dramatic supernatural encounter on the Damascus Road, spending much of the next three years in the Arabian desert (Galatians 1:17–18), most likely alone, and then enduring another ten years of rejection, failure, and, most likely, excommunication from his community (Galatians 2:1). The biblical story reveals how seasons of wilderness are the painful gift God allows his sons and daughters to walk through because God is so committed to making us like himself.

During that time, I came to realise God had taken the prayers I had prayed and the songs I had sung in the months building up to my gap year much more seriously than I had. In my journal I had written, *'God I want to give you my whole life, I want to serve you with everything I am.'* I had sung wholeheartedly that I wanted to live all my life for Jesus, and to surrender all my ambitions, my hopes and plans for the future, into his hands.

The reality was that God's plans and purposes for my life were beyond my wildest imaginings. He knew the only way I could become who he created me to be was if I was changed, shaped, moulded, enlarged. I needed the 'hidden' work that can only happen in the wilderness to take place inside of me if I was going to fulfil the glorious destiny God had for my life.

The good news is Jesus never calls us to follow him into anything he has not already experienced or endured. The Gospels reveal Jesus as our model for wilderness endurance. Matthew 4:1 says, 'Then Jesus was led by the Spirit into the wilderness to be tempted by the devil.' It's important to note the context of this verse – it comes directly after Jesus' baptism. Now pay attention to the structure of this verse: 'led by the Spirit … into the wilderness … to be tempted by the devil.' Sometimes the Spirit leads us to places we do not expect him to.

As Matthew goes on to describe Jesus' wilderness experience, he presents Jesus to us as the fulfilment of Israel's story, overcoming where Adam had failed in the Garden of Eden and where the children of Israel had failed in the wilderness. But Matthew also wants us to realise that Jesus identified with all the temptations and sufferings each of us will experience through our own wilderness sojourns. The writer to the Hebrews picks up this theme stating that Jesus learned obedience through his own wilderness experiences:

> *Son though he was, he learned obedience from what he suffered and, once made perfect, he became the source of eternal salvation for all who obey him.*

HEBREWS 5:8–9

These are staggering verses. Through the testing ground of wilderness suffering, Jesus the Son of God, in the fullness of his humanity, provided humankind with an example of how to endure the wilderness seasons of our lives in order that we might become all we were destined to be. John Stott rightly reminds us how we need to pay serious attention to this, 'if suffering was the means by which the sinless Christ became mature, so much the more do we need it in our sinfulness.'*

What type of 'wilderness' seasons do we go through? Unlike Jesus, wilderness seasons for us are often associated with the consequences of disobedience or patterns of sin. But they should not always be understood as a place of punishment. Rather, the wilderness can be understood as a place of opportunity. A place the Spirit leads us into. A season of life we are called to endure when our false attachments are revealed and where new patterns of holy love can be scribed upon our hearts. A space where something new can be formed in us, all part of the preparation for the great inheritance that lies ahead for us. In the narrative of Scripture, the wilderness is not understood as our final destination. God's leading of the children of Israel out of Egypt is paradigmatic for us. A great inheritance is ours to lay hold of beyond the wilderness. Yet there is no way around the wilderness. All true cruciform leaders go through it, if we are going to be entrusted to steward authority in the kingdom of God.

Reflecting on my gap year and the many years of ministry experience since, I have come to realise God will not patronise his children. He doesn't comfort us with platitudes or clichés for the sake of making us feel better about ourselves. God's parenting is not the helicopter style of the twenty-first century Western world – flying in whenever we encounter difficulty. He is gentler than you could ever imagine but he will never indulge us by diluting his love into mere 'mollycoddling'. God's love is a consuming fire. He is zealous for us and for our destiny. As Chris Green says, 'God is not jealous of us', but 'jealous for us, desiring above all things for us to know the fullness of the joy intended for us in Christ.'** The truth is, God is more committed to the process of you becoming like him

*John Stott, *The Cross of Christ* (InterVarsity Press, 1986), p295.
** Chris EW Green, *Sanctifying Interpretation*, p106.

than you are, which means he will never compromise the process of formation to get you there.

Since my gap year I have lived through a number of other wilderness experiences; seasons of struggle, grief and disappointment more difficult than I could have ever imagined. Yet as a naïve teenager, hidden away in a street kids' shelter in one of the most dangerous cities on the earth, I learned lessons about God, myself and leadership which would stay with me for the rest of my life. I discovered a knowledge of God and with that a holy resilience no seminary or university could ever have taught me. This revelation has helped me endure excruciatingly painful seasons of life and ministry. In short, I would never be the person I am today without the gift of wilderness.

SHOW YOURSELF APPROVED

The Apostle James, the brother of Jesus, wrote to the churches under his care and said, 'Consider it pure joy, my brothers and sisters, whenever you face trials of many kinds, because you know that the testing of your faith produces perseverance' (James 1:2–3). James, along with the first Apostles, wanted to encourage the believers of the early church because he knew everyone would at some point endure testing of 'many kinds'. Yet, building on their experience as Jesus' disciples, the Apostles also promoted a period of testing, particularly for leaders. Could it be that they had become aware of how potentially destructive they could have been as leaders, had Jesus not taken the time to shape and challenge them?

To his young apprentice, Timothy, Paul said:

Do your best to present yourself to God as one approved, a worker who does not need to be ashamed and who correctly handles the word of truth.

2 TIMOTHY 2:15

And when it came to Timothy appointing leaders in the churches, Paul was even more explicit, 'And let them also be tested first; then let them serve … ' (1 Timothy 3:10, ESV).

Interestingly, the word 'approved' was the same word used in Paul's day to describe the practice of 'testing' metals in order to measure their purity. Paul wanted Timothy to see how the characteristics of a leader's lifestyle would be the 'proof' of whether they qualified for leadership or not. Encouraging Timothy to present himself as one 'approved' was his way of saying to Timothy: 'Let the people you lead bear witness to the fruit of your formation, the visible results of the testing you have gone through.' Nothing less than authentic Christlikeness would do.

Paul was, of course, talking from experience. After Paul had planted and established one of the first churches in Thessalonica, he wrote to them months later saying:

> On the contrary, we speak as those approved by God to be entrusted with the gospel. We are not trying to please people but God, who tests our hearts.

1 THESSALONIANS 2:4

Notice that word 'approved' again. Paul had lived by this principle of 'provenness' before his churches for many years. He wanted his churches to respect his leadership authority, not because he was impressive and popular but because he had undergone a sober assessment before God. This assessment was the process of spiritual formation he had submitted to, under the guidance of the Holy Spirit, shepherded by other mature leaders, to 'prove' genuine Christlikeness. Paul goes on to describe to the believers in Thessalonica more specifically the type of fruit this process should produce.

> Surely you remember, brothers and sisters, our toil and hardship; we worked night and day in order not to be a burden to anyone while we

preached the gospel of God to you. You are witnesses, and so is God, of how holy, righteous and blameless we were among you who believed.

Through all the trials and triumphs Paul had experienced before the Thessalonian church, his motives had been 'proven' worthy. The evidence? A 'holy, righteous and blameless' life. Now Paul wanted all those he was raising up into positions of leadership to follow this pattern.

Timothy was encouraged to go through this same sober assessment, committing himself to the refining work of the Spirit. Wisdom had taught Paul this process could not be rushed and so he advised Timothy to take his time bringing people into leadership. Therefore, 'let them also be tested first; then let them serve' (1 Timothy 3:10, ESV).

We will discover the core elements of this testing process below – context, character, capacity, charism and commission – but first, to highlight the importance of this principle of 'provenness' further, it's worthwhile going back in the biblical narrative to a strange story in the book of Exodus concerning Aaron's two sons Nadab and Abihu.

NADAB AND ABIHU

Aaron, the brother of Moses, had been called by God to be the High Priest of Israel and his sons were given the privilege of serving alongside their father in the Tabernacle. Moses, under the Lord's command, had prepared Aaron and his sons thoroughly for their ministry, anointing them and setting them apart for the Lord on behalf of the children of Israel. They were leaders chosen by God to reflect his own nature so there could be no room for entitlement or pride. The terms were clear. With this awesome privilege came great responsibility: 'Even the priests, who approach the LORD, must consecrate themselves, or the LORD will break out against them' (Exodus 19:22).

Following the pattern God had commanded them for presenting sacrifices, Aaron's sons had the role of guarding the altar. If they did so faithfully, the fire of God's presence would come upon the sacrifice, consuming every part of it (Leviticus 9:24). This would serve as a powerful revelation of God's favour and acceptance of the Israelites' sacrifice.

Unfortunately, two of Aaron's sons, Nadab and Abihu, did not pay careful heed to God's instructions. The consequences, as the verses below describe, were fatal.

> *Aaron's sons Nadab and Abihu took their censers, put fire in them and added incense; and they offered unauthorised fire before the LORD, contrary to his command. So, fire came out from the presence of the LORD and consumed them, and they died before the LORD.*

LEVITICUS 10:1–2

It's hard to deduce the exact reasons why Nadab and Abihu's wrongdoing resulted in such catastrophic consequences. God had explicitly said concerning the altar 'You shall not offer unauthorised incense on it' (Exodus 30:9, ESV). The word 'unauthorised' here has also been translated as 'alien' or 'strange'. We are left to conclude that Nadab and Abihu didn't follow God's pattern wholeheartedly and their act of worship did not flow from a place of intimate reverence for God but from the place of entitlement and presumption. This was an offering of 'strange fire'.

This story points to other incidents throughout the Bible of individuals who made mistakes which, on the surface, look like they led to disproportionate consequences. Moses' striking of the rock (Numbers 20:6–12); Saul's presumptuous sacrifice (1 Samuel 13:7–14); David's transportation of the Ark back to Jerusalem on a cart (2 Samuel 6:1–11); Peter's declaration that he would not allow Christ to suffer (Matthew 16:21–23); Ananias and Sapphira's 'white lie' about their property dealings (Acts 5:1–11). All of these decisions resulted in severe consequences for the respective individuals. Studying these individual incidents in Scripture, I came to realise a common denominator. In each case the leader(s) acted in ways which, at face value, appeared to be in God's name, for the purposes of God's kingdom, but underneath some form of motivation for self-promotion loomed large – their own craving for approval, a strong impulse to maintain control, a need to appear more godly than they really were. Using God's name to prop up your own agenda. This is the essence of strange fire. God does not like it.

Within the current leadership crisis of the Western church today we may not be witnessing the extreme consequences Nadab and Abihu experienced but we are witnessing the tragic results of too many leaders offering 'strange fire'. As selfish ambition, entitled attitudes, human control and abuses of power are being laid bare, we are being reminded that when leaders use their positions of influence for their own gain in God's name, God will act, particularly in those situations when power is being used to use and abuse others. This is why cruciform leaders should understand their wilderness seasons as a gift. It's in our own best interests to be tested. We are capable of doing too much harm. The extent of our brokenness and our propensity towards pride is much greater than we often think it is. Cruciform leaders therefore understand the *daily* need to join with the psalmist and say:

> *Search me, God, and know my heart;*
>   *test me and know my anxious*
>   *thoughts.*
> *See if there is any offensive way in me,*
>   *and lead me in the way everlasting.*

PSALM 139:23–24

I remember a time in my late twenties when increasing opportunities to lead and preach began to come my way, both within my own church and further afield. On one hand, being noticed and wanted by others felt good. On the other hand, though, I had become aware of the moral failure of a number of significant Christians leaders. Witnessing the damage this had done on multiple levels shook me significantly. I was conscious of the shadows lurking in my own heart. I didn't like it, but I also didn't want to admit it. I had an overwhelming experience of the fear of the Lord at this time, and a sobering reminder that one day I would stand before God and give an account of my leadership.* I felt like I was being tested. Again. Called to die. Again. As I sat before the Lord, I found myself praying these words:

> 'God I want to serve you all my life. I want to do great things for you. So much of me feels born to change the world. But I am acutely aware of how I could mess this up and hurt a lot of people. So please, as much as I desire more of the opportunities coming my way, don't give me anything beyond what you can trust me with. I trust my life into your hands – please only give me what you have given me grace to steward humbly and faithfully.'

It was such a hard prayer to pray. I knew at the time it would mean certain opportunities would pass me by. I knew it would mean I wouldn't be elevated in the sight of others as quickly as I wanted to be. I knew it would mean watching others go ahead of me. At times over the years, I have even regretted praying that prayer. But twenty years later I am so thankful to God that he challenged me to relinquish my need for recognition. I knew these wise words from Martyn Lloyd-Jones were for me, 'the worst thing that can happen to a man is to succeed before he is ready'**

Leaders of the church of Jesus Christ are nothing less than God's ambassadors – under-shepherds of the Great Shepherd, servants who represent God's name and God's nature. It's the most awesome privilege to be entrusted with the care of God's church. But make no mistake, this is God's church. It is Jesus' bride. And he is a jealous lover. Jesus reminded us emphatically that the triune God cares too

---

* Consider Hebrews 13:7.
** This is quoted often by RT Kendall and is sourced from his book, *Holy Fire: A Balanced, Biblical Look at the Holy Spirit's Work in Our Lives* (Charisma House, 2014), p8.

much for those he has entrusted to our care to allow us to take advantage of them for our own fame or gain.

> *... when you receive the childlike on my account, it's the same as receiving me. But if you give them a hard time, bullying or taking advantage of their simple trust, you'll soon wish you hadn't. You'd be better off dropped in the middle of the lake with a millstone around your neck.*

MATTHEW 18:5–7 (MSG)

Nadab and Abihu found out the hard way the mandate of leadership in God's house is not to be messed with. The stakes are too high. With great privilege comes great responsibility. Those who teach and lead will be judged more strictly (James 3:1). God does not expect leaders to be perfect or sinless, but he does expect us to work hard to keep our hearts pure and to hold our calling in the fear of the Lord so we can be Christlike examples to the people under our care. When we stand before Jesus, the questions he will ask us will have nothing to do with our platform or profile. Rather, following quickly after the question 'Do you love me?' we looked at in Chapter 2, will come a question about the spiritual health of those he entrusted into our care. How will you answer? How much has your life and leadership contributed to them becoming like Christ? How have you loved them and laid your life down for them? How did you prefer them over your own best interests? Were you more concerned about them fulfilling their destiny than you were of your own career trajectory? When I think of the challenging nature of these questions, I find myself immensely grateful for the times of testing I have gone through. I give thanks to God for those seasons of hiddenness, where my motives and intentions have been refined in the crucible of suffering, as the fear of the Lord gripped my heart, admonishing me and driving me to my knees, to relinquish my sense of independence and control at the foot of the cross.

IMPORTANT KEYS IN THE TESTING PROCESS

I want to take the remainder of this chapter to explore four main elements of the testing process of leadership which I believe are consistent with a biblical understanding of Christian leadership: context, character, capacity and charism. My hope is that this will help provide helpful language and a framework for church leadership teams to use as they seek to discern whether emerging leaders have shown themselves 'approved'.

1. CONTEXT (LOCAL CHURCH)

It's no secret that twenty-first century Western society is defined, among other things, by radical individualism and image-obsessed performance. The more shocking thing is how far this culture has permeated the Western church. As a result, leadership today is often discerned through the lens of gifting, stage presence and online influence, meaning we subconsciously judge an individual's sphere of leadership without any relational context. Meanwhile, the triune God has never stopped believing in family, intimate relationship and community. Churches today must therefore be careful not to outsource their leadership development to agencies who do not prioritise the kingdom family paradigm. The local church has and always will be the primary place of discipleship for any Christian, never mind a leader. As my friend Adam Cox puts it, we are found by a Father and formed in a family. Discipleship is never a privatised concept in the kingdom of God.

To be clear, I am a strong advocate for immersing emerging leaders in robust theological training environments, and these often happen best outside local church environments. For a season this is healthy and formative. But we must find creative ways to ensure our streams of theological development are woven into the familial and experiential learning of the local church. There are wonderful examples of this today. Places like Westminster Theological Centre,

Union School of Theology and St Mellitus College in the UK or Moody College in the USA combine rich theological input with on-the-ground ministry experience. Training is provided in flexible ways that encourage people to stay connected to a local learning community. This approach to leadership development provides wonderful opportunities for emerging leaders to sharpen their theological acumen while being incubated in intentional relational spaces, shepherded by elders who walk through all the seasons of life with them.

The Apostle Paul knew his young apprentice Timothy had an obvious leadership call on his life, an anointing for a much wider sphere of influence than the local church. Yet Paul was passionate about Timothy 'proving' this leadership first and foremost in the immediate locale he found himself in, instructing him to: 'set an example for the believers in speech, in conduct, in love, in faith and in purity' (1 Timothy 4:12). Paul knew that for Timothy, and for all the leaders he was raising up, being rooted in a local church is the emerging leader's greatest test. The crucible of community is where all the best sanctification happens. It is here young leaders should be encouraged to give themselves to training in all of the unglamourous parts of the kingdom family. This is where leaders grow in real-life spiritual maturity, holy grit and emotional resilience as they learn to navigate all the relational dynamics and intergenerational tensions that exist in the wounded, wonderful and, at times, slightly weird local church community.

I remember years ago as a young leader on my way to graduating with a Masters in Divinity, I began to receive a considerable number of invitations to speak in different churches. Aware of this, Uncle Phil pulled me aside one day. He quipped, '*Al, remember sometimes people want your gift more than they want you. Think about who you give yourself to.*'

This is an example of the kind of input that flows from the heart of a true shepherd. Phil wanted me to know he was still committed to who I was becoming irrespective of whether I gave a good preach or not! He was not being controlling. Rather, he was more interested in the longer-term process of the person I was becoming than he was in the popularity I was gaining. And he could say these words with authority and gravitas because he knew me. He had been walking with me for many years, shaping me and discipling me, watching my development in the exhilarating highs and devastating lows of serving alongside him in our local church.

And yet, as the years went by, there came a point when it became clear that I was leading alongside, not under, Phil. I'd been a 'son' to him in the Lord for years; now he was treating me like a 'brother'. I'd been a student and now I was a peer. There had been times I was sorely tempted to muscle my way in front of Phil. But each time God confronted me strongly on this. *Be Number 1 at being Number 2*' were the words I heard the Spirit say. Of course, it was a privilege to follow someone I respected so much even if the struggle within me was real. But God was gracious and patient with me. So was Phil. I came to joyfully accept this was part of my development into Christlikeness. I needed to humble myself. Submit to the process in the local context. Learn how to serve someone else's vision. This is all part of the cruciform way.

I say all this to demonstrate how this type of formation can only happen in the local church. 'Saints are always made somewhere', my friend Daniel Grothe states in his wise and brilliant book, *The Power of Place.*' Having our lives planted in a specific place and in a particular community is central to God's design for our fulfilment, friendships and fruitfulness. All the great saints down through church history understood that without the rootedness of a local context there will be no genuine long-lasting fruit. The people God has surrounded us with are the ones he intends to use to shape us more into the image of the Son.

* Daniel Grothe, *The Power of Place: Choosing Stability in a Rootless Age* (Thomas Nelson, 2022).

2. CHARACTER

One of the main appeals at the heart of this book is for Christian leaders to address the imbalance in churches where competency has been emphasised over character. The first few chapters have therefore focused on developing character in terms of surrender and servanthood. There are two essential elements which need to be explored when considering the development of character in a leader. Time, and integrity in all of life.

Time

It takes time to make a Christian leader because it takes time and devotion to be transformed into the character of Christ. Paul made it clear to Timothy, it is only when the qualities of Jesus are observed in a person's life should they be considered for leadership. In 1 Timothy 3:1–9, Paul lists the Christlike qualities which Timothy should be looking for in emerging leaders. But as we have already seen, after these qualities are listed, Paul adds a detail that is so often missed. 'They must first be tested' (1 Timothy 3:10). Even when there is clear evidence of the fruit of the Spirit in a potential leader's life, they still need to be tested before they are to be considered for senior leadership in the church. Importantly, that process of testing – of proving or approving – will take time. Paul clearly did not expect leaders to be perfect, but he knew the formation period in a leader's life should not be rushed. Because what leaders establish in a decade can be lost in one day. In another place Paul says it even more plainly:

> Don't appoint people to church leadership positions too hastily. If a person is involved in some serious sins, you don't want to become an unwitting accomplice.

1 TIMOTHY 5:22 (MSG)

In 2021, *Christianity Today* released a hugely popular podcast series called 'The Rise and Fall of Mars Hill'.* In it the show host Mike Cosper took his listeners inside the tumultuous story of Mars Hill Church in Seattle where, under the leadership of their now infamous pastor Mark Driscoll, the church experienced remarkable growth and then spectacular decline. Over the course of nineteen episodes Cosper elucidates a number of salient points around themes which dovetail with many of the issues this book seeks to address – money, celebrity, power, ego. One of the 'bonus episodes' on this podcast shifts focus and takes a look at another significant leader within Western evangelicalism in the last twenty years, Joshua Harris. Harris was what Collin Hansen called 'an evangelical boy wonder' after his landmark book *I Kissed Dating Goodbye* sold millions of copies when Harris was only nineteen years old. By all accounts, Harris was an entirely different personality to Mark Driscoll, but similar to Driscoll, he became a rising star in the charismatic reformed world. Both Harris and Driscoll were gifted communicators and as Cosper points out they achieved a significant level of national attention before they were thirty years old. This involved leading megachurches, writing books and headlining popular Christian conferences. In different ways, however, the years that followed for both Driscoll and Harris tell a sad story. As 'The Rise and Fall of Mars Hill' podcast narrates, Driscoll was stepped out of leadership in Mars Hill for a range of spiritual abuse and anger issues, and Harris resigned as Senior Pastor of his own church, separated from his wife and declared publicly that he no longer identified as a Christian.

There is much nuance and context, and many complex sensitivities to both these stories, and time does not allow me to unpack this further. I believe both Driscoll and Harris desired to do good and to honour God with their lives and their ministry. But it's hard not to connect the insane profile both these men achieved

* This podcast series can be found on various podcast platforms including Apple Podcasts, found at: podcasts.apple.com (accessed 7 March 2025).

at such a young age with the breaking down of their ministries and the damage left behind in their wake. Being thrust into the national spotlight at this stage of their development undoubtedly exposed unformed parts of their identity and character. The formation process – that 'long obedience in the same direction'* – had been short-circuited. The 'testing' process had been rushed. More time should have been taken.

I grieve over stories like these of Harris and Driscoll. I grieve for the people who have been damaged by this type of dysfunctional leadership. We can do better. But I also grieve for Driscoll and Harris because I recognise so much of my own sin and brokenness in their stories. All of us are much more of a mixed bag, a complex combination of light and shadow, than we project to those around us. Of course, Harris and Driscoll made mistakes they should repent of, but I do not think they went into Christian leadership intending to hurt people. Somehow, in the celebrity culture of Western Christianity, their brokenness was manifested at a global scale. As Cosper provocatively poses throughout this series, maybe we are all part of the problem?

In all of life

Paul wrote to another of his young apprentices, Titus, concerning the establishment of elders in the church in Crete, saying:

> *An elder must be blameless, faithful to his wife, a man whose children believe and are not open to the charge of being wild and disobedient. Since an overseer manages God's household, he must be blameless – not overbearing, not quick-tempered, not given to drunkenness, not violent, not pursuing dishonest gain. Rather, he must be hospitable, one who loves what is good, who is self-controlled, upright, holy and disciplined.*

TITUS 1:6–8

---

* This phrase, originating with Friedrich Wilhelm Nietzsche was popularised in Christian formation literature by Eugene Peterson who used it for the title of one of his books: *A Long Obedience in the Same Direction* (Special Edition – IVP Formatio, 2024).

Notice how the testing period for an emerging leader involves the intentional observance of Christlike qualities in all aspects of their lives – community relations, church life, marriage and family life. Unfortunately, too many leadership titles are being given out in the church today, before evidence of the life of Christ has been testified to in a potential leader's work environment or family life. Again, we are too enamoured of gifting and not enough of character in the 'ordinary' parts of life. But the New Testament is unflinching on this: if a person's gift is taking them where their character cannot keep them, they are not yet ready for leadership. Or, as a wise mentor once said, 'what a person builds with their gift they can destroy with their character'. The church is crying out for leaders who model godliness and faithfulness in every area of their life.

My friend Mark Sayers argues in his book, *Platforms to Pillars*, that today the church is crying out for more 'pillars' and fewer 'platforms'.[*] By pillars he is referring to elders – men and women of gravity and grace who are courageous and discerning in their local churches, prepared to confront any traces of control and counterfeit success seeding themselves into their community. Women and men who faithfully witness to the life of Christ on the school run and in the supermarket, far away from the spotlight of the platform. These are the kind of pillars the local church community should be established on.

3. CAPACITY

A third significant part of the testing process for Christian leaders, often missed or misunderstood, is the principle of capacity – the emotional, spiritual, relational availability of an emerging leader. A few years ago, I listened to a talk from Jon Tyson at a conference in England. At the end of his talk there was some time for Q&A.

---

[*] Mark Sayers, *Platforms to Pillars: Trading the Burden of Performance for the Freedom of God's Presence* (Moody Publishers, 2025).

One person asked the question, *'Jon, what are your top tips for church planting?'* I still remember Jon's reply. Steering away from all the culturally savvy answers everyone was expecting a church-planter in downtown Manhattan to give, he said three things:

- *Number 1: Do you have a heart for the lost? There's no point even thinking of planting a church if you don't want to see people come to know Jesus.*
- *Number 2: What is your pain threshold? If you are married, what is the pain threshold of your spouse?*
- *Number 3: Does change delight and excite you or does it beat you up and terrify you?*[*]

Planting and leading churches advances the kingdom of God against the kingdom of darkness and the opposition that will inevitably be stirred up has the potential to break you. If you are not prepared for it, it will hurt you badly. You may have all the external attributes, you may be a brilliant communicator, you may be theologically astute, you may have the gift to gather people, you may even have a great team, but if you aren't prepared for the intensity of spiritual warfare which will come your way at every level, quite frankly you are going to struggle to stay spiritually and emotionally fit, never mind physically and mentally healthy for the long term.

Let me put it like this: I am an amateur runner at best. I do it not because I like it but because I need to! Recently I was training to run 100k over the course of a week alongside my wife Rachel, to raise money for our new church building. In the early parts of the run my body was holding up well and I even found myself enjoying it! But as I went beyond the 15k mark, I began to feel twinges of pain in various places in my body. First my knees, then my lower back and then my hip-flexors. All these parts of my body began

* Jon Tyson episodes are available on Spotify at: open.spotify.com (accessed 12 March 2025).

sending messages to my brain, 'please stop soon!' It felt like every weakness in my body was revealed. The intensity of road-running had exposed the fault lines in my physical make-up due to the wear and tear of a previous life dedicated to semi-professional football.

Experience has taught me that long-distance running is a good metaphor for frontline church leadership. There is joy in the journey and the prize at the end will be an experience better than we can comprehend. But the struggle along the way is real. A clear sense of calling and a healthy dose of pragmatism is what is needed if we are going to make it. Any potential leader in the church must prepare themselves for the enemy's assault against them and their family. He or she must be aware of the resilience needed to absorb other people's pain, the steely determination required to persevere when you aren't witnessing the results you expected and the fortitude that is essential to remain soft-hearted even as you are receiving stinging criticism from others. Church leadership is intense. Contrary to what you may have been sold this is a call to the twilight not the limelight.

With that in mind the testing period for an emerging leader should involve serious discernment, all part of the 'sober assessment' which Paul encouraged Timothy to undertake.

The following questions may help in this discernment process:

- Is there a clear sense of being called by God 'in season and out of season' to leadership in the church?
- Is there a compelling level of energy towards service and a willingness to sacrifice?
- Is there evidence of good practices and boundaries – a disciplined devotional life, the practice of sabbath rest, scary levels of accountability with soul-friends and a well-developed prayer muscle?

- Are these boundaries flexible enough to give over-and-above what is required in a 'normal' working environment? If married, is there evidence of grace from one's spouse to release their partner to serve the body of Christ?

One of the most awkward moments in the New Testament appears to be centred on this issue of capacity. In Acts Chapter 15 we are told of a sharp disagreement which took place between Paul and Barnabas just as they were about to embark on another mission trip together. Barnabas wanted to bring their young apprentice John Mark with them. Paul disagreed because, 'he had deserted them in Pamphylia and had not continued with them in the work' (Acts 15:38). Paul didn't think John Mark had the capacity required to lead. Was Paul too harsh? Was Barnabas too soft? There is no simple answer to this question. What we can conclude from this episode, however, is that frontline church leadership is tough and demanding and not for the fainthearted. Paul made sure his other young assistant Timothy knew what he was getting himself into when he said, 'join with me in suffering for the gospel' (2 Timothy 1:8).

You have to be ready to give everything. But Jesus is worth it.

4. CHARISM

So far we have focused on the dangers of emphasising gifting over character, but it's important we don't swing the pendulum too far in the other direction. The New Testament leaves us in no doubt, the first kingdom families planted across the Mediterranean basin were, at their core, charismatic communities. For the earliest believers, following Jesus meant becoming as Jesus was – born of the Spirit, filled with the Spirt and empowered by the Spirit. Jesus had told the disciples to wait on the Spirit's infilling presence before their mission began. The early church therefore understood themselves as individuals and a community baptised into the Holy Spirit and endowed by the Holy Spirit with a variety of gifts. We will unpack the topic of spiritual gifts in Chapter 6 but, in this context, with our focus on the testing ground of emerging leaders, it is important to state that cruciform leaders are those upon whom an obvious gift of the Spirit has been granted or imparted. '*Charism*', the word we translate into 'gift' in English, is the idea that someone has been granted divine grace from God for the building up and equipping of others. Leaders in the church should therefore be people flowing in an obvious anointing of the Spirit. If not, they may be morally upright people, but they will lack the power of the Spirit required for breakthrough. Spiritual gravity and spiritual gifting are required. Above natural talents, popularity, gender or social standing – the first Apostles were men and women gifted by God to proclaim the gospel and lay foundations for the church. Naturally then, as they looked to develop and install future leaders in the churches, the Apostles searched for evidence of the endowment of the Spirit upon those emerging from within their communities.

One other thing to note on spiritual gifts at this point. The gifts of teaching, preaching, miracles and prophecy are often gifts we would and should associate with leaders in the church, but again, the challenge we have today is not dissimilar to Paul's day. Human beings have a propensity to develop an unhealthy attachment to the more public and prominent gifts. The examples of Driscoll and Harris above remind us that the testing process involves discerning whether leaders can steward these God-given charisms, particularly in today's celebrity culture. Our attention should not primarily focus on how good these gifts are in emerging leaders, but how they are being used! The question is, does the fruit of these gifts ultimately result in the formation of disciples in the way of Jesus? This is where the charisma of the Spirit will always lead the cruciform leader – the equipping of the saints to fulfil the Great Commission.

CONFIRMATION AND COMMISSION

I believe a mixture of the criteria above – context, character, capacity, charism – should aid the discernment process required for 'testing' potential leaders. Assimilating this thinking into our leadership development pathways will enable us to create healthy environments where emerging leaders can 'show themselves approved'. While in one sense the process of development never stops for any leader, the process of 'testing' should ultimately lead to moments of confirmation and commission when leaders in training are affirmed and honoured for their commitment to a season of apprenticing and simultaneously released into their divinely orchestrated assignments. These moments are often intentional occasions when mature elders, through the laying on of hands, confirm the calling of God upon those who have been raised up under their care, commissioning them into the fullness of their destiny. Think of Jesus breathing upon his disciples the empowering presence of his own Spirit as their apprenticing process came to an end. This was their moment to step forth into a new level of authority and influence. Think of Paul's words to Timothy, reminding him of a particular significant moment of impartation and commissioning in his life:

> *Do not neglect your gift, which was given you through prophecy when the body of elders laid their hands on you.*

1 TIMOTHY 4:14

In the same way, elders not only recognise the maturation point of an emerging leader's process of development, but as they lay their hands upon them, they impart fresh grace upon their lives, releasing them to serve the body of Christ in the power of the Spirit.

PRACTISING THE CRUCIFORM WAY

Consider the questions and readings below in discussion, reflection, journalling and prayer.

ONE:

Then Jesus was led by the Spirit into the wilderness to be tempted by the devil.

MATTHEW 4:1

Reflect on this verse together describing what happened after Jesus' baptism.

- Why do you think the Spirit will sometimes lead us into the wilderness?
- Take time to share some of your own personal 'wilderness' experiences and how these have become 'a painful gift' to you in the long term.

TWO:

And let them also be tested first; then let them serve …

1 TIMOTHY 3:10 (ESV)

Do your best to present yourself to God as one approved, a worker who does not need to be ashamed and who correctly handles the word of truth.

2 TIMOTHY 2:15

Reflect on two of Paul's exhortations to his apprentice, Timothy.

- What has been the process of 'testing' in your own journey towards leadership and how has this been significant for you?

THREE:

I believe a mixture of ... context, character, capacity, charism – should aid the discernment process required for 'testing' potential leaders. Assimilating this thinking into our leadership development pathways will enable us to create healthy environments where emerging leaders can 'show themselves approved.'

- Discuss or reflect on the importance of context, character, capacity and charism within the testing process of emerging leaders.
- How does this outwork itself in your church community?

CHAPTER 5

A SPIRITUAL PARENT

Then Jesus came to them and said, 'All authority in heaven and on earth has been given to me. Therefore go and make disciples of all nations, baptising them in the name of the Father and of the Son and of the Holy Spirit, and teaching them to obey everything I have commanded you. And surely I am with you always, to the very end of the age.'

MATTHEW 28:18–20

In the early hours of Friday 30 September 2011 my life changed forever. Weighing 8.2lbs, our baby girl Anabel burst into our lives. Nothing prepared me for the overwhelming force of emotions which would surge through me as I watched my wonderful wife Rachel bring our own little creation into the world. Since then, Rachel and I have been blessed with two more beautiful and irrepressible children, Erin and Finn. We are officially outnumbered!

It is hard to find words to describe how parenthood changes a person's life, but everyone agrees it does. One's whole world gets flipped upside down as the new normal – which can only be described as holy chaos – begins to unfold. As someone once said, 'having kids is like having a bowling alley installed in your brain!' And yet everyone also agrees having children is one of the greatest privileges a human being can experience. There is an indescribable sense of wonder, awe and sacred mystery that comes through the birth of every son or daughter.

For any parent the sheer delight of holding a tiny human who now carries their literal DNA on the earth is matched by a tremendous sense of responsibility as they begin to contemplate who their child will become for all the years which will follow.

The rest of a parent's life is spent dreaming, worrying, praying, hoping, planning, watching, nurturing and letting go, because their own life is now, in some mysterious way, entwined forever with their child's. There is a beautiful line in the book of Genesis where Judah describes his father's relationship with his youngest brother Benjamin. He says Jacob's 'life is closely bound up with [Benjamin's] life' (Genesis 44:30). This is what parenthood has done to me. I have found my soul bound up in the lives of Annie, Erin and Finlay – small humans I love more than my own life; three kids who elicit a depth of love from me that I didn't know I was capable of. Of course, the challenges are real – some days all too real. Children keep us on our toes and on our knees. And even though they sometimes make choices I would not have made – after all, they have free will; who knew?! – I am wholeheartedly invested in who they are becoming.

Reflecting on how parenthood changes us is a helpful way to frame how the Apostles understood leadership. The Apostles would have been aware of the many references in the Hebrew Scriptures which reveal how Yahweh led his children as a loving parent. The psalmist declared, 'As a father has compassion on his children, so the LORD has compassion on those who fear him' (Psalm 103:13). Through the prophet Hosea, God declared, 'When Israel was a child, I loved him, and out of Egypt I called my son' (Hosea 11:1), and through the prophet Isaiah, God passionately cried, 'Can a mother forget the baby at her breast and have no compassion on the child she has borne? Though she may forget, I will not forget you' (Isaiah 49:15)!

These beautiful word pictures of Yahweh's tender love for Israel were brought to full expression in Jesus; 'Whoever has seen me has seen the Father' (John 14:9, ESV), he declared to his disciples. He then went on to assure them that through the fellowship of the Holy Spirit he would never leave them as orphans (John 14:16–18). In the days ahead, as the Spirit was poured into the lives of the Apostles, they in turn would overflow with the Father's love in their service to the first churches.

MOTHERS AND FATHERS

During the early years of parenting my own kids, I felt the Holy Spirit prompt me to read through the New Testament again, this time focusing on the Apostles' tone, their manner of speaking and the relational interplay rather than the doctrinal treasures my reformed evangelical upbringing had conditioned me to give primary consideration to. Not unlike my own parenting experience, this process changed me in a profound way. I'd never perceived the love and care the Apostles showed towards the churches they served before, and it captured my heart. I was deeply moved by how the Apostle John addressed the believers in his young churches as 'my little children' (1 John 2:1; 3:18; 4:4). I found myself weeping as l realised the depth of emotion Paul carried in his heart for the believers in Thessalonica – the same emotions a gentle nursing mother or an encouraging father would experience towards their own children (1 Thessalonians 2:6–12). I began to feel Paul's aching desire to be with his sons and daughters in the Lord when absent from them. I was challenged by his commitment to pray diligently for them, 'My dear children, for whom I am again in the pains of childbirth until Christ is formed in you,' (Galatians 4:19), and I was inspired by the Apostle Peter's exhortation to the elders of his churches to 'be shepherds of God's flock that is under your care, watching over them – not because you must, but because you are willing' (1 Peter 5:2).

Reading the apostolic letters this way marked me. Through the lives and words of these first leaders of the church I felt my life was being imprinted in a life-changing way by the Spirit of the Servant King. In all of this I came to realise that the Apostles understood biblical leadership through a posture of gentleness – the gentleness of a loving parent whose heart is tender to their children. As I once heard theologian Lucy Peppiatt explain, when Paul used the word 'gentleness' to describe his relationship with the early churches, he was not referring to a feminine quality but a Christlike one. Remember, none of the Apostles encouraged the emerging leaders of the first churches to become great speakers or dynamic leaders. Instead they were urged to imitate the Apostles as fathers and mothers of the children of God. Listen to more words from the Apostle Paul:

> *Even if you had ten thousand guardians in Christ, you do not have many fathers, for in Christ Jesus I became your father through the gospel. Therefore, I urge you to imitate me.*

1 CORINTHIANS 4:15–16

The inner posture of the cruciform leader is one shaped by parenthood. Of course, that's not to say one must experience parenthood to be a cruciform leader. From what we know, the Apostle Paul did not have children. Neither did Jesus. Some of the best spiritual mothers and fathers I know are single people or couples who have not had biological kids. What makes them incredible spiritual mothers and fathers is that they have allowed their hearts to be touched by their heavenly Father in such a life-changing way that they have given the rest of their lives to adopting others into their hearts.

The Apostles understood this way of leading as a natural expression of the authority Jesus had bestowed upon them. Imitating the heart of the Father, they were convinced that each person was a beautiful manifestation of God's workmanship and a creative expression of God's own nature. Jesus taught them that everyone had been given something of incredible worth. Each person was entrusted with a divine assignment to reflect his glory. The Apostles therefore understood that any giftedness they had been given by God was to be used to help unlock the God-given destiny of others. As Paul explained in his letter to the Ephesians, the functioning essence of true apostolic ministry is, 'to equip his people for works of service, so that the body of Christ may be built up' (Ephesians 4:12). In another one of Paul's letters, to the church in Rome this time, he said:

I long to see you so that I may impart to you some spiritual gift to make you strong – that is, that you and I may be mutually encouraged by each other's faith.

ROMANS 1:11–12

This is the perfect example of the heart and motives of a true cruciform leader – the passionate desire to supply what is lacking in the faith of younger believers, not because they have all the answers but because this is what parents do for their kids – they leverage the best they have to release their children into the fullness of their destiny. The authentic parent has no desire to establish their own empire or build their own platform. As a wise man once told me, 'Young men and women may build their ministries, but fathers and mothers always build families.' Cruciform leaders are mature spiritual mothers and fathers who are not threatened by those being raised up around them. Rather, as loving parents, they serve their sons and daughters in the Lord, helping them to fulfil their purpose in life through that healthy parental mixture of love and challenge.

WHAT WILL YOU DO WITH WHAT YOU HAVE BEEN GIVEN?

To help us understand more deeply how the first Apostles understood this central aspect of their leadership, it is worthwhile returning to one of Jesus' parables. In popular culture an age-old debate rumbles on – are leaders born or made? Jesus, I believe, asks a different question – what will you do with what you have been given? Through the Parable of the Talents (Matthew 25:14–30), Jesus frames the gift of leadership, and every other gift for that matter, within the broader biblical theme of stewardship. This parable is the story of a wealthy man, who is about to leave town for a considerable length of time. Master to three servants, he gathers them before he leaves and distributes his wealth, 'each according to his ability' (Matthew 25:15). One of the servants is given five talents, one is given two talents, and one is given one talent. While the master is away, two of the servants diligently go and invest their talents. When the master comes back and asks for his talents back, the one who was entrusted with five talents is able to give him back ten and the one who was entrusted with two talents gives him back four. The first two servants are affirmed as good stewards and invited to share in more of the master's inheritance.

> *Well done, good and faithful servant! You have been faithful with a few things; I will put you in charge of many things. Come and share your master's happiness!*

MATTHEW 25:21, 23

In contrast, we are told that the third servant who was given one talent went away and buried it. When the master came back, this particular servant could therefore only give back the same one talent. The master was angry with the third servant's attitude. Really angry.

> *You wicked, lazy servant! … you should have put my money on deposit with the bankers, so that when I returned I would have received it back with interest.*

MATTHEW 25:26–27

The Parable of the Talents brings the dynamic theme of stewardship that runs throughout the whole biblical narrative into sharper focus. The children of Abraham, four thousand years before Jesus told this parable, had been called by God to carry the seed of blessing to all nations. Jesus was now reframing this principle to say that everyone has been entrusted with something. Our heavenly Father has placed the treasure of heaven in each one of his image-bearing children. Everyone is called to steward what they have been given diligently and invest wisely. Further, the parable teaches us that when we surrender the results of what we have invested to the will of God (our master) he will entrust us with even more. Interestingly the Parable of the Talents ends with the master taking the one talent from the third servant who had wasted it and giving it to the first servant who had proved himself faithful. 'For whoever has will be given more, and they will have an abundance' (Matthew 25:29), Jesus concludes.

In the rest of this chapter, we will discover that the Apostles developed a theology and an ecclesiology in line with Jesus' Parable of the Talents which, in short, was built upon the principle that everyone has been entrusted with something. The phenomenal way the Jesus-movement spread across the world throughout the first century was famously described by Roland Allen as 'The Spontaneous Expansion of the Church'* and one of the essential factors contributing to this growth was that the Apostles understood every believer as an empowered agent. Pentecost had brought with it the radical reality of 'the priesthood of all believers' which meant anyone now 'in Christ' was qualified to carry the authority of the kingdom.

In light of this, the Apostles embodied the loving parenthood of God towards the first believers by encouraging them to receive God's grace as empowerment unto service; teaching them that each one had not just been gloriously saved but uniquely gifted by God as a precious son or daughter and entrusted with special heavenly

---

* Roland Allen, *The Spontaneous Expansion of the Church* (Wipf & Stock, 1997).

attributes to manifest the presence of their heavenly Father on the earth. Therefore, the Apostles taught, each one should seek to invest those gifts wisely – using them for the building up of the body of Christ and the advancement of the kingdom of God in the world.

Listen to how the Apostle Peter's words of encouragement to the churches echoed the same themes resident in the Parable of the Talents, approximately thirty years after he'd first heard it from Jesus: 'Each of you should use whatever gift you have received to serve others, as faithful stewards of God's grace in its various forms' (1 Peter 4:10).

HILDA AND CAEDMON

Let me remind you of a beautiful story in church history that provides a wonderful example of the type of 'equipping' leadership I am referring to above. It involves one of the great saints in history who is often overlooked, Hilda of Whitby.* Hilda was the great-niece of an Anglo-Saxon king called Edwin and became a Christian under the Roman Bishop Paulinus. But it was the Celtic saints and their vibrant Christianity who truly shaped Hilda's faith. Hilda was influenced by Aidan, one of the original founders of Lindisfarne, a famous monastic community in the North-East of England and she eventually became the abbess of another monastery that was planted, not far away, in Whitby. Hilda helped create a culture in Whitby where social distinctions had little meaning and, in line with the practices of the Celtic churches, the community at Whitby intentionally invited people from the wider community to come and feast with them. It became a well-established custom at these feasts for each guest to take a turn to sing a song. At the community meal in Whitby, an older man called Caedmon, who wasn't thought to have

---

* I am indebted to Michael Mitton's work in Michael Mitton, *Restoring the Woven Cord* (BRF, 2010) for the use of this story.

an active faith, often attended. Caedmon had gained a reputation for leaving the gathering once the harp was about to be passed to him to sing a song. On one of these occasions, he left to avoid having to sing and went out into the night to look after his sheep. As he fell asleep that night, he had a vivid dream which changed his life. He dreamt a man came and stood before him and said to him, 'Caedmon, sing me a song.' Caedmon was alarmed – because he knew he couldn't sing – or, at least, that is what he thought. 'I can't sing,' Caedmon replied. The man continued to look at him and said, 'but you will sing for me,' and then directed him to sing a song about creation. Caedmon suddenly found himself singing some of the most profound things about God's creation in a beautiful melody. After this Caedmon awoke. Amazed at what had happened he went to see Hilda about his experience. Hilda encouraged Caedmon to sing what God had given him before a few of her mature leaders and they all agreed that what Caedmon had been given was a gift from God. Caedmon was invited into the community at Whitby and was discipled in a way that encouraged him to integrate theology and doctrine into poetry and song. Caedmon spent the rest of his life doing this and he became one of the great Celtic poets.

This story reminds us that like Caedmon, each person has a God-song inside of them, a spiritual gift that the Father has uniquely endowed them with. But it also encourages us to be like Hilda, a leader who understood her role as an equipping leader, one who is called to release the songs resident in the hearts of those entrusted to her care. Like the first Apostles, Hilda reveals the beautiful ministry of spiritual mothers and fathers, those who help unlock the glorious destiny of sons and daughters in the Lord.

THE BODY OF CHRIST AND BUILDING OF GOD

The 'every-member-ministry' principle which pulsed through the life of the early church is particularly evident in Paul's letters to his churches. In these pages Paul taught the believers to centre their communities not around a dominant leader but the unifying and empowering presence of the Holy Spirit (see Philippians 2:1–2; Ephesians 4:2–16). Paul's favourite way of describing this dynamic reality was through the metaphor of a 'body'. He believed the church is a living organism of many members connected to, and flowing from, Christ, who is the head. Paul focuses on 'the body of Christ' theme in his letter to the Romans (Romans 12:3–8) and his first letter to the Corinthians (1 Corinthians 12:12–31). I've selected some of these Scriptures below:

> *For just as each of us has one body with many members, and these members do not all have the same function, so in Christ we, though many, form one body, and each member belongs to all the others.*

ROMANS 12:4–5

> *Just as a body, though one, has many parts, but all its many parts form one body, so it is with Christ. For we were all baptised by one Spirit so as to form one body – whether Jews or Gentiles, slave or free – and we were all given the one Spirit to drink. And so the body is not made up of one part but of many.*

1 CORINTHIANS 12:12–14

It's clear Paul rejoiced in the kaleidoscopic beauty of the early church's unity-in-diversity. He, along with the other Apostles, longed for every member of the kingdom family to fulfil their God-given destiny, believing when each one was uniquely mobilised in their gifts the body of Christ would move more effectively throughout the world. But Scripture also makes clear that Paul received specific divine wisdom about particular leadership gifts God coded into the kingdom family. The letter to the Ephesians is one of the letters where these gifts are most obviously laid out. This provides the church with enduring inspiration around the different types of leadership God has given to his church and the reasons they have been given. In Ephesians 4:11, Paul specifically identifies apostles, prophets, evangelists, pastors and teachers. In the next chapter we will unpack these gifts and the ways they should be embodied. As we do, we will see the underlying principle of spiritual parenthood at the heart of all New Testament leadership. This further emphasises the kingdom family macro-theme I outlined in Chapter 1 and how vital it is to understand Christian leadership through this lens. One clear example of this is Paul's second letter to Timothy where he acknowledges the parental (and grandparental!) influence in Timothy's own spiritual formation:

> *I am reminded of your sincere faith, which first lived in your grandmother Lois and in your mother Eunice and, I am persuaded, now lives in you also.*

2 TIMOTHY 1:5

It is clear from Paul's letter to Timothy and Titus that the intergenerational nature of the transmission of faith was fundamental to the ongoing movement of the gospel in the world. Thomas Oden in his commentary on the Pastoral Epistles says:

> To these two women [Lois and Eunice] we rightly credit the transmission of faith to Timothy, the precondition of his transmission of faith to countless others. In Timothy we have a young man from a transitional, cross-cultural family charged with transmitting the faith intergenerationally ... When preaching asks how Christian mission is to be revitalised today, nothing is more central to the answer than being a good parent.[*]

---

[*] Thomas Oden, *First and Second Timothy and Titus: Interpretation: A Bible Commentary for Teaching and Preaching* (John Knox Press, 1989), p126, 133, quoted in Jeff Reed, *Living in God's Household, First Principles from the Pastorals* (Independently published, 2014), p50.

THE HOUSEHOLD OF FAITH

Before we dig deeper into more of Paul's revelation of the different leadership gifts, there are a couple of preliminary things it is good to be aware of.

First, we must notice how Paul switches metaphors in Ephesians, supplementing the image of a 'body' he uses in his other letters with the visual representation of a 'building' – a holy temple.

In [Christ] the whole building is joined together and rises to become a holy temple in the Lord. And in him you too are being built together to become a dwelling in which God lives by his Spirit.

EPHESIANS 2:21–22

Second, Paul wants the churches to know he is not merely outlining some of his own ideas about church leadership structures. Rather, Paul says:

This grace was given me: to preach to the Gentiles the boundless riches of Christ, and to make plain to everyone the administration of this mystery, which for ages past was kept hidden in God, who created all things.

EPHESIANS 3:8–9

What is the 'mystery' Paul is referring to? It is nothing less than the church – the beautiful new humanity in Christ (see Ephesians 2:14–16), people from every tribe and tongue, now being formed together as one family. So, in these verses, Paul wants the believers to know that his unique apostolic mandate was to articulate ('make plain') how the kingdom family, the newly formed fledgling church, one new humanity in Christ ('this mystery'), was to be established, organised and built up ('administration'). The word 'administration' here is the English translation of the Greek word, *oikionomia* – which is actually a combination of two Greek words: *oikos* meaning 'house' and *nomos* meaning 'management' (or 'law'), giving us 'household management'. Paul therefore understood himself entrusted by God with a special ability to bring 'household management' to the new kingdom family. He had been endowed with supernatural insight into the design of Christ's church and how it should take shape in the world.

This was obviously a bold claim by Paul but one we should not take lightly – and in Chapter 6 we will delve deeper into Paul's revelation discovering normative principles which can be applied to the church down through the ages. In other words, there are things Paul describes in his letters which can be applied in every culture and in every generation. Cruciform leaders should therefore endeavour to become fluent in these biblical principles if they want to fulfil their calling as authentic spiritual mothers and fathers of God's people.

But as I close out this chapter, I want to draw on the work of Henry and Richard Blackaby as a helpful conclusion. Father and son, Henry and Richard have collaborated together for many years, writing and speaking on different areas of Christian leadership. In one of their most important books, *Spiritual Leadership: Moving People on to God's Agenda*, they argue for the clear distinction which must be drawn between general leadership principles and the spiritual leadership that is aligned with biblical principles.* At the heart of their work they remind us that leaders can achieve all their goals yet miss God's will. Spiritual leaders, however, those shaped in the cruciform way, do not use people to achieve their ends; their people are the end. They are spiritual mothers and fathers who lay down their lives to equip the saints.

My own father Alan, who I am named after, has embodied this to me more than anyone else I know. Dad is my hero and my best

---

* Henry & Richard Blackaby, *Spiritual Leadership: Moving People on to God's Agenda* (Broadman & Holman, 2001).

friend. Everything I know about 'fathering' and equipping others – both with my own kids and in the church – I have learned from him. One thing that stands out for me and marks my dad as a true 'spiritual father' is the fact that he has always and consistently wanted me to go beyond him. Dad is a church elder and an anointed Bible teacher in his own right – he's watched me grow over the last twenty-five years in increased leadership authority and influence in the very church where he also serves as an elder and leader. Yet never once in my life have I felt he was insecure or threatened by me. It has only ever been the opposite. Encouragement, advice, prayerful support and the odd spiritual kick on the butt! Dad has leveraged every ounce of his own greatness to help supply my destiny more than his own. He has championed me every day of my life. My dad has shown me, more times than I can count, a window into the Father heart of God. And it is for this reason more than any other that I still want to be like him when I grow up.

I have been deeply blessed to have had such an incredible role model of spiritual parenting in my own dad, but I am reminded that for us all, no matter the individuals we may have known and valued, no example can be of greater importance or relevance to the cruciform leader than Jesus. We do well to remember Jesus' words to the disciples, 'Anyone who has seen me has seen the Father' (John 14:9). Jesus, the best leader the world has ever known, was the perfect parent.

PRACTISING THE CRUCIFORM WAY

Consider the questions and readings below in discussion, reflection, journalling and prayer.

ONE:

Imagine yourself as one of the servants in the Parable of the Talents.

- Prayerfully ponder Jesus entrusting you with his talents and asking you the question *'[insert your name], what will you do with what I have given you?'* How would you respond?

TWO:

My dear children, for whom I am again in the pains of childbirth until Christ is formed in you …

GALATIANS 4:19

Be shepherds of God's flock that is under your care, watching over them – not because you must, but because you are willing.

1 PETER 5:2

Even if you had ten thousand guardians in Christ, you do not have many fathers, for in Christ Jesus I became your father through the gospel. Therefore, I urge you to imitate me.

1 CORINTHIANS 4:15–16

Spend some time reading and reflecting on these verses from the Apostles Peter and Paul which speak about the parental nature of their leadership.

- In what ways do these verses encourage and challenge you to adopt the posture of a spiritual parent in your leadership?

THREE:

As a wise man once told me, 'Young men and women may build their ministries, but fathers and mothers always build families.' Cruciform leaders are mature spiritual mothers and fathers who are not threatened by those being raised up around them. Rather, as loving parents, they serve their sons and daughters in the Lord, helping them to fulfil their purpose in life through that healthy parental mixture of love and challenge.

Reflect on these words from Chapter 5.

- Take some time to discuss who, specifically, God might be calling you to spiritually parent in this season. Practically, what will this mean or look like for you?

AN EQUIPPER OF SAINTS

The image of the body of Christ describes what is at once perhaps the most attractive and the most radical features of the early church – the spirit of mutual submission and interdependence that flowed between each of her members. While the picture of a beautiful, egalitarian, countercultural society never fails to warm our hearts when we read this passage, it would be wrong to assume this meant there was no leadership, no structure or no order in the first churches. In one sense everyone could be a leader in the early church because every believer was understood as an empowered agent of the kingdom of God. But what is equally clear from the Book of Acts and the New Testament epistles is that leadership was also understood as a distinct gift. Those who had been graced with a recognisable gift 'to lead' and a discernable call upon their lives to lead God's people were encouraged to do so. In his letters to the Christians in Rome, Paul listed certain gifts God had given to the church – prophecy, service, teaching, encouragement, generosity, leadership, mercy (Romans 12:6–8). Regarding those gifted to lead, Paul added, they should 'do it diligently' (verse 8). It's unequivocally clear that Paul understood the body of Christ required godly and intentional leadership. Throughout his letters he said a lot about the damage of bad leadership in the church. But he also knew the damage of no leadership. Leaders need to lead.

As we move forward, we will shape our reflections on the gifts of leadership, as outlined in the New Testament, around these three questions:

- *Why* was the gift of leadership needed and required in the early church?
- *What* were the different leaderships gifts and in *what* ways were they expressed?
- *How* do we steward these gifts of leadership wisely?

WHY?

Let's return to Ephesians, this time to some verses from Chapter 4, to discover more.

> *So Christ himself gave the apostles, the prophets, the evangelists, the pastors and teachers, to equip his people for works of service, so that the body of Christ may be built up until we all reach unity in the faith and in the knowledge of the Son of God and become mature, attaining to the whole measure of the fullness of Christ.*
>
> *Then we will no longer be infants, tossed back and forth by the waves, and blown here and there by every wind of teaching and by the cunning and craftiness of people in their deceitful scheming. Instead, speaking the truth in love, we will grow to become in every respect the mature body of him who is the head, that is, Christ. From him the whole body, joined and held together by every supporting ligament, grows and builds itself up in love, as each part does its work.*
>
> EPHESIANS 4:11–16

We will describe the different types of leadership gifts later in this chapter but, for now, let's focus on verses 12–16. From these we can conclude that Paul was convinced leadership was granted to help supply the destiny of others. Leadership in the early church was never to be used to exert control, maintain an institution, or wield power. As a leader in the church, I am genuinely sorry if this has been your experience. But I hope as we review the lives of those who shepherded the first churches into the life of Christ, it will help restore some of your confidence in leadership again. Inspired by the empowering way Jesus had discipled them, these faithful men and women understood their leadership gift as catalytic and generative. They knew they were put on this earth to equip the saints. It was axiomatic for Paul that 'the work of the ministry' was to be done by the saints, the 'everyday' Christian – not the paid professionals. As Hans Kung put it:

> The charisms of leadership in the Pauline churches did not … produce a ruling class, an aristocracy of those endowed with the Spirit who separated themselves from the community and rose above it in order to rule over it.[*]

For a start you don't get the dramatic expansion the early church experienced if leaders function within a hegemony of power. You only get such movemental impact if leaders are prepared to lead like spiritual parents – mothers and fathers who live for the joy of releasing spiritual sons and daughters to go further than they ever could. Ray Stedman, in his book *Body Life*, explains how the word 'equip' in Ephesians 4:12 comes from the original Greek word *katartismon*, from which we get the English word 'artisan' – 'an artist or craftsman, someone who works with their hands to make or build things.'[**] Stedman expounds further that *katartismon* originally appears in the New Testament at the point when Jesus first called his disciples as they were 'mending' their nets (Matthew 4:21 ESV). He wants us to notice that there is a beautiful connection to be made here. Stedman argues that Paul is using *katartismon* in Ephesians 4:12 to imply just as the

---

[*] Hans Kung in Alan Hirsch and Tim Catchim, *The Permanent Revolution, Apostolic Imagination and Practice for the 21st Century Church* (Jossey-Bass, 2012), p283.
[**] Ray C Stedman, *Body Life: The book that inspired a return to the church's real meaning and mission* (Discovery House Publications, 1972).

disciples were preparing, shaping and strengthening their nets for the service of the seas, the primary reason God gives gifts of leadership to the church is so they can equip – mend, fix, shape up, craft and form – the people of God into saints, ready 'for the work of the ministry'.

Paul wanted leaders in the church to clearly understand that any gifting God had graced them with to lead was to be leveraged for the greatness of others. Yes, Paul encouraged members of the local churches to submit to their leaders but if that leadership was ever expressed in superiority, heavy-handed control or manipulation, the church was encouraged to dismiss these leaders as 'hired hands'. This style of leadership is the antithesis of the cruciform way. As Chris Green says to those whom God has called to serve the church in a leadership role:

> We take on the ecclesial vocation always only on behalf of others – never instead of them, much less against them. We are the called-out ones whose lives are dedicated entirely to collaboration with God's work for those who have yet to hear or to submit to the call. The elect are elected always for the sake of the non-elect ... we find ourselves called out from them, but only because we have been singled out by God to share in the work of making room for them.[*]

A worthwhile reality check for most leaders is to ponder what it will be like to stand before Jesus and give an account for our days on the earth when we had the privilege of serving his bride, the church. We would do well to remember that when standing face to face with the Servant King, we will not be asked how big our church was, how amazing our gifts were, or how wide our reach was. Rather, Jesus will want to know how faithful we were to the people he entrusted into our care (1 Corinthians 3:8–9) and how committed we were to them becoming like Jesus. Neil Cole reminds us frankly of the true measurements of success.

* Chris EW Green, *Sanctifying Interpretation: Vocation, Holiness and Scripture* (CPT Press, 2020), p21.

Ultimately, each church will be evaluated by only one thing – its disciples. Your church is only as good as her disciples. It does not matter how good your praise, preaching, programs, or property are; if your disciples are passive, needy, consumeristic, and not radically obedient, your church is not good.*

With this in mind I believe the real questions any leader should be asking him- or herself are: What level of spiritual health and maturity have those under my care in the Lord reached? How are the people I am leading experiencing my leadership? Will I be able to say like Jesus in some of his final words on earth as he prayed to the Father, 'While I was with them, I protected them and kept them safe by that name you gave me' (John 17:12)?

WHAT?

Now that we have established the main reasons *why* God gave gifts of leadership to the church, we are ready to explore *what* types of leadership gifts the New Testament outlines. Before we proceed, though, there are a few important characteristics of leadership structures in the earliest churches it is worthwhile acknowledging.

Firstly, it's clear the principle of apostolic authority and spiritual oversight was pivotal to the development of the church, yet there does not seem to be a strict nor standardised structural norm. For example, we aren't told that Antioch rigidly followed Jerusalem's leadership structure or that Ephesus followed Antioch's.

Secondly, while there is a clear pattern of leaders passing on the Jesus tradition (in different parts of the apostolic letters this is called 'the faith', 'the deposit' or 'sound doctrine') to emerging leaders, there is no sign of a 'formal' book of ordination for clergy.

Thirdly, in different contexts different terminology is actually

* Neil Cole, *Ordinary Hero: Becoming a Disciple Who Makes a Difference* (Baker Books, 2011), p185.

used for leadership. The different terms are: *episkopos* – overseer, guardian; *diakonos* – deacon, servant; *presbuteros* – elder, older man; *doulos* – slave; *sunergos* – co-worker. In Corinth, one of Paul's earliest letters, we see him highlight apostles, prophets, gifts of administration and teachers (1 Corinthians 12:27–30). This then seems to provide the basis for the other leadership gifts Paul describes in his letter to the Ephesians. In Acts 20:28, Luke, quoting Paul, refers to 'overseers' and 'shepherds'. In Philippians 1:1, Paul addresses 'overseers and deacons'. In Titus 1:5–7, the terms 'overseers' and 'elders' seem to overlap. And in 1 Peter 5:1–14, 'elders' are encouraged to serve as overseers or shepherds.

Fourthly, leadership was not chosen on the basis of positional power, gender, status or affiliation. The glorious consequence of charismatic ecclesiology was that men, women, Jews, Gentiles, slaves, non-slaves, rich and poor all came into leadership. Becoming a leader in the body of Christ was discerned primarily through evidence of the anointing of the Spirit and the Christlike characteristics of servanthood, sacrifice and suffering.

All these realities point to the fact that leadership emerged in the early church charismatically and organically. Rather than imposing top-down structures of power and control on the spreading movement of churches across the Mediterranean basin, the Apostles paid attention to discernible patterns of the Holy Spirit. In doing so, they discovered God's design for the household of faith and could apply these patterns with sensitivity to different contexts and cultures. In other words, leadership structures were initially put in place to serve the movement of the Spirit rather than the other way around. The Apostles were caught up in the life of the local churches, but their lightness of touch allowed for the empowerment of the body and the activation of spiritual gifts through its members. In turn, the local churches were able to grow into maturity and their influence could continue to spread.

Further, while the Apostles were wholeheartedly committed to their local churches, they also knew they were not called to stay in once place forever, but to expand the gospel into new geographical territories and cultures. As they moved into these new areas preaching the gospel, many people responded, pledging allegiance to Jesus. As a result, the foundation-laying work of the kingdom family started again. In order to sustain the dynamic sense of movement, the Apostles realised a distinctive new element needed to be added into their ministry – the work of raising up leaders within the local church to care for and disciple these new believers. Paul, in particular, seems to have crystallised a type of apostolic pattern – expanding the kingdom, establishing the churches, entrusting leadership.*

It became clear that two types of leaders would needed if this pattern was going to be sustained.

LOCAL ELDERS

Local elders were the men and women identified by the Apostles as spiritual mothers and fathers, who would provide authority and oversight for churches in specific locales. Luke describes this principle emerging through Paul and Barnabas' apostolic ministry: 'Paul and Barnabas appointed elders for them in each church and, with prayer and fasting, committed them to the Lord, in whom they had put their trust' (Acts 14:23). As Paul's ministry unfolded throughout the years it appears that his belief in the appointing of local elders only strengthened. Writing to his younger apostolic apprentices, Timothy and Titus, in the final years of his ministry, we can see how Paul came to view the installation of elders in the local churches which he cared for as vitally important.

To Timothy, Paul said, 'the things you have heard me say in the presence of many witnesses entrust to reliable people who will also

* Jeff Reed, *Unfolding the Great Commission: First Principles from Acts*, The First Principles Series 3 (BILD, 2006), p61.

be qualified to teach others' (2 Timothy 2:2). To Titus, who was stationed at the fledgling church in Crete, Paul said, 'The reason I left you in Crete was that you might put in order what was left unfinished and appoint elders in every town, as I directed you' (Titus 1:5).

It is clear from these examples that Paul viewed the 'establishing' process of a church as incomplete until local elders had been raised up and appointed. Therefore, in his letters to both Titus (Titus 1:5–9) and Timothy (1 Timothy 3:1–7), Paul dedicated time to describe in detail the qualifications potential elders should meet. Interestingly, when we explore these passages in detail, we see characteristics that map easily onto the traits of loving and committed parents, confirming the emphasis of our previous chapter. Among the different spiritual qualities Paul listed in these passages, 'managing' one's own home in a godly, responsible way was seen as evidence that a potential elder could spiritually parent within the local church. Paul knew it was the spiritually mature mothers and fathers in a local church, not simply the gifted charismatic leader, who would provide the healthiest form of oversight a local church needed.

Identifying such individuals in the local kingdom family is critical if the church is going to stay true to her original foundations. It was these men and women to whom the Apostles could pass on the traditions of Jesus, commissioning them to build the new churches on these truths and serving the new believers as mothers and fathers in the Lord.

'TRANSLOCAL' LEADERS

As the story of the early church unfolds, we become aware of particular women and men called by God to serve not only in their local church but the wider church as the gospel movement advanced in new contexts and cultures. These leaders were gifted by God to be more mobile, attending to the needs of multiple churches and pioneering into areas where the gospel had not yet been preached.

Timothy and Titus, who we have mentioned above, are good examples of this second designation of leaders. Crucially, Timothy and Titus had first been 'tested' and 'proven' in the local context and Paul had recognised both the gift and the capacity within them to serve a wider body of churches. Paul's letters to Timothy and Titus were written for this distinct purpose – to help his young apprentices understand what was required as they followed Paul in the pioneering and establishment of multiple churches.

It was the synthesis of this twofold nature of leadership (local and 'translocal') in the early church that allowed for its dynamic movement and effective sustainability. Jeff Reed put it like this:

> Paul's intention was to set a pattern for networks of churches in the future to be both under the care of local elders and the future Timothys – Pauline teams if you will – moving among the churches. Both types of leaders were critical to the first-generation network of churches under Paul and both would be needed down through the centuries as churches multiplied across the empire and around the world.[*]

As we dive deeper into Paul's epistles, we become aware of the different types of leadership gifts that many who were called to such a translocal ministry were entrusted with. There are two passages in Paul's letters written to the churches of Corinth and Ephesus which I believe are particularly instructive for us regarding these gifts.

> *Now you are the body of Christ, and each one of you is a part of it. And God has placed in the church first of all apostles, second prophets, third teachers, then miracles, then gifts of healing, of helping, of guidance, and of different kinds of tongues.*

1 CORINTHIANS 12:27–28

---

[*] Jeff Reed, *Living in God's Household, First Principles from the Pastorals* (Independently published, 2014), p25.

These verses in Corinthians are fascinating given they come at the end of Paul's 'body of Christ' passage. We have already drawn attention to how Paul's 'body' metaphor beautifully describes every member of the body performing their own unique part in a spirit of interdependence and mutual submission. 'Just as a body, though one, has many parts, but all its many parts form one body, so it is with Christ' (1 Corinthians 12:12). Yet, a few verses later Paul introduces the language of 'first' and 'second' when referencing certain gifts. What is Paul doing? Is this not a contradiction of the striking imagery he has just used to describe the equality and complimentary nature of every part of the body?

The answer is no! Paul does not view these 'first' and 'second' gifts as the highest ranks, akin to a 'chain-of-command' type structure in a more corporate leadership setting. Rather, Paul had received insight into the divine ordering of certain leadership gifts. If the church was to remain true to the apostolic call – fulfilling the Great Commission of Jesus – Paul believed certain gifts needed to lead the way. Experience and divine revelation had shown Paul that the church was established around the presiding gifts of apostles, prophets and teachers. All the gifts were equally important, but they could only all function effectively together if certain gifts were released to pioneer a way forward and create room for all the other gifts to play their part. As Jon Thompson describes, the gift of apostleship and prophecy 'aren't first in order of importance but in order of impact'.* While many of the other spiritual gifts are more centred around the individual, gifts like apostleship, prophecy and teaching are more community-orientated. Leaders who operate in these gifts should not be elevated more than others but, provided these gifts are stewarded humbly, they should effectively open up a playing field for all the other spiritual gifts to operate and flourish.

* Jon Thompson, *Convergence: Why Jesus Needs to Be More than our Lord and Savior to Thrive in a Post Christian World* (Independently published, 2018).

This principle of divine ordering when understanding spiritual gifts is only strengthened further in Paul's letter to the Ephesians. In Chapter 2, Paul refers to the prominent roles of apostles and prophets laying essential foundations for the establishment of God's household:

> *Consequently, you are no longer foreigners and strangers, but fellow citizens with God's people and also members of his household, built on the foundation of the apostles and prophets, with Christ Jesus himself as the chief cornerstone.*

EPHESIANS 2:19–20

Then, as we return to Ephesians 4, note how Paul adds to the gifts mentioned in Corinth – apostles, prophets and teachers – another two – pastors and evangelists – in verse 11.

> *But to each one of us grace has been given as Christ apportioned it. This is why it says:*
>
> > *'When he ascended on high,*
> > *he took many captives*
> > *and gave gifts to his people.'*
>
> *(What does 'he ascended' mean except that he also descended to the lower, earthly regions? He who descended is the very one who ascended higher than all the heavens, in order to fill the whole universe.) So Christ himself gave the apostles, the prophets, the evangelists, the pastors and teachers …*

EPHESIANS 4:7–11

The designation of gifts Paul describes here are categorised by some streams of the church as 'the fivefold gifts',* because five distinct gifts are mentioned, and together they are often known as the

---

* Numerous scholars choose to identify only four designations here, coupling the pastor and teacher into a pastor-teacher type.

'Ascension Ministry of Christ'. Considerable debate across different traditions of the church has taken place throughout the centuries concerning the function and priority of these gifts today. I recognise and respect that not everyone reading this book may share my views on this. Nevertheless, I hope we can at least find common ground in the spirit of service I believe all of these gifts should be stewarded in.

In Ephesians 4:8–11, Paul reveals the insight he has received from the Holy Spirit concerning the continuation of Christ's ministry on the earth after Christ's ascension. The picture Paul paints is of the victorious cosmic Christ, raised from the dead to rule triumphantly over all, longing 'to fill the whole universe' (verse 10) with his presence. God's universal plan for the world is therefore still continuing and this can happen because Jesus has bequeathed these five core attributes of his ministry on the earth into his church. In other words, Jesus is continuing to work on the earth today, but now it is not through his unique, solitary, physical body limited by time and space but through his Spirit-filled, corporate, multi-faceted body all around the world. If the church is the embodiment of Christ's presence in the world post-ascension, then these five gifts expressed through his people – apostles, prophets, evangelists, pastors and teachers – bring the shape and definition to Christ's ministry in the world. Alan Hirsch, who has written extensively on this topic, says:

> Ephesians 4:11 is nothing less than the ministry of Christ expressing itself in and through the body of Christ ... Anything less than a fivefold ministry is a misrepresentation of the ministry of Christ and by consequence, then leads to a misrepresentation of Christ in the world.*

It should go without saying that Jesus is the archetype of each of these gifts. He is the chief Apostle, the great Shepherd, the One

---

* Alan Hirsch and Tim Catchim, *The Permanent Revolution: Apostolic Imagination and Practice for the 21st Century Church* (Jossey-Bass, 2012), p89.

who taught like no other, the ultimate Prophet and the exemplar Evangelist who came to seek and save the lost. If cruciform leaders are those who follow Jesus, then they will be leaders who are familiar with each of these characteristics of Jesus' ministry.

FIVE GIFTS

With all of this in mind we will now take a brief look at each of the five gifts below, exploring the distinctives of how each gift operates and makes a particular contribution to the church and her impact in the world.

Apostle

I have already acknowledged, indeed argued strongly about, the distinctiveness of the original Apostles. These first leaders of the church who walked with Jesus and encountered him as resurrected Lord provide us with the inspiration for the type of cruciform leadership we are called to. But while I believe the unique role of the original Apostles (including Paul) is unequivocally unrepeatable, throughout Acts and the Epistles it is clear that many more apostles emerged and were recognised.[*] Today, we may not share in the unique apostolic authority of the original Apostles but we do share their apostolic mission and, as the eminent New Testament theologian Gerald Bray points out, the Greek word for apostle – *apostolos* – embraces the ideas of both authority and mission without difficulty.[**] The literal meaning of *apostolos* is 'sent one' and so it follows that the primary role of the first Apostles was to ensure the church stayed true to the fulfilment of Jesus' final words:

[*] James (Galatians 1:19), Barnabas (Acts 14:3, 14), Epaphroditus (Philippians 2:25), Silas and Timothy (1 Thessalonians 1:1; 2:6), Andronicus and Junia (Romans 16:7), and others (1 Corinthians 15:7; 2 Corinthians 8:23).
[**] Gerald L Bray, *The Pastoral Epistles: I & II Timothy,* The International Theological Commentary (T&T Clark, 2025), p160.

> *Therefore go and make disciples of all nations, baptising them in the name of the Father and of the Son and of the Holy Spirit, and teaching them to obey everything I have commanded you.*

MATTHEW 28:19–20

In short, the apostolic gift pulses with the overall vigour of the Great Commission. Apostles are therefore usually characterised by a pioneering spirit, leading out from the front through the proclamation of the kingdom into 'unreached' areas and people groups, with signs and wonders following. They plant new kingdom families, establishing these fledgling churches in the ways of Jesus and laying biblical foundations which allow a 'household of faith' to grow up in Christ. They help expand the churches' mission in the world, establish new churches and entrust leadership to those they have invested in.

Paul described his apostolic ministry as that of a 'master builder' (1 Corinthians 3:10, ESV). The Greek word here is *architekton*, which is where we derive the English word 'architect' from. We discovered earlier in this chapter that Paul was entrusted with revelation to reveal and administer the mystery of the church, therefore his way of describing his apostolic gift in architectural terms is not a surprise. It follows then that when we see leaders bringing the divine wisdom needed for the organisational health of the church, we are most likely witnessing this apostolic gift. As we referenced above, the only reason that the gift of apostle comes first in the list (1 Corinthians 12:28), is not because the apostle is most important but because he or she creates a 'field of influence' where all the other gifts can function. The apostle's role should therefore never be authenticated by claims of personal position or personal prestige but by suffering and Christlike sacrificial living.

Prophet

The prophetic gift is given to the church to encourage God's people to maintain covenant faithfulness. All through the Bible, prophets were raised up to communicate the heart of God to the people of God in a clear and compelling way. These were and are men and women able to discern God's heart on the one hand and the current cultural reality of God's people on the other. Their words speak to the gap that exists between these two realities and pulse with longing for true and sincere alignment. An authentic prophetic message will bring the people of God into an immediate and convincing sense of divine focus. Often the prophetic gift manifests wisdom or knowledge beyond what is naturally or rationally known because it has the supernatural ability to hear and see what the Spirit is saying.

Evangelist

The evangelistic gift enables an individual to transmit the gospel fluently and simply. Those who lead in this sphere of influence are usually able to win a hearing for the gospel much more easily than others and are more comfortable sharing the gospel than others. This gift is often found in those with naturally outgoing personalities, who are therefore better able to interest and enlist people into the gospel movement.

Pastor

The pastoral gift nurtures spiritual development and formation among the community of Christ. Pastors, sometimes known as 'shepherds', lead God's people into Christlikeness while being committed to every aspect of their wellbeing throughout the process. The pastoral grace also imparts community health into the kingdom family and is motivated by how the flock relates to one another. In short, those who lead with a strong pastoral gift will reveal a passion to see a loving, healthy family being formed among the people of God.

Teacher

The teaching gift is given to mediate wisdom and understanding to the people of God, leading them into a clearer comprehension of their standing and purpose in Christ. I believe the teaching gift operates best in its relationship to the other gifts, bringing depth and substance to the revelation of God. For example, often after an inspired prophetic word is delivered or an apostolic vision is presented, an anointed teacher is needed to ground this divine insight. Here, the teacher establishes deeper layers of understanding from God's word in a way that ultimately leads to transformation. Because these women and men have been gifted by God to know how to 'rightly handle the word of truth' (2 Timothy 2:15, ESV), they will articulate to the believers how they should respond to God's word and how the culture of the kingdom should be incarnated in their lives.

OTHER SPIRITUAL GIFTS

While I have focused on the spiritual gifts highlighted at the end of 1 Corinthians Chapter 12 and in Chapter 4 of Ephesians, it is important to acknowledge there are many other spiritual gifts listed in the New Testament which God has placed within his body, the church.* We should remind ourselves of these great words from Paul, 'God has placed the parts in the body, every one of them, just as he wanted them to be' (1 Corinthians 12:18).

The reason I have placed more emphasis on these passages is because these gifts are usually the ones most associated with leadership in the church. Individuals whom God has obviously graced with the different 'fivefold gifts' we have outlined above will usually develop as leaders in the church. If they are not natural leaders already, they will often have been supernaturally endowed with a measure of spiritual leadership from God, enabling them to at least lead in the context of their particular gift(s). However, the bottom line for any leader in the body of Christ: whatever gifts you have been graced with by God from the variety of passages outlined above, you are fundamentally called to use your gifts to release others into theirs.

* See Romans 12:6–8, 1 Corinthians 12:4–11 and 1 Peter 4:10–12.

HOW?

Now that we have explored 'why' spiritual gifts are given and 'what' they look like, it's important to finish this chapter reminding ourselves 'how' they should be stewarded. As I've acknowledged above, different denominations debate the function and use of these gifts today. I fully accept this. However, I would contend our theological differences about them aren't our main problem today. Across the global church almost all streams believe in the need for leadership gifts of some sort or another. Our real problem is *how* leaders have stewarded these gifts in the past. Here, we have common ground.

THE WAY OF JESUS

Notice the order of Ephesians 4:11 one more time, 'So Christ himself gave the apostles, the prophets, the evangelists, the pastors and teachers ...' If Christ gave these gifts to his church, then it follows when leaders operate in these gifts they should look like Christ. Once we stop viewing our leadership giftings through a Christological lens we are no longer operating biblically and have likely become a danger to others and ourselves. Marcus Barth said:

> The task of the special ministers mentioned in Ephesians 4:11 is to be servants to that ministry which is entrusted to the whole church. Their place is not above but below the great number of saints who are not adorned with resounding titles.*

Not above but below. Yes! Notice how Paul understood his apostleship as he introduced himself in his letters to his young apprentice Titus, 'Paul a servant of God and an apostle of Jesus Christ' (Titus 1:1). Any understanding of Paul's calling as an Apostle was predicated on a life of servanthood. Cruciform leaders first and foremost understand

---

* Marcus Barth quoted in Darrell L Guder, *Called to Witness: Doing Missional Theology* (Eerdmans, 2015), p145.

themselves as servants of God stewarding the gifts God has given them for the release of others into their destiny.

DIVINE ORDER

We have already shown that early church ecclesiology was not characterised by rigid forms of hierarchy but rather prioritised divine ordering of the kingdom family through Christlike servant-hearted leaders. It's clear in Paul's churches the apostolic gift acted as a fulcrum around which the other gifts operated and supplemented. As each of these five leadership gifts served together to equip the saints, every member of the body would begin to function in harmony and in unison. While a definite Spirit-inspired pattern emerged among the first wave of churches, it's important to repeat the point – this pattern was never understood as a flat, copy-and-paste process. There was great flexibility and fluidity in how these principles were outworked in different contexts as the Apostles discerned the Spirit's leading. The believers were therefore encouraged to respect and honour their leaders as they poured themselves out on behalf of Christ and his church.

MUTUAL SUBMISSION

This will be the subject of much of the next chapter but, suffice to say, the only way there could be fluency among all the members of the body of Christ was if each member adopted the posture of humility and submission, preferring and honouring one another in the love of Christ. Cruciform leaders model, before the wider body of Christ, a posture of sacrificial (agape) love – the only spirit through which all the gifts can truly function and flow together.

One of the beautiful characteristics of the leadership structure of the early church, and one often missed, is how local elders and those with translocal leadership giftings submitted mutually one to another. Neither saw themselves 'above' the other nor 'in control of the other' but rather recognised the sphere of influence each was called to and moved together in loving partnership. For all the problems the first churches endured there is a stunning unity-in-diversity dynamic at the heart of New Testament ecclesiology which provides an uncomfortable reflection for contemporary models.

NON-COMPETITIVE

Mutual submission means there can be no room for competitiveness in the body of Christ. Going back to the Parable of the Talents the question to ask is not, 'why do some get five talents and some only get one talent?' The real question Jesus is asking is *'What will you do with what you have been given?'* Insecurity makes us prone to comparison which in turn allows jealousy to take root in our hearts. When we sense this spirit rising within us, we would do well to pray for those who we are comparing ourselves to. And remember the one who got the five talents has a greater responsibility to give back ten! 'From everyone who has been given much, much will be demanded; and from the one who has been entrusted with much, much more will be asked' (Luke 12:48).

Cruciform leaders have cultivated lives of confident sonship and daughterhood in the love of the Father. They have no time for comparison because they recognise comparison as the thief of joy. Instead, they steward their gifts in the fear of the Lord, seized by a holy ambition to give back to the Lord more than they were ever given.

RELATIONAL AUTHORITY

Jesus' life and discipleship methods bear witness to the truth that the kingdom of God always moves at the speed of relationship. Jesus showed us that authority in the kingdom of God is never primarily expressed through position or title but friendship:

> *I no longer call you servants, because a servant does not know his master's business. Instead, I have called you friends, for everything that I learned from my Father I have made known to you.*

> JOHN 15:15

Love is the true muscle of spiritual authority and therefore leadership gifts are never used to control but to release. It's interesting that the Apostle Paul recognised the basis of his relationship with the churches not in terms of positional authority but relational partnership. The move towards a more institutional leadership power base over the centuries has stifled the dynamism the early church enjoyed, creating a chasm between leaders and the laity of the church. As Barry A Harvey put it, 'In Christendom the fundamental division is not between church and world, but between clergy and laity.'*

Henri Nouwen, lamenting the increasing aloofness of leaders he witnessed through his lifetime, said, 'Somehow we have come to believe that good leadership requires a safe distance from those we are called to lead.'** This is not the leadership of Jesus. Cruciform leaders naturally smell of the sheep. They are not cloistered away in their own offices or overly consumed with church committee meetings but are found in homes, in coffee-shops and on the road with those God has entrusted to their care. They understand that people (like sheep!) do not like to be driven towards a vision but are gently led to the place of pasture and sustenance.

GROWING YOUR GIFT

I hope it is clear by now – the way you increase your influence in leadership has less to do with how gifted you are and more to do with stewarding well what you have been given. Throughout my time as a leader, I have watched many young disciples, those who are perhaps not as naturally gifted as their peers, become some of the best leaders I know, entrusted with greater levels of influence than they ever desired. How does this happen? Simply because they have been faithful to their calling from God to serve his church and,

* Barry A Harvey, *Another City: An Ecclesiological Primer for a Post-Christian World* (Trinity Press, 1999), p71.
** Henri JM Nouwen, *In the Name of Jesus: Reflections on Christian Leadership* (Darton, Longman & Todd, 1989), p43.

in the kingdom of God, it is faithful stewardship that is rewarded, not performance. I will leave the final words of this chapter to the Apostle Paul:

This, then, is how you ought to regard us: as servants of Christ and as those entrusted with the mysteries God has revealed. Now it is required that those who have been given a trust must prove faithful.

1 CORINTHIANS 4:1–2

PRACTISING THE CRUCIFORM WAY

Consider the questions and readings below in discussion, reflection, journalling and prayer.

ONE:

And he gave the apostles, the prophets, the evangelists, the shepherds and teachers, to equip the saints for the work of ministry, for building up the body of Christ …

EPHESIANS 4:11–12 (ESV)

Revisit Ephesians 4:11–16, and ponder these words describing Paul's instructions to the church of Ephesus.

- Discuss or reflect on how effective your leadership and discipleship process is at 'equipping the saints for the work of the ministry'.
- Do you agree with his suggestion that leadership is granted 'to help supply the destiny of others'? How are you outworking this in your context? What discipleship processes are in place in your community to enable this?

TWO:

Recall how Chapter 6 deals with the reality of the movemental nature of the church.

- Reflect on how this dynamic impacts your own context of church leadership.
- Are there ways that you are encountering the healthy tension of both raising up local leaders and releasing those with translocal gifts?

THREE:

Discuss the current gift mix active in your leadership setting.

- What gift muscles are strong and what are weak?
- Take time to call out the gifts in one another and pray over each other. Reflect on the importance of how these gifts are stewarded and how you can best support one another in this.

CHAPTER 7

A TEAM PLAYER

*A new command I give you: love one another. As I have loved you,
so you must love one another.*

JOHN 13:34

Reflecting back on twenty-five years of church ministry, there are two commitments that I have learned to prioritise, and these have greatly influenced my effectiveness as a leader. They sometimes surface as deep, soulful longings. These two commitments are God-given vision and authentic friendship.

Moreover, I have come to realise I need them both together – one without the other results in leadership that is lopsided and not fully empowered.

- *Vision without friendship*: The vision of a future outcome or an end goal can be energising and consuming, and we can be motivated to work hard towards it; yet pursuing vision at the expense of friendship can lead to loneliness and lack of joy.

- *Friendship without vision*: The thrill of deep connection with those we want to be on the road with can be appealing; yet without vision, if we aren't running towards a goal together, we can become bored and irritated with friends.

When God-given vision and true friendship come together in my life, I am never more effective. For most of the last twenty-five years I have worked in teams and environments where these two values have converged. It was in my early twenties that I first realised how important this combination was. Over the years we have run a number of short-term mission trips to Uganda, the Pearl of Africa, to a beautiful church community in a village called Jandira in the African bush, an hour outside the capital Kampala. As part of this, a deep friendship and partnership developed between ourselves and Pastor Richard, who leads the church, and with others in the community. Our teams' daily work pattern would begin with assembling in the morning for devotions; then dividing up to serve in children's programmes, craft classes, building projects, discipleship classes or sports activities; then closing out the day with a meal alongside our Ugandan brothers and sisters and sharing testimonies of how God was moving among us.

A few days into each trip, as the team's daily rhythm was established and new relationships started to form, I would experience a gentle epiphany. Looking around the village, there would be barefooted Ugandan children screaming with joy alongside some of our team members when a goal was scored in a football match; one of our young female team members sitting under a tree praying privately with an older Ugandan lady; boys from our church passing bricks to local builders as they built alongside one another, laughing uproariously together as they tried to communicate across their different languages. Or in the school classrooms there would be a handful of our schoolteachers sitting with the local teachers sharing their wisdom and equipping them with new resources, while outside the classroom some of our teenage girls would be surrounded by young Ugandan girls, singing songs they had taught one another full of the sweetest harmonies.

At the sight of all this, I would find myself almost forced to stand still, to pause and take in the wonder of what I was witnessing. I would sit down on a stone under the relentless African sun, hot tears rolling down my cheeks but joy rising up inside. Surely God was in this place. I was beholding nothing less than the genius of God, a glimpse of reality of the one new humanity in Christ.

Reflecting on the visceral memory of these times in Uganda, I realise this was my younger self encountering the dynamic intersection of those Holy-Spirit inspired themes – movement and family – that we described in Chapter 1; themes which shape God's mission in the world. Every person on our team was playing their part, falling in love with people of a different colour, language and culture. In the intensity of those short-term mission trips, with all the tensions and dynamics of team life, I became aware that this is what my whole being was wired for – playing my part in fulfilling God's vision for the world alongside those who have become my friends.

JESUS

Jesus' life pulsed with both vision and friendship.

- Vision: In Jesus we see a life resolutely focused on fulfilling his life's purpose and calling, a life of uncompromising obedience to his Father's will. He 'set his face to go to Jerusalem' (Luke 9:51, ESV); he did 'only what he [saw] the Father doing' (John 5:19), initially refusing to be distracted by a Canaanite woman as he was sent to the lost sheep of Israel (Matthew 15:24); and he worked to see the establishment of the kingdom of God on the earth.

- Friendship: At the same time, Jesus' life was one of open-hearted love and intimate friendship – healing the lame and lepers and raising the sons of widows; eating with tax collectors and staying with fishermen and calling them friends. Jesus was the most secure individual who ever lived and yet everything about him embodied team and community.

Let's unpack two noteworthy areas of Jesus' life to explore this more deeply.

Firstly, as 'the image of the invisible God' (Colossians 1:15), Jesus displayed the exquisite fellowship which exists at the centre of God's eternal nature. God is Love. Jesus demonstrated this not just by doing 'loving' things but by revealing to humanity that God is a loving community. The Maker of the heavens and the earth is three-in-one; an Eternal Family, living and moving together in vibrant harmony. The most vivid example of the inseparable operations of the triune God revealed through the life of Jesus is when John the Baptist baptised Jesus.* At this moment the four gospel accounts record how all three persons of the Trinity were present. Jesus the Son undergoes baptism as a model for all of humanity, the Father is heard declaring Jesus' beloved sonship, and the Holy Spirit, in the form of a dove, anoints Jesus for ministry. This sacred moment in history emphatically confirmed what the biblical story had always been pointing towards – the mutual submission and self-giving love which defines the essence of the triune God. Jesus' life and ministry as recorded in the gospels only confirms this further. Wholly surrendered to the power and presence of the Holy Spirit, Jesus constantly refers to his oneness and partnership with the Father in all he does.

Secondly, Jesus offered his followers an invitation into the heart and essence of the triune God. After three years of cultivating Trinity-love among them, Jesus prayed for them to understand the depths of what he was bidding them into:

> *I pray also for those who will believe in me through their message, that all of them may be one, Father, just as you are in me and I am in you. May they also be in us so that the world may believe that you have sent me.*

JOHN 17:20–21

* Matthew 3:13–17; Mark 1:9–11; Luke 3:21–22; John 1:32–34.

Incredibly, the followers of Jesus were called to become an extension of the triune family on the earth. Catching even a glimpse of the mystery of Trinity-love helps one understand the passion for intimate friendship that Jesus displayed as he discipled his followers. I am more and more moved by the way Jesus invited his disciples into the big vision of the kingdom of God without ever compromising the genuine friendship he wished to enjoy with them. In other words, Jesus' friends were never the victims of his vision. His approach to team-life flowed from the essence of who he was, who God is. Jesus was open-hearted. Vulnerable. Invitational. Jesus gave the disciples access to every area of his life. He was bound to them. They were never treated as mere subjects, recruited simply to 'get the work done'. Rather, Jesus viewed them as intimate comrades who would walk alongside him in the fulfillment of the Father's good purposes.

In all of this, Jesus set an example he wanted his disciples to follow. 'A new command I give you: love one another. As I have loved you, so you must love one another' (John 13:34).

Friendship over function is the Jesus way. It's not just about getting the job done but how you do it that really counts. Patience is required. Think of Jesus slowly nurturing this team-based approach among a bunch of ego-fueled, competitive and ambitious young men. Commissioning them into their first mission experience, Jesus made sure to send them out together, two by two; not one of them was sent out alone:

> *Then Jesus went around teaching from village to village. Calling the Twelve to him, he began to send them out two by two and gave them authority over impure spirits.*

MARK 6:6–7

> *After this the Lord appointed seventy-two others and sent them two by two ahead of him to every town and place where he was about to go.*

LUKE 10:1

The results of the mission were better than the disciples could have expected – they healed the sick, preached the gospel effectively and drove out demons. Yet, alongside all of the wonderful demonstrations of power the disciples witnessed flowing through their hands, Jesus wanted them to experience something even deeper in their hearts – the joy of being part of the mission of God with one another, together – and the eternal significance of that, of having their names 'written in heaven' (see Luke 10:20). He wanted them to glimpse the beauty of genuine partnership – the thrilling experience of honouring one another's distinct gifts and abilities in a kingdom enterprise, carrying out a God-given vision together. As we turn the pages from the Gospels to the book of Acts, we witness the incredible fruit of Jesus' team-based apprenticing in the remarkable one-mindedness of the early church.

THE EARLY CHURCH

The first church, founded on the love of Christ, was a stunning reflection of team. Try to read the following oft-quoted description of community life in the early church like you are reading it for the first time:

They devoted themselves to the apostles' teaching and to fellowship, to the breaking of bread and to prayer. Everyone was filled with awe at the many wonders and signs performed by the apostles. All the believers were together and had everything in common. They sold property and possessions to give to anyone who had need. Every day they continued to meet together in the temple courts. They broke bread in their homes and ate together with glad and sincere hearts, praising God and enjoying the favour of all the people. And the Lord added to their number daily those who were being saved.

ACTS 2:42–47

Every time I read these words, I feel them in my bones! Every one of us was created to be a part of such a community – a colony of heaven on the earth. The biblical word for this 'oneness' Luke describes in the verses above is *koinonia*, a much stronger word than our English translation 'fellowship'. *Koinonia* speaks to the idea of a deeply shared passion and collective mission, undergirded by sacrificial love. Contrary to the way our hyper-individualised Western society understands the idea of 'community' or 'team' today, in the early church relationships are never merely transactional or tokenistic. The depth of community the first kingdom family formed reminds us as brothers and sisters in Christ that we are so much more than associates who merely require each other's skills to achieve a goal. Rather, we are surrendered sons and daughters of Jesus, covenanted to one another in sacrificial love, reflecting the love of the Trinity to the world.

The apostolic instructions of the Epistles further emphasise the *koinonia* foundations of the church which Luke has described in Acts. As we have discussed in the previous chapter, Paul received special revelation about God's plan for the church. In his letter to the Ephesians (2:14–16), Paul magisterially described how Jesus' death and resurrection had brought about a glorious new reality on the earth – one new humanity. Jew and Gentile, master and slave, male and female had all become one in Christ. Paul had glimpsed into the heart of God, witnessing the divine kaleidoscopic beauty of people from every tribe and tongue united in Christ. The beauty of this vision was so splendid it had ruined him for the rest of his life. He would never see anything on the earth, as glorious as the family of God, united in Jesus. And he would never live for anything less than this reality. It's no wonder then that Paul constantly uses sibling language throughout his letters to refer to the believers in the churches. He uses the term *adelphos* or 'brothers and sisters' 127 times. Paul's letters exhibit the heart of a cruciform leader contending for what Christ died for – a multicultural, multiethnic family, surrendered to the Lordship of Jesus. Further, they reveal how Paul understood the only way this could be achieved was through the effective functioning of teams made up of cruciform leaders who modelled *koinonia* – siblingship in Christ.

Did this come easily? Absolutely not. But did they do it? Yes! The New Testament provides us with some of the best examples of effective, healthy, functioning teams while at the same time including all the tensions and dramas too. Most Christians today are ignorant of the challenges the Apostles faced as the early church broke into new cultural, social, economic and political spaces. Scholars, like James Dunn in his epic book *Unity and Diversity*, have helped bring the complexities to light.

> No longer is it possible to conceive of first century Christianity as a clearly defined entity, easily extractable from its historical context like a nut from a shell, the historical reality was much more complex.[*]

For a moment try to imagine Jews and Greeks, Arabs and Cretans, soldiers and peasants, wealthy Roman citizens and slaves all coming to faith. What would a local fellowship of believers made up of all these so-called opposing sectors of society have looked like? Scot McKnight, in his book *A Fellowship of Differents*, helps paint a picture. Arguing that local churches were made up of on average around thirty people, McKnight lists who could have been there:

- a craftworker in whose home they meet, along with his wife, children, a couple of male slaves, a female domestic slave, and a dependent relative

- some tenants, with families and slaves and dependents, also living in the same home in rented rooms

[*] James DG Dunn, *Unity and Diversity in the New Testament: An Inquiry Into the Character of Earliest Christianity* (SCM Press, 2005), p4.

- some family members of a householder who himself does not participate in the house church

- a couple of slaves whose owners do not attend

- some freed slaves who do not participate in the church

- a couple homeless people

- a few migrant workers renting small rooms in the home.

McKnight goes on to say:

> Add to this mix some Jewish folks and perhaps an enslaved prostitute and we see how many 'different tastes' were in a typical house church in Rome.*

I hope you are getting the picture – the diversity of the early church was staggeringly beautiful, but its unity was hard won. The integrity of the biblical authors shines through in this regard because they refuse to give us an airbrushed account of the first churches. Rather we are granted the honour of a 'ringside seat', invited to pay attention to the many points of tension which existed in the early church between leaders and within the communities. It is as if the Apostles want us to know that the outworking of the unity Jesus prayed that his followers would share together (John 17) wasn't easy, but at the same time that's exactly what it means to be a part of the church.

The idea of unity in diversity was as radical a concept then as it is now. In contemporary society, the church included, we are more divided than ever around race, gender, wealth, politics and status. The New Testament has something to teach us about how we live with the tension in a godly way. In his dissertation, a friend of mine, Roger Ellis, has stated that many see 'diversity as an end in and of

---

* Scot McKnight, *A Fellowship of Differents: Showing the World God's Design for Life Together* (Zondervan, 2015), p15, citing Peter Oakes, *Reading Romans in Pompeii: Paul's Letter at Ground Level* (SPCK, 2009), p96.

itself, but in the New Testament Christ remains the goal. Jesus is both the source and advocate of both diversity and unity.'*

In other words, the unity of the early church was not a token acceptance of difference or a 'woke' form of tolerance. It was a steely determination towards covenantal love. The first believers were resolutely committed to one another and to the unity of their faith in Jesus. They chose to relinquish self-centred and deep-seated manmade traditions in exchange for life in the Spirit. The one-mindedness the early church achieved in the midst of immense cultural complexities, is, I believe, one of its most beautiful and underrated qualities. Numerous accounts throughout the first few centuries reveal how it was the loving unity of the first Christians which made the rest of the culture sit up and take notice. The world had never seen anything like this level of love and commitment before.

It was this foundational understanding of the church as family – the one new humanity in Christ, bound together in covenantal love – which influenced the Apostles' leadership style and motivated them to build these teams. The Apostles modelled this unity among themselves and the teams they sought to establish, creating a culture where each member was recognised and their gifts honoured. Leaders today need to reflect again on this example, repenting of ungodly rivalry and competitiveness and returning to genuine gospel partnership in a spirit of unity. This is the way of the cruciform leader – shared leadership in a spirit of mutual submission and committed friendship. The only competitiveness the New Testament allows room for is connected to the level of honour we can show one another. 'Love one another with brotherly affection. Outdo one another in showing honour' (Romans 12:10, ESV).

This is the way of the Three-in-One God.

* Roger Ellis, 'A Comparative Study of the Churches in Jerusalem and Corinth Paying Particular Attention to their Emerging Ecclesiology, and how this is Shaped by their Different Contexts', MA Dissertation (WTC, University of Chester).

MODELLING TEAM

COVENANTAL CO-WORKERS

Often, when we think of Paul, we picture him as a dynamic missionary filled with theological zeal, adopting a no-nonsense approach to pastoral issues. Many presume he was difficult to like. But we've seen so much evidence of a man consumed with love for the churches; a spiritual father carrying a burden for his 'children in the Lord' who were constantly in his heart. Further, while at times Paul no doubt came across as strong-minded and forthright, the overwhelming evidence points to a co-labouring comrade brimming with wholehearted affection for those he ministered alongside. He makes countless references to his friends and co-workers. The esteemed New Testament theologian, Ekhard Schnabel, researched thirty-eight co-workers among the hundred names associated with Paul throughout the New Testament.* This list includes names such as Priscilla and Aquila, Urbanus, Timothy, Titus, Epaphroditus, Clement, Justus, Philemon, Mark, Aristarchus, Demas, Luke, Andronicus and Junia, Phoebe and Chloe.

Scot McKnight insightfully points out how Paul used the word *agape* when he refers to this circle of co-workers and associates. McKnight argues Paul could have used *philia*, another Greek word for 'love' which is more commonly used in the context of friendship.** Why did Paul use *agape* then? Because *agape* defines the essence of covenantal love that Paul knew he and his co-workers had been graciously invited to experience together in the Spirit. Paul wanted his friends to know the nature of his relationship with them was defined by the same deep affection and rugged commitment God has always had for his people. Following in the footsteps of Jesus,

---

* Ekhard J Schnabel, *Early Christian Mission* (IVP Academic, 2004).
** Scot McKnight, *Pastor Paul: Nurturing a Culture of Christoformity in the Church* (Brazos Press, 2019).

who had formed his team around the self-emptying embodiment of sacrificial love, Paul sought to establish his teams on the same *agape* root.

We often skip over Paul's affectionate references to his co-workers in order to get to what we have been led to believe are the 'meatier' theological sections of his epistles. But if we read these verses a little more thoughtfully, noticing the tender tone of Paul's voice and the intentional choice of his words, we will begin to realise the same love Jesus had for his disciples was burning in the heart of the Apostle for his co-workers in the gospel. It's fascinating that on one occasion, after describing to the Corinthians an opportunity for extending the gospel, Paul writes how he actually turned down this particular opportunity. Why? Because it seems the strength he would have needed to fulfill this opportunity, flowing from partnership with Titus, was not in place at that time.

> *Now when I went to Troas to preach the gospel of Christ and found that the Lord had opened a door for me, I still had no peace of mind, because I did not find my brother Titus there. So, I said goodbye to them and went on to Macedonia.*

2 CORINTHIANS 2:12–13

This gives us great insight into how Paul valued kingdom partnership. But the New Testament also reveals how Paul was on the receiving end of such *agape* love. Luke highlights the role of one of the Bible's best examples of a team player, Barnabas, whose name means 'son of encouragement'. Luke identifies Barnabas as Joseph, a Cypriot Levite, who sold his field and gave all the proceeds to the local church. Barnabas evidently became an important figure in the early Jerusalem church and Luke later describes him affectionately as 'a good man, full of the Holy Spirit and faith' (Acts 11:24) and it seems many came to faith through him. After Paul's dramatic conversion on the Damascus Road, many of the believers had been wary of him, given his former zeal for persecuting Christians. But Barnabas had observed how Paul witnessed to his own conversion in Damascus and was convinced Paul's life had been transformed by the love and power of Christ. Barnabas vouched for Paul and recommended him before the other Apostles, who then welcomed him. Paul was able to move around and preach freely in Jerusalem, until he began to debate with some Hellenistic Jews, who turned against him and tried to kill him. The disciples had to spirit Paul away to Caesarea and sent him off to Tarsus. He then endured a number of years in seclusion.*

Years later, when the gospel had spread further into Gentile territory and the church in Antioch had experienced a move of the Holy Spirit, Barnabas discerned that Paul was needed – perhaps he even sensed this was the moment Paul had been supernaturally saved and prepared by God for, preaching the gospel to the Gentiles. Barnabas sought Paul out and took a risk on him when it seems others had forgotten him. He brought Paul to Antioch where, under their shared leadership, the church there flourished. One year later Barnabas and Paul's relationship would go to a new level when, after a time of prayer and fasting, the Antioch church's leadership heard the Lord say to them, 'Set apart for me Barnabas and Saul for the work to which I have called them' (Acts 13:2). In obedience, the church sent Barnabas and Paul out to proclaim the kingdom of God and partnering together they pioneered a new wave of gospel expansion.

It is clear that Barnabas was the ultimate team player. Barnabas championed the gifts of others, sought out those on the margins, gave people a second chance and was willing to leverage any greatness of his own so others could fulfil their destiny. I often wonder, in the long term, how much Barnabas's example influenced Paul's own understanding of relationships.

* You can piece together the story of Barnabas and Paul in Acts: Acts 4:36–37; 9:27–30; 11:24; 13:1–3.

LEADERS NEED FRIENDS

As we will see, Paul and Barnabas had different personalities and different giftings, but in different ways their lives confirm the same, often undertaught principle: leaders need friends. Jesus never called us to lead on our own. This is why Jesus called his disciples friends not servants. This is why Jesus sent the disciples out in twos. This is why Jesus himself took a day off to hang out with his team. This is why Jesus, in his most difficult hours, asked his closest comrades to be with him. In all these ways Jesus modelled how leaders, no matter how gifted, anointed or successful they are, are still human beings – image-bearers created for fellowship with the Father and friendship with others. Leaders may need the complimentary gifts of their co-workers to get the work done but they need the friendship that comes with this more. Jesus knew the greatest gift the disciples would have in their life of kingdom-mission was one another.

One of the ways I have been blessed to experience this team-based leadership approach is through my friend Pete Greig, founder and leader of 24-7 Prayer – a movement I have been a part of for all of my adult life. Pete is an outstanding leader, graced with a unique anointing from God to steward a global movement of prayer, mission and justice in over half the nations on earth throughout the last twenty-five years. Pete would be the first to admit that the staggering impact 24-7 Prayer has had around the world is because of the team of gifted and committed people God has gathered around him. But what Pete himself has embodied so well throughout these years is leadership defined by friendship. Over the years, as we have gathered for important meetings to discuss all the opportunities and challenges that come with stewarding a global movement, Pete has always emphasised the priority of the meeting after the meeting. In practice this means we work hard during the day, digging into big conversations around theology, structural redesigns, fundraising and event-planning. These times are important; they help push us forward and prevent drift – culturally and theologically – given all the complexities connected to a multicultural, global movement. But it's the stuff that happens in between the agenda items and after our 'work' conversations that Pete has encouraged us to be even more committed to – those spontaneous moments of connection around coffee breaks, the stimulating conversations in the corner of a pub, the laughing together in a hot tub or around a fireplace in one another's homes. It is in these moments, when we choose to take ourselves less seriously, that the real magic happens. Over the years, I have come to treasure these times of deep soul connection and loving camaraderie with other faithful leaders of the 24-7 Prayer movement – precious brothers and sisters from Germany, Czech Republic, Holland, South Africa, Macedonia, USA. These men and women inspire me, for they have chosen the path of radical discipleship in the way of Jesus, and it is a joy to call them my friends.

THE DIFFICULT CONVERSATIONS

But what do we do when friends disagree? What about the difficult conversations leadership teams who travel through the seasons of life together will inevitably need to face? As I've alluded to throughout this book, the New Testament gives us a window into lots of the real-life gritty drama that comes along with committed, covenantal love. Let's briefly look at two examples of this.

Paul wrote openly to the Galatians about a disagreement he had with the elders of the Jerusalem church after they had come down to check on the emerging new community in Antioch (Galatians 2:11–21). The dispute centered around long-standing Jewish customs of table fellowship and how these should be applied now that numerous Gentiles had become fellow participants in the new covenant through saving faith in Jesus. The dispute ended with a confrontation between Paul and Peter, and from what we can piece together, it seems it didn't end well.

On another occasion in Acts, Luke tells us of a disagreement between those best of friends and co-labourers we have just described above, Paul and Barnabas (15:36–41). The bone of contention here centred around their young apprentice John Mark and how committed to the cause – how reliable – he really was. The difference in opinion between Paul and Barnabas was so strong they ended up separating. Paul took Silas with him on his next missionary trip and Barnabas took John Mark in a different direction. While the result meant two missionary teams were now extending the kingdom in different parts of the world there is no getting away from the fact that this was a complete relational breakdown and an altogether sorry episode.

These examples shatter some of the romanticism many Christians hold concerning the early church. But if we are prepared to acknowledge our own quirkiness, insecurities, short-temperedness and propensity to want our own way, maybe we shouldn't be surprised about these two examples above. For all the Apostles' brilliance they were still imperfect human beings after all. Just imagine trying to steward all the complexities and sensitivities that come with a dynamic and diverse people movement. It was overwhelmingly tough. Inevitably at times it put a strain on their relationships. Take note: the places where you will experience the most intense forms of spiritual warfare in your ministry are around the relationships you hold with those who you lead alongside.

Yet, as the story of the early church unfolds throughout the New Testament, it becomes clear how the Apostles overcame these challenges. They kept choosing *agape* love. Yes, they weren't perfect. But these men and women were also mature enough to repent, to hold their hands up when they got it wrong and to embody a graceful magnanimity which allowed them to transcend their differences. They continued to choose the way of Jesus. Listen to Peter's words about Paul some years after their Antioch confrontation:

> *Bear in mind that our Lord's patience means salvation, just as our dear brother Paul also wrote to you with the wisdom that God gave him.*

2 PETER 3:15

Think about this: Paul had confronted Peter (Cephas) publicly – 'When Cephas came to Antioch, I opposed him to his face, because he stood condemned' (Galatians 2:11). Yet Peter could still speak of Paul as a 'dear brother', a sure sign of the mutual respect they continued to share for one another. The tensions between Paul, Barnabas and John Mark were also restored. As Scot McKnight highlights, when Paul later wrote to the Corinthian church, 'Or is it only Barnabas and I who have no right to refrain from working for a living?' (1 Corinthians 9:6, ESV), 'he is implying that he and Barnabas are back on the same page.'* John Mark is referenced in Paul's later letters three times (Colossians 4:10; Philemon 24; 2 Timothy 4:11). In his letter to Timothy, Paul states, 'Get Mark and bring him with you, because he is helpful to me in my ministry' (4:11). It's clear that over time John Mark had become a treasured co-worker and friend of Paul.

These situations of relational dysfunction, which I'm sure each of us can identify with, provide examples of the commitment and humility we need to resolve tension in our teams. At a time when many church leaders are shamefully airing their disagreements and schisms in public, these are beautiful examples to us of what true reconciliation of difference in the Spirit of Christ should look like. Despite the Apostles' imperfections, their understanding of covenantal love meant they ultimately learned how to say sorry, forgive one another and listen more intently to each other's hearts.

ESTABLISHING TEAM

THE POWER OF PLURALITY

Another essential element to the team dynamic of the early church, and the reason her leaders would contend so strongly for unity

---

* Scot McKnight, *Pastor Paul: Nurturing a Culture of Christoformity in the Church* (Brazos Press, 2019), p49.

despite their diversity, was their belief in the principle of plurality. In my reading of Acts and the Epistles, it is my observation that the Apostles always established the churches they planted around more than one leader. While certain individuals may have been recognised as carrying the spiritual authority to 'lead out' from the front, at best, these leaders were recognised as a type of 'first among equals' but expected to operate in a spirit of mutual submission with the rest of the leadership team. The first church in Jerusalem provides us with a good example of this. Peter, James and John all seem to have had different spells as 'first among equals' in the Jerusalem church, rotating with fluidity.* Yet at no point were any of them not in submission to a wider team of elders. Rather they continued to discern God's will together. The life of leadership in the early church was shared. The Apostle Peter, when writing to the elders of some of his first churches, referred to himself as a 'fellow elder' (1 Peter 5:1), further proof that the Apostles, while outstanding leaders in their own right, never allowed themselves to be identified as the singular dominant leader. The 'itinerant' element to the Apostles' ministry was never demonstrated in an independent way. Their understanding of the church as family and their fellow leaders as siblings was so foundational to their thinking and practice that they made it their ambition to operate in harmonious unity. The Apostles resisted the pyramid structures of the world and instead yielded to the accountability of committed relationships and the council of elders. It is hard therefore to argue that New Testament leadership practice promotes anything less than leadership in plurality. This is a principle we must work hard to see restored in the Western contemporary church. In our current leadership crisis, we are quick to place all blame on the leader after 'a fall from grace' rather than the church structure in which the leader is working. Of course, we could never rush to excuse a leader's individual sin, but often

* Peter: Acts 2; James: Acts 15; John is less obvious but general consensus is that he had great influence in Jerusalem also.

the systems and culture the leader is working within have been a significant contributing factor to the leader's downfall. We need to create better relational structures built on a healthy balance of trust and robust process. In this context, gifted leaders can be released to pioneer and envision others, while supported by a culture that encourages joyful submission to a team of committed brothers and sisters in Christ.

On the occasions I have experienced leaders operating in plurality, mutually yielding to one another, complimenting one another's gifts and holding each other to account in a culture of covenantal love, the result has been a church body empowered towards the mission of God and a confident family, secure in the unity of their spiritual mothers and fathers who are shepherding them. This is the manifold wisdom of God.

THE GOAL OF ONENESS

As the Apostles of the first churches modelled plurality among their own translocal teams, they also recognised a key element of their work was to establish a vision of one-mindedness at the heart of their local churches. Loving one another in *koinonia* community sat right at the heart of the Apostles' doctrine. Listen to Paul's words to the Philippians:

> *Therefore if there is any encouragement in Christ, if any consolation of love, if any fellowship of the Spirit, if any affection and compassion, make my joy complete by being of the same mind, maintaining the same love, united in spirit, intent on one purpose.*

PHILIPPIANS 2:1–2 (NASB)

Notice how practical Paul is here, detailing the different elements of unity the believers should seek to 'maintain' if they were to stay true to the covenantal nature of the kingdom family. I have summarised these elements as 'one mind', 'one heart', 'one spirit' and 'unto one purpose'.

- One mind – 'being of the same mind'
- One heart – 'maintaining the same love'
- One spirit – 'united in Spirit'
- One purpose – 'intent on one purpose'

It seems Paul had come to realise that flourishing churches and mature leadership teams could only happen if these different aspects of 'oneness' had been formed. Let's finish the chapter by exploring each one of these aspects as they provide a helpful scheme for leaders today seeking to develop more effective and healthy teams and churches that demonstrate the cruciform way.

One Mind ('being of the same mind')
The Greek work for 'mind' here is *phroneo*, and literally means 'to think or be minded in a certain way'. Paul is encouraging the church to have a collective mindfulness about their purpose, goals, and faith; to work hard to achieve an alignment of vision and values. The Apostles' doctrine was the ultimate plumbline which would foster one-mindedness theologically among the early churches. This was crucial for the unity of the spiralling movement of churches multiplying across the Mediterranean basin at a time when all sorts of heresies, false gospels and conspiracy theories were threatening the spread of its growth. Yet just agreeing on who Jesus was (and is) isn't necessarily enough to assume that a team will function healthily together. The Apostles were pragmatic enough to accept that wherever there are human beings there will inevitably be disagreements and differences. So, their encouragement was not just to believe in Jesus but to practise the way of Jesus, starting with their relationships with one another.

The Jerusalem Council, described in Acts Chapter 15, is a terrific example of the attitude and effort required to achieve such a collective one-mindedness. There, we witness the hard-earned wisdom and unity which is born out of a process of corporate discernment undergirded by covenantal love. The Apostles teach us how we must work hard to listen well to one another and be prepared to relinquish our own traditions if we are to discern what the Spirit is doing today. We should learn how to humble ourselves and realise the mind of Christ is in the body of Christ not simply in one dynamic leader. We are to learn the way of Christ from one another.

Many churches today are committed to one another relationally but haven't gone through the robust conversations and biblical reflection needed to establish one-mindedness around shared theology, vision and values, and their missional objectives. This lack of clarity leads to a divergence of vision, plateaus of unmet expectations among the church body and an ineffective use of time and resource. On the other hand, when leaders take the time to reflect on 'what', 'where' and 'how' the Spirit is leading them in a context of corporate discernment, a dynamic sense of shared vision can be established which releases the body into effective missional purpose.

One Heart ('maintaining the same love')

We now know Paul loved to use the word *agape* when speaking about his brothers and sisters. Here, in his letter to the church in Philippi, he uses the word again as a reference to the wholehearted affection and sacrificial love Jesus calls all his followers to. Paul had experienced how sibling love among the diverse and intercultural family of God is tested and challenged. He therefore strenuously exhorted the church to pay attention to anything which might threaten their affection for one another. Jesus had showed the disciples *agape* love is not merely a feeling. *Agape* is grittier and far more robust than the 'tolerance' and 'equality' our twenty-first century postmodern, post-Christian culture prides itself upon. Paul longed for the believers to demonstrate this type of love to one another, to consistently choose to serve others when there are no rewards, to refuse to allow offence to take root in one's heart and to decide that a life built upon secret sacrifices is the way the church will heal the world.

This type of one-heartedness between brothers and sisters needs to be cultivated, 'maintained' and guarded through the various seasons of life. That means building margin into our lives to eat together. It means committing ourselves to the difficult conversations. It means growing in the Scriptures together. It means paying careful attention to the seasons of life our fellow team members are going through and, where appropriate, changing our cadence to keep pace together. It means discerning the gift-mix and gift-tensions which make up your team and being mature about how these can complement each other even when we step on one another's toes. It means praying consistently with one another. It means being quick to say sorry. No church or leadership team is going to go the distance without this muscle of *agape* love strengthening the joints and sinews of the relationships that exist at the heart of it.

One Spirit ('united in spirit')

This gets at the idea of inner harmony. The word Paul uses here is *sympsychos* which is actually a compound word (i.e. made up of two words), *syn* ('together with') and *psychos* ('soul, self, inner life, or the seat of the feelings and desires'). Putting these together helps us understand how Paul longed for the Philippian church to be united in Christ in all their desires. This can only happen through the free-flowing ministry of the Holy Spirit among the kingdom family. Make no mistake – other spirits will want to fill the spaces between believers and especially between the members that make up the leadership teams which oversee our churches. Pride, competitiveness, offence, manipulation, religion, and all sorts of other counterfeit spirits are looking to take territory. One of the gifts of the Holy Spirit every leader should therefore ask for is 'the discerning of spirits'. Cruciform leaders build their teams around patterns of prayer and worship, the Eucharist and the constant invitation of the Spirit's ministry. Through these practices they help create a culture defined by the sweet fellowship of the Holy Spirit, first and foremost celebrating who we are in God and in doing so cultivating an atmosphere of mutual affection among the family of God.

One Purpose ('intent on one purpose')

As we grow in a unity of spirit, one-hearted love and one-minded vision, we are ready to move towards 'one purpose' together. It is impossible to hold onto one purpose together without these other elements of oneness in place. This one purpose should always result in our co-labouring with Christ in the fulfilment of the Great Commission (Matthew 28:16–20). When any other form of 'purpose' supersedes this purpose, we have tragically missed the mark and diverged from the church's true vocation in the world.

From these elements of oneness that Paul encouraged, we can see further proof for the principle of plurality and the team ethic at the heart of New Testament ecclesiology. Along with the other Apostles, Paul believed relational alignment was central to their divine assignment. Staying in step with one another was part of what it meant to stay in step with the Spirit. The Apostles exemplified what Jesus had first embodied: the cruciform way is a shared leadership journey. Navigating the spaces between relationships is not a distraction from the cruciform leader's work, *it is their work*. Ruth Haley Barton summarises it well:

> Life in community can never be about merely getting the job done – as important as it is. It must always take into account how we get the job done and whether we are transformed or deformed in the process.*

Cruciform leaders are those committed to this type of healthy culture. The New Testament principles of team, plurality and shared leadership journey must exist at the centre of this. This will not be

---

* Ruth Haley Barton, *Life Together in Christ: Experiencing Transformation in Community* (InterVarsity Press, 2014), p113.

easy in our increasingly fragmented society. The great Irish poet John O'Donohue, reflecting on contemporary Western civilisation, says:

> The commercial edge of so-called progress has cut away a huge region of human tissue and webbing that held us in communion with one another. We have fallen out of belonging.*

Cruciform leaders understand that the Church of Jesus Christ should be the antidote to this. They are convinced that our original design carries the echo of our maker, the triune God who is perfect in oneness. And they believe that through God's grace, Christ's passion for us to become one new humanity, participating with him in the redemption of the world, can become a reality.

GETTING PRACTICAL: TOP TIPS

To finish this chapter, here are a number of practical ways leaders can create environments and practices to help foster healthy teams as we move towards a shared sense of purpose together.

1. Intentionally create margin to be in one another's lives without agenda. Build in 'hanging out' moments to your annual calendar, to ensure as leadership teams you are relating to one another first and foremost as friends, celebrating the 'highs' and carrying each other through the 'lows' of life together.
2. Build in key planning times to become clear on your vision and shared missional objectives as a church. These times, often best offsite, should be a mixture of prayer and prophecy and 'blue-sky thinking' which then results in setting key and realistic shorter-term objectives. This will foster a clear one-mindedness among your team and congruency of vision and values.
3. Develop a culture of self-reflection, personal growth and healthy self-awareness. Encourage people where possible to

* John O'Donohue, *To Bless the Space between Us: A Book of Blessings* (Convergent Books, 2008), pxiv.

get coaching or spiritual direction to help them understand their own life stories and personality traits better and how these impact others in their teams.

4. Take time to name and nurture one another's spiritual gifts. Celebrate the gift mix that exists between your team and acknowledge where there may be tensions. Encourage a culture where everyone is flowing in their spiritual gifts.

5. Learn how to recognise seasons and major events in one another's lives. Very seldom will any two members of your team be in the same place on their journey with Christ or experiencing the same life circumstances. Learn how to acknowledge this and give space for people to be honest, sharing stories with one another and praying for each other.

6. Create a culture where difficult conversations can be had, even expected, but friendship will remain. Encourage people to hold their opinions lightly but their friendships tightly. Get external help from trusted and skilled leaders to facilitate these conversations where possible.

7. Learn to be clear with one another as leaders about expectations and the required capacity you are agreeing to. These expectations should seek to find a balance between understanding the flexible boundaries required due to the rigours of senior church leadership while ensuring there are rhythms which cultivate an emotionally healthy spirituality among leaders.

8. Ensure there is definition and recognition around the different meetings and roles which exist within your church culture. Defining the 'why' and distinct function of each team can really help the effectiveness of your meetings.

9. While acknowledging and honouring the unique role of each team (e.g. Elders, Staff, Board) it is also helpful a few times a year to bring all of these teams together to discern key decisions for the church. This demonstrates a mutual

submission, ensuring a 'flatness' in structure and empowers everyone in the decision-making process. While reaching complete consensus on decisions can sometimes be tough, the benefits of allowing everyone to feel heard are hard to deny.

10. Beware of the enemy. Guard your unity. Be prayerful and vigilant.

11. Beware of the futility of the cult of personality above team. Be aware of the ungodliness of craving to be No.1 or elevating leaders. Build in spiritual disciplines that give space for confession and repentance.

PRACTISING THE CRUCIFORM WAY

Consider the questions and readings below in discussion, reflection, journalling and prayer.

ONE:

A new command I give you: love one another. As I have loved you, so you must love one another.

JOHN 13:34

Reflect on this verse from the Apostle John.

As a leadership team or in your journal, explore the quality or depth of your love for one another in this season.

TWO:

Take note: the places where you will experience the most intense forms of spiritual warfare in your ministry are around the relationships you hold with those who you lead alongside. Yet, as the story of the early church unfolds throughout the New Testament, it becomes clear how the Apostles overcame these challenges. They kept choosing *agape* love. Yes, they weren't perfect. But these men and women were also mature enough to repent, to hold their hands up when they got it wrong and to embody a graceful magnanimity which allowed them to transcend their differences. They continued to choose the way of Jesus.

Reflect on these words from Chapter 7.

- How good are you as a team at having difficult conversations?
- In what ways do the examples of Paul and Peter, and Paul and Barnabas challenge you?
- How are you practising 'mutual submission'?

THREE:

If you have any encouragement from being united with Christ, if any comfort from his love, if any common sharing in the Spirit … then make my joy complete by being like-minded, having the same love, being one in spirit and of one [purpose].

PHILIPPIANS 2:1–2

Take time reflecting on the various elements of unity described by Paul to the Philippian church.

- As a leadership team or in your journal, honestly describe the level of 'oneness' you are experiencing together in each of the areas explored in the chapter:

  1. One mind – 'being of the same mind'
  2. One heart – 'maintaining the same love'
  3. One spirit – 'united in the Spirit'
  4. One purpose – 'intent on one purpose'

CHAPTER 8

A FOCUSED FOLLOWER:

KNOW YOUR ENEMY

I am sending you out like sheep among wolves. Therefore be as shrewd as snakes and as innocent as doves.

MATTHEW 10:16

I was lost. Buried in a street kids shelter in the back streets of Johannesburg, separated at the age of nineteen from the people and things which had helped shape and form my identity, my gap year wasn't unfolding the way I thought it would. The truth was, God hadn't gone anywhere; I was just struggling to find him in the deconstruction of my world. But in the midst of my intense homesickness and first experience of identity crisis, I became aware of something else going on. Something working against me. A merciless resistance, taking advantage of my loneliness and the vulnerable state of my homesick soul. Tormented, I was driven into a dark spiral of introspection, wondering at times if I was losing my mind. Shame-filled regrets from the past and fear about the future flooded my head. As I wrestled with these thoughts, I had to face an uncomfortable truth – my faith muscles were nowhere near as strong as I thought they were and my authority in prayer was much less developed than it needed to be if I was going to become a leader of substance in the kingdom of God. The temptation to give up and go home was strong.

Yet somewhere deep inside I knew I couldn't give up; I had to stick it out. Slowly but deliberately, I began to teach myself how to activate the spiritual weaponry Paul encouraged the Ephesian church to clothe themselves in. As I endured the 'wild animals and angels' (Mark 1:13) of this lonely 'wilderness' experience, I learned self-control: how to bring my mind and body into submission in the fruit of the Spirit and how to stand with confidence on the promises of Scripture, stare the devil in the eye and courageously speak the name of Jesus.

Martin Luther once said:

> he who prays is fighting against the devil and the flesh. Satan is opposed to the church … the best thing we can do, therefore, is to put our fists together and pray.[*]

Experiencing my first intense round of spiritual warfare while still a teenager, this is what I had to learn – put your fists together and pray. In all the fragility of that testing gap year, with whatever strength in my spirit I could find, I hung on.

I made it. Just about.

By the end of the gap year the reality check I needed had truly taken place, and the youthful naivety with which I had approached mission and ministry had been tempered. I now knew something of what I was getting into! The cost of leadership in the kingdom of God was greater than I could have ever imagined. Only a foundation of holy grit, formed by the sustaining grace of God, would enable me to stay the course of long-term fruitful and faithful Christian ministry. My spiritual acumen had been sharpened. To endure the different seasons of leadership which lay ahead was going to require a steely sense of commitment and resilient backbone.

* Martin Luther, *Luther's Works*, ed. & tr. Theodore G Tappert (Fortress Press, 1967), 54: Table Talk.

I came back from that year knowing my life needed more focus, more intentionality and the spiritual rigour of 'training in righteousness.'

THE COST OF LEADERSHIP

In the years since that gap year, I have gone through seasons more intense and more difficult than my nineteen-year-old self could have conceived. This is because life is tough. Leaders are no different from anyone else in this regard; every Christian, in fact every person, faces times of severe testing, grief and trouble in our broken world. Jesus wasn't just talking about leaders when he prophesied, 'In this world you will have trouble' (John 16:33).

Yet I am convinced there is a dimension to some of the challenges and tribulations I have experienced in my life precisely because of the leadership vocation I hold within the church. Let me caveat what I am about to say by first stating that as a leader I've had the privilege of seeing God do 'immeasurably more than all we ask or imagine' (Ephesians 3:20), witnessing stunning demonstrations of God's miraculous love and power in many different parts of the world. But it would be disingenuous not to admit that I have also experienced pain and struggle, immeasurably more than I could have ever imagined. In fact, looking back at the last twenty-five years of leadership, I would surmise: the 'immeasurably more' I have seen God do in and through my life has almost always come through situations that were immeasurably more painful than I could have ever imagined! Thanks be to God for his redeeming grace. But it's been tough!

I've become convinced over these years that cruciform leaders are called to embody the paradox which sits at the heart of the gospel. We die so we might live. We endure tribulations, bearing in our bodies the marks of Jesus (Galatians 6:17), so that God's redemptive healing can be displayed to the world. We keep standing in the face of Satan's attack, knowing that even though we carry the scars of battle, one day these wounds will be transformed into trophies, testifying to a love more powerful than death itself. This is the life the cruciform leader is called to – following Jesus through the death-unto-life cycle which is the essence of the kingdom of God. Louis Berkhof powerfully reminds us how central suffering was to Jesus' whole ministry, not just his death:

> In view of the fact that Jesus began to speak of His coming sufferings towards the end of His life we are often inclined to think that the final agonies constituted the whole of His sufferings. Yet His whole life was a life of sufferings. It was the servant-life of the Lord of Hosts, the life of the Sinless One in daily association with sinners, the life of the Holy One in a sin-cursed world. The way of obedience was for Him at the same time a way of suffering.[*]

To be clear, I am not saying cruciform leaders should desire tribulation or hard times, nor should they ask for it. That's not biblical, that's just morbid. But as the inevitable tribulations of life come to each of us, cruciform leaders are those who understand these seasons as an opportunity to know Christ, not just in the power of his resurrection but in the fellowship of his suffering (Philippians 3:10).

The bottom line is cruciform leaders are focused on becoming like Christ in every season of life – the good, the bad and the ugly. They know they are not called to some kind of intense religious stoicism or asceticism, Jesus was way too much fun for that! But they do recognise that, like Jesus, they are called to set their faces like flint and fulfil the mission the Father has assigned them. Even if it costs them their lives. As Lesslie Newbigin put it:

> this suffering is not the passive acceptance of evil; it is the primary form of witness against it. It is the way in which we follow Jesus along the way of the cross … the final surrender is not defeat but victory.[**]

[*] Louis Berkhof, *Systematic Theology, 6th ed.* (Banner of Truth, 1971), pp321–322.
[**] Lesslie Newbigin, *The Open Secret: An introduction to the Theology of Mission* (Eerdmans, 1995), p107.

The extraordinary determination which pulsed through the life of Jesus in the form of sacrificial love is the perfect example of the holy focus every cruciform leader should seek to emulate: as surrendered sons and daughters who know how to passionately celebrate the goodness of God and groan with all creation as it awaits its full redemption. Because our forerunner Jesus experienced both the suffering of the cross and the resurrection from the dead, we can know his 'abundant life' (John 10:10) not just in the limelight of victory but also the twilight of apparent defeat. Even here his love and presence reside.

STRATEGIES OF DARKNESS

The sober reality every leader called to serve God's church must face is that if you want to lead like Jesus you need to know there is a target on your back! Remember, Paul did not ask his young apprentice Timothy to join him on the bright lights of the platform but in suffering for the gospel. I am convinced many of you reading this book are currently underestimating the degree of spiritual warfare surrounding your lives and your churches. One of the main reasons we must become focused followers of Jesus is because Satan systematically targets those called to lead God's people. We dare not become naïve to this fact. Let's take a moment to remind ourselves of the seriousness of the battle we are engaged in.

Woven into the entire biblical narrative from beginning to end is an insidious agency of evil diametrically opposed to God's good plans for creation and humankind. The Bible personifies this agency of evil and calls it *'the Satan'*. Satan and his evil forces are intent on desecrating God's creation. CS Lewis famously declared: 'There is no neutral ground in the universe: every square inch, every split second, is claimed by God and counterclaimed by Satan.'*

* CS Lewis, *Christian Reflections* (Eerdmans, 1967), p33.

Spiritual warfare is not incidental in the biblical story. It is central to the whole narrative. The whole Christian life can be justifiably presented as an act of war against Satan and his demonic forces. Lesslie Newbigin states powerfully how this is the very motive of our mission:

> I think that the deepest motive for mission is simply the desire to be with Jesus where he is, on the frontier between the reign of God and the usurped dominion of the devil.*

It should come as no surprise to us that Satan hates the church – the bride of Christ – the people through whom God is recreating the world. Central to Satan's sinister strategy to dismantle the church is to take out its leaders. And he is ruthless. Jesus was clear about this, calling the devil a thief who comes to 'steal and kill and destroy' (John 10:10). I have a mentor called Andrea who puts it like this: the enemy traces through your life and your history, seeking for an occasion to take advantage of. In other words, Satan wants to find something in your life you are particularly sensitive to – something in your past, present or future; usually something that makes you feel shame, fear or unforgiveness – and when he finds such 'an occasion' he will double down with fury for the sole aim of crushing you. He has no mercy.

Understanding the ruthless nature of Satan's strategy to 'steal and kill and destroy' means it's vital that emerging leaders are prepared for the onslaught of spiritual warfare that comes with leadership in the church. Again, Jesus refused to insulate his disciples from the realities of the battle that lay ahead. 'I am sending you out like sheep among wolves. Therefore be as shrewd as snakes and as innocent as doves' (Matthew 10:16). Numerous other times throughout the disciples' apprenticeship Jesus referred to ways in which his followers would endure hardship for the sake of the gospel and how

* Lesslie Newbigin, *A Word in Season: Perspectives on Christian World Missions* (Eerdmans, 1994), p129.

Satan would seek to hinder the advancement of the kingdom of God. The book of Acts and the Epistles build upon these warnings of Jesus, confirming the reality that wherever the people of God are demonstrating the kingdom of God, a desperate counterattack of darkness is taking place. We are, after all, standing between the living and the dead, rescuing people from hell – both their present hellish reality and the hell that is to come. To say the devil doesn't like the church's rescue mission in the world is the quintessential understatement.

When we dig deeper into the book of Acts and the Epistles, we discover some specific strategies Satan uses against the church:

- Satan opposes ministry opportunities which would have advanced the gospel. For example, Paul told the Thessalonians he wanted to get to them numerous times, but Satan blocked their way (1 Thessalonians 2:18).
- Satan works to slander church leaders, seeking to destroy their reputations with the aim of discrediting the gospel (1 Timothy 3:7).
- Satan incites division and unforgiveness among churches (Romans 16:17–19).
- Satan's kingdom seeks to deceive believers and pollute the churches with falsehood (1 Timothy 4:1–7).
- Satan is continually at work to bring trials to Christians in order to discourage them (1 Thessalonians 3:5).

Understanding the systematic way Satan seeks to dismantle the church and hijack its mission in the world, Paul exhorted the young churches to be aware of the enemy's schemes and 'to pray without ceasing' (2 Corinthians 2:11; 1 Thessalonians 5:17). This is why in Paul's letter to the church in Ephesus – the place where he experienced the most intense spiritual warfare – he described so graphically the items of armoury every Christian needs to stand against such attacks. 'Put on the whole armour of God, that you may be able to stand against the schemes of the devil' (Ephesians 6:11, ESV).

But why is it that leaders are of particular interest to the enemy? Leaders are those who take their positions on the frontlines of the battlefield, going beyond the enemy's battle lines to establish territory for the kingdom of God. Therefore, it follows that if Satan can wound them badly enough to take them out of the battle, he will more effectively hinder the advancement of the kingdom of God on the earth. Satan knows if he can discredit a leader then the impact on the wider church and community has the potential to be devastating. He is desperate not to lose territory and he knows a confident-in-Christ church, led by courageous Spirit-filled leaders, possesses the power to take it off him. Therefore, he frantically seeks ways to maintain control of his domains, by distracting the church from her mission in the world and sabotaging her witness in the world through the toppling of her leaders.

Paul, of course, had years of firsthand experience of this type of frontline leadership so he knew what his younger apprentice Timothy would have to endure. Listen to these exhortations to his spiritual son:

Timothy, my son, I am giving you this command in keeping with the prophecies once made about you, so that by recalling them you may fight the battle well.

1 TIMOTHY 1:18

Join with me in suffering, like a good soldier of Christ Jesus. No one serving as a soldier gets entangled in civilian affairs, but rather tries to please his commanding officer. Similarly, anyone who competes as an athlete does not receive the victor's crown except by competing according to the rules. The hardworking farmer should be the first to receive a share of the crops. Reflect on what I am saying, for the Lord will give you insight into all this.

2 TIMOTHY 2:3–7

Paul wanted to prepare Timothy for those times in battle when, metaphorically speaking, it would feel like he had climbed out of a bunker only to be shot at from all directions. Yet ultimately, Paul wanted to equip Timothy to stare the enemy in the eye and not be intimidated. His advice to this young leader he loved as his own son was to recall the prophecies once made about him. Paul knew if Timothy could meditate on the precious words of God which had been spoken over his young life, he would activate the main weapon he needed to combat the enemy – confidence in his sonship.

This is where we return to Jesus' wilderness temptations for our ultimate example of spiritual combat, which no doubt formed the backdrop to Paul's encouragement to Timothy. If we look closely at the way the synoptic Gospel narratives are constructed, we will discover Jesus' wilderness experience came directly after his baptism. This is not an accident. For while we often focus on the fasting element of Jesus' forty days in the wilderness, we can miss the fact that for forty days Jesus was also feasting on the last words he heard from his Father at his baptism, 'You are my beloved Son; with you I am well pleased' (Mark 1:11, ESV). Ponder this for a moment – while Jesus was abstaining from physical food during this gruelling period of preparation for ministry, he was inwardly digesting the words of fatherly love spoken over him, confirming his position as his Father's beloved Son. Flowing from this place of secure identity, Jesus rebuked Satan, dismantling every attack he endured with words of holy Scripture. In this way, Jesus taught us that victory over the kingdom of darkness comes, not by shouting and screaming at the devil, but by standing strong in your God-given identity. Knowing who you are and whose you are is enough to make the demons tremble. Paul knew if Timothy could practise what Jesus had modelled – confident sonship formed by the word of God – he would overcome. Paul is reminding him: *Recall the word of God spoken over you, Timothy, and you will fight the battle well.*

Timothy would have to learn, like I did during my gap year, that because the enemy had come for Jesus, he would come after those who love Jesus too. Paul wanted Timothy to count the cost of this. But crucially, he also wanted Timothy to rejoice in the even greater reality – that because Jesus overcame the enemy in the wilderness and ultimately on the cross, we can overcome him too. We can overcome the tormenting thoughts, the false accusations, the ongoing health problems, the persecutions, the divisive tactics of darkness. I know some days it doesn't always feel like we are winning, but never forget, one day, 'The God of peace will soon crush Satan under your feet' (Romans 16:20).

CONTESTED AUTHORITY

Coming into the lived reality of this victory and authority in Christ, though, does not come overnight. Remember the principle we learned through the Parable of the Talents, discussed in Chapter 5: the level of authority we walk in is connected to our level of faithful and effective stewardship. Only as we prove ourselves with the measure we have been entrusted with, can we grow in authority and influence in the kingdom. But we must also recognise that growing in authority in the kingdom will also be contested. There is an element of truth in the old saying, 'with every new level is another devil'. Our authority in Christ is always something the enemy will constantly seek to undermine. We must fight for it. Following in the footsteps of Jesus we must orientate our whole lives towards an ever-deepening identity in the Father's love. The disciplined pursuit of such, in a world full of forces competing for our identity, is the pathway to a lived victorious reality. This is why Jesus told the disciples to 'Watch and pray so that you will not fall into temptation. The spirit is willing, but the flesh is weak' (Matthew 26:41).

The church fathers also have much to teach us in this area of contesting. Building on the example of Jesus and the teachings of the original Apostles, theologians like Irenaeus, Athenagoras and Origen, among others, developed a clear 'warfare' worldview.[*] It is clear from their writings that they regarded everything in our present world as part of a cosmic struggle between God and Satan. For them the Scriptures point to a world existing between humans and God that is filled with intelligent, free spiritual beings – a vast array of angels – many of whom act as God's messengers, but many others who have sided with darkness. Those who have joined ranks with Satan are diametrically opposed to the work of God through his church and every committed Christian should therefore expect to do combat against these demonic forces. This 'warfare' theology, so central to the life of the church over its first few hundred years, is displayed most vividly in the lives of the earliest monks who began retreating to the Egyptian and Syrian deserts in the third century.

The accounts of the life of St Anthony, often considered the father of monasticism because he was one of the first to 'flee from the world' to the wilderness, paint him as a paragon of spiritual warfare. St Athanasius, a wonderful saint himself, famously records the details of St Anthony's battles vividly. In his classic text, *The Life of St Anthony*, Athanasius writes that when people would visit St Anthony in the desert:

> They heard tumults and many voices and clangor as of weapons. At night they saw the mountain alive with wild beasts. They also saw him fighting as with visible foes, and praying against them.[**]

[*] Athenagoras: In *Plea for the Christians* he suggests that Christians are in opposition to spiritual powers by refusing idolatry. Irenaeus: In *Against Heresies* he taught that Jesus had come to undo Adam's failure by resisting Satan's temptations and ultimately defeating him on the cross. He believed that Christians should hold fast to the apostolic teaching to resist heresies which he saw as part of Satan's deception. Origen: In Origen's *Homilies on Joshua*, Origen allegorises the conquest of Canaan as the believer's struggle against sin and demonic opposition and in *Contra Celsum* he argues that demonic forces are actively at work in the world to lead people away from God.
[**] St Athanasius, *Life of St Anthony of Egypt* (CreateSpace Independent Publishing Platform, 2016), p64.

But like the tactics Jesus had employed in the wilderness, St Anthony's life of prayerful discipline enabled him to endure.

> And it was truly remarkable that, alone as he was in such a wilderness, he was neither dismayed by the attacks of the demons, nor, with all the animals and creeping things there, did he fear their savageness. But, as Scripture has it, he truly trusted in the Lord like Mount Sion, with a mind unshaken and unruffled. Thus the demons rather fled from him, and the wild beasts, as is written (Job 5:23), kept peace with him.*

'A mind unshaken and undisturbed.' As cruciform leaders, this is what we can come to know.

GUARD WHAT YOU HAVE BEEN GIVEN

It was in consideration of the intensity of the battle a Christian leader should expect to endure that Paul called Timothy to a life of unbending focus. He described the call of leadership Timothy had been entrusted with as a treasure or a 'good deposit' (2 Timothy 1:14). One can detect a measure of sobriety and the fear of the Lord in Paul's tone as his exhortations to Timothy continue throughout his letters to him:

> *Watch your life and doctrine closely. Persevere in them, because if you do, you will save both yourself and your hearers.*
>
> 1 TIMOTHY 4:16

> *Timothy, guard what has been entrusted to your care.*
>
> 1 TIMOTHY 6:20

> *Guard the good deposit that was entrusted to you – guard it with the help of the Holy Spirit who lives in us.*
>
> 2 TIMOTHY 1:14

---

* *Ibid.*

Paul was experienced enough to know that there would be days ahead for Timothy when his spirit would be willing but his flesh weak. He knew the fire of God in his life needed to be carefully tended to because, if it wasn't, the 'strange fire' of carnal desire would be fanned instead. He knew that such untamed flames in a leader's life result in a raging and damaging fire where many more casualties can get burned in the process. So guarding the good deposit God had entrusted Timothy with over the long haul would require a life of extraordinary focus. 'Watch your life … closely' (1 Timothy 4:16), Paul instructed him.

I remember when I was younger my uncle Phil warned me about putting myself in tempting positions. This was his line: *'Al, I trust you, but I don't trust your flesh, because I don't trust my own.'* Like the Apostle Paul, years of experience had taught Uncle Phil, when it comes to the old nature, it doesn't get any easier. Until Jesus returns, my self-centred nature will never be improved nor fully removed. Therefore, I have had to learn how to master it; to grow in the grace-empowered ability to bring my carnal passions and desires to the cross of Christ daily, exchanging them there for new creation.

The current leadership crisis in the West has revealed too many leaders who have not known how to 'guard what has been entrusted to them'. Many of you will be familiar with Dietrich Bonhoeffer's phrase 'the cost of discipleship', taken from the title of his seminal book which thousands of Christ-followers over the last century have been challenged by. But the reality we are facing today, across the Western Christian church, is that we are actually counting the cost of non-discipleship.

The enemy, the perennial scheming opportunist he is, has taken advantage of the untested or underdeveloped characters of many Christian leaders and tragically their secret sins have been brutally exposed. This is a sobering pattern the New Testament does not shy away from – not every leader makes it. Judas is the obvious case within Jesus' own band of emerging leaders. But the Apostle

Paul also endured the disappointment of watching those he had invested in and co-partnered with over years fall away. One of these was Demas, who started well but couldn't stay the course. In two early letters, Colossians and Philemon, Paul refers to Demas as a fellow worker in the gospel. But by the time Paul was writing to Timothy, later in his life, he says, 'Demas, because he loved this world, has deserted me and has gone to Thessalonica'. Hymenaeus and Alexander are two others who Paul said, 'suffered shipwreck with regard to the faith'. These are sad stories. And sadder still is that each of us can think of modern-day equivalents. Some of them are our friends. But facing the disappointment of his fallen friends only strengthened Paul's exhortations to his emerging protégé, Timothy: 'fight the battle well, holding on to faith and a good conscience'. Timothy would have to learn how to 'put his fists together and pray', for the call to cruciform leadership is ruthlessly contested. One has to commit oneself to an extraordinary level of focus.[*]

Thankfully, Paul's advice does not stop at headline exhortations. He gets practical with Timothy, encouraging him to establish a number of holy habits in his life – spiritual disciplines which can be traced back to Jesus' own life practices. It's obvious from the tone of Paul's letters and the metaphors he used to inspire Timothy – a soldier, an athlete and a farmer – that Paul is expecting him to integrate into his life a disciplined path towards ongoing spiritual transformation and increasing maturity. Each of Paul's word pictures imply intention, obedience, discipline, perseverance. If Timothy is going to stay the course over the long haul, learn how to resist the enemy and stay faithful 'in season and out of season', then he is going to need to develop a thoughtful plan regarding his own leadership development (2 Timothy 2:3–7; 4:2).

What might this look like?

---

[*] You can trace these developments in the following Scriptures: Colossians 4:14; Philemon 24; 1 Timothy 1:18–20; 2 Timothy 2:17–18; 4:10.

A FORMATION FRAMEWORK

The monastic stream of the church has been instrumental down through the ages in helping Christians understand their primary sources of temptation. Traditionally these have been summarised as 'the world, the flesh and the devil'. Down through the ages wise sages have developed certain practices and habits, through lives of rigour and discipline, which have helped equip Christians to resist these three-pronged attacks they will inevitably face. They refer to this type of well-ordered spirituality as 'a rule of life'. The mothers and fathers of the church took seriously Paul's warning to the Corinthian church – 'we urge you not to receive God's grace in vain' (2 Corinthians 6:1) – that it was possible to receive God's grace as divine favour and miss the empowerment which came with it for transformation. They responded to the divine invitation to become more anchored in the presence of the triune God by integrating rhythms of intentional spiritual disciplines into their lives. This way they were empowered for ongoing transformation, less distracted by the noise of the world around them and more rooted in their authority in Christ to overcome the evil one. Today the ancient practice known as 'a rule of life' is described in more contemporary language as 'a formation framework'. While neither Jesus nor Paul used these specific terms, it's clear that Jesus modelled a disciplined pursuit of his Father's presence, and it is apparent that this is what Paul had in mind when he commanded Timothy, 'train yourself to be godly' (1 Timothy 4:7).

Dallas Willard, a great writer and teacher of spiritual formation in the last fifty years, was convinced that as followers of Jesus we need to have this type of intentional plan to aid our development in Christlikeness.

> We cannot adopt [Jesus'] form of life without engaging in his disciplines – maybe even more than he did and surely adding others demanded by our much more troubled condition.[*]

[*] Dallas Willard, *The Spirit of the Disciplines: Understanding How God Changes Lives* (Harper One, 1999), p29.

If Jesus, the Son of God, valued certain spiritual disciplines to help him orientate his life in the love of the Father, then, Willard contends, it is appropriate we should follow suit. To be clear, Willard was not promoting spiritual practices at the expense of the Spirit's grace-filled encountering presence. The church down through the ages has learned this lesson the hard way – when discipline becomes more important than devotion the result is a monstrous religion empty of the Spirit, doing much more damage than good. Willard knew any spiritual discipline, no matter how rigorously practised, will bring zero transformation if it does not lead us into the grace of God and the transforming power of the Spirit. Willard's well-known formula for the process of spiritual formation, *VIM* (Vision, Intention and Means), always frontloaded a vision of Christlikeness. The vision is always Jesus.

But like the church fathers and mothers down through the ages, Willard also knew this vision of Christlikeness needed backing up with intentionality and a means. Spiritual discipline should never become a substitute for the grace of God but the two are not mutually exclusive. 'Grace is opposed to earning, not to effort',* Willard contends. The parables of Jesus which described the scandalous and radical nature of God's grace also included themes of stewardship, discipline and preparation. Grace is always and forever the undeserved favour of God towards a sinful humanity, but it is also the supernatural force which empowers his image-bearers towards their ultimate destiny – becoming like Jesus. So the questions every believer, never mind every leader, should be asking themselves are:

- How am I positioning myself to receive and live out of God's grace in a distracted and chronically anxious world?

* Dallas Willard, *The Great Omission: Reclaiming Jesus' Essential Teachings on Discipleship* (Monarch Books, 2014), p34.

- Given my propensity to be tempted in all sorts of directions, how am I ensuring that I do not receive God's grace in vain?

It's important to strike a balance here. As overcomers in Christ, we do not need to be intimidated by Satan, but equally we should be aware he has studied us. As I have already pointed out, the enemy has done his homework on us, looking for the weaknesses in our character, our personalities and our histories. As leaders we are too prone to temptation, too easily seduced by fame and too quick to adopt a sense of entitlement to presume we don't need to do the deep interior soul work. The good news is that Jesus already knows this about us and is patient with us as we are formed in Christlikeness. But we need to be intentional about how we hold our weaknesses in the light of God's face, allowing him to heal, transform and mature us in the beauty of his presence. As James KA Smith says:

> If the heart is like a compass, an erotic homing device, then we need to (regularly) calibrate our hearts, tuning them to be directed to the Creator, our magnetic north.*

Time does not allow us a deep dive into every spiritual discipline the church has adopted for the purposes of Christlike formation over the past two millennia, but in the next chapter I will focus on four main areas of life I believe all cruciform leaders should pay particular attention to, which integrate the most well-known spiritual practices of church history together in a helpful formation framework.

Before we get to this, however, I want to re-emphasise the reason why such a framework is crucial. I want to encourage you to reflect a little more on the most important dimension of a Christian leader's life, the dimension which will help you overcome Satan's resistance more than any other. To do so we return to a topic we discussed in Chapter 1 – the importance of holding on to our first love.

* James KA Smith, *You Are What You Love: The Spiritual Power of Habit* (Brazos Press, 2016), p20.

FIRST LOVE

In around 95 AD, the Apostle John, the last living disciple of Jesus, had been exiled to the island of Patmos. Here John experienced a stunning vision of heaven's throne room, revealing the all-conquering nature of Jesus' death and resurrection. Flowing from this scene John also received vivid, prophetic insight concerning many things which were, and are, to come. All of this is recorded in the Bible's final book, Revelation.

John's revelation begins, however, with a vision of the risen Jesus walking among seven lampstands which represent seven churches in the Roman province of Asia. John would have been familiar with these churches and records instructions Jesus gives him for each one in the form of a circular letter. Part of this letter was addressed to the church in Ephesus, which, against human standards, was arguably the most successful of all the churches John addresses. Jesus' words to the believers in Ephesus began with a clear and genuine commendation for their hard work, perseverance and good doctrine. But then Jesus says these harrowing words:

> Yet I hold this against you: you have forsaken the love you had at first. Consider how far you have fallen! Repent and do the things you did at first. If you do not repent, I will come to you and remove your lampstand from its place.

REVELATION 2:4–5

These are words which should evoke the fear of the Lord into the heart of every Christian leader, for they reveal an uncomfortable truth – we can be doing all the right things, we can be saying all the right words, we can even be witnessing the growth of our churches and the favour of others, yet Jesus can hold something against us. What could this be? Quite simply but very seriously, it is a lack of love. The spiritual temperature of our hearts will drastically drop once we begin to forsake our 'first love'. The worrying dimension to this is that most leaders often aren't aware when this has begun to take place. They are so conditioned to the function of ministry that they haven't recognised the diminishing nature of their friendship with Jesus. And this is the most dangerous place for any Christian leader, because if the enemy can rob a leader of anything, it will be their intimacy with Jesus.

To be clear, Jesus is not demanding we love him in some type of insecure way, nor is he trying to control us in the Machiavellian style of some leaders. Rather, as we learned from Jesus' interaction with Peter on the Galilean shoreline in Chapter 2, Jesus is passionate about 'first love' because Jesus wants us, more than he wants our leadership. Knowing Jesus intimately is God's greatest desire for us because love is the centre of who God is. A diminished love for Jesus in our lives reveals a lack of genuine knowledge of Jesus. As Jesus taught Peter: in the kingdom of God, to be loved is to be truly known and to be known is to be truly loved. When the flame of 'first love' begins to flicker and gutter in our lives it exposes a lack of full surrender and therefore implies we have found love in other places. More often than not, these 'other loves' in a leader's life bend back towards themselves. In other words, they have become more interested in the illusion of themselves – the idealised ego image – they are projecting to the world around them, than who they are becoming in Jesus. Satan rejoices when leaders fall for this age-old narcissistic trap as he gains a significant foothold in their lives.

Despite the impressive qualities of the Ephesian church, Jesus had to expose this grievous reality – the affection of their hearts for him had been stolen. Perhaps they had come to love the church they had built more than they loved Jesus. Such self-love is the root of pride, and we would do well to remember God 'opposes' pride (1 Peter 5:5).

I write this as the leader of a church which at one point in our history allowed ourselves to be seduced by the excellence of what we had built. We didn't realise it at the time but in the process of building an 'amazing' church we lost our first love. We had started out as a small group of Jesus followers who were unpolished and naïve but passionate for the presence of God and winning the lost. For all our imperfections, God honoured our hunger and the purity of our hearts. The first ten years were a crazy adventure of risk and faith, and we witnessed miraculous provision, many salvations and powerful demonstrations of the kingdom. God had led us from a handful of hungry believers gathering to worship in my Uncle Phil's living room to a 30,000 square foot multifunctional building attracting over 300 people.

But somewhere along the way we began to be seduced by what we thought it meant to be successful. We had established multiple ministries, we had introduced impressive systems and structures, our worship teams were striving for excellence, and the Sunday experience we produced was exceptional. Yet something was missing. The numbers were good, but the genuine kingdom breakthrough was small. The worship sounded amazing, but the spiritual temperature was cold.

And then, during one Sunday service in this season, as my Uncle Phil was standing in worship, he sensed the Lord ask him:

'Phil, what are you doing?'
Slightly affronted by this question, Phil answered defensively,
'I'm building your church, Lord. What do you think I am doing?'
A few seconds later Phil sensed the gentle rebuke from the Lord:
'Phil, when did I ever tell you to do that?'
Phil scrambled around for an answer and the best he could do was quote Jesus' own words back to him:
'Jesus, you said, "I will build my church."'
Sensing the conviction of the Spirit, Phil knew he had set himself up for what the Lord would say next.
'Exactly Phil, I will build my church.'

It was as if the Lord was saying to Phil and the rest of our leadership:

'Take your hands off controlling your version of my church. I am the head of the Church. You proclaim the gospel. I will build my church.'

We knew we had to repent, and quickly. Many things had to change in our church leadership and culture. But most of all we had to restore our first love. Jesus, not the model or success of the church we were building, was what deserved our worship alone. We began gathering our church body around the presence of God again, relinquishing control and surrendering every human agenda. As we did, a fresh fear of the Lord was instilled.

It was a painful season, but a necessary refocusing. Our love for Jesus had been reduced to a smouldering wick but God was true to his word. As we turned our hearts to him, he did not 'snuff out' that wick (Isaiah 42:3; Matthew 12:20), but gently fanned first love into flame again.

And the irony was, as we laid our best attempts to build the church at the feet of Jesus and returned to our first love and the mission of Jesus, within a year the church grew to double what it had been before. The Lord was building his church.

I never want to make that same mistake again.

Contrary to the church in Ephesus, the enduring picture of Mary of Bethany sitting at the feet of Jesus provides us with the perfect image of 'first love'. Luke records this scene in Chapter 10 of his Gospel. Martha, Mary's sister, had 'opened her home' (10:38) to Jesus and got busy making sure the house was in order and dinner preparations were in hand for the Rabbi and his disciples. Mary, on the other hand, was sitting at Jesus' feet during these preparations, engrossed with the words and very presence of Jesus in her home. Martha became irritated with Mary's lack of assistance and her irritation could be contained no longer as she appealed to Jesus, her words filled with passive aggression: 'Lord, don't you care that my sister has left me to do the work by myself? Tell her to help me!' (Luke 10:40).

No matter how many times I read this passage, Jesus' reply never fails to challenge me: 'Martha, Martha, you are anxious and troubled about many things, but one thing is necessary. Mary has chosen the good portion, which will not be taken away from her' (Luke 10:41–42, ESV).

Mary has chosen the good portion. Mary has made the main thing the main thing. Mary has discovered the essence of first love – prioritising love over work, relationship over transaction, being over doing, devotion over duty. Her attention to Jesus' presence in her life reveals the heart of genuine worship, the beginning and end of all things. At the feet of Jesus is the place where all genuine authority in Christ is found and the source of every Christian's victory over Satan. Jesus promised Mary's actions and desire for his presence 'will not be taken away from her' (Luke 10:42) and the same promise is given to every follower who prioritises 'first love'. Jesus will always give us his undivided attention as we turn our hearts to his.

And yet could we also argue Mary needed Martha? Makoto Fujimura in his delightful book *Art and Faith: A Theology of Making*, writes:

> Mary's intuitive response requires her sister, Martha, to respond pragmatically in order to host Jesus. In other words, Mary cannot be herself without Martha.[*]

Mary and Martha. There is no need for a false dichotomy here, Fujimura contends. Jesus loved Martha too and maybe Martha's practical, rational traits are too often overlooked. 'It is wrong to simply pigeonhole Martha as an overly busy do-gooder', Fujimura writes. Fujimura wants to make the point that Mary and Martha's personalities should not be presented as dualities opposed to one another but as complements. If Mary represents the contemplative and devotional, Martha presents the active and rational. What is important here is

* Makoto Fujimura, *Art and Faith: A Theology of Making* (Yale University Press, 2020), p108.

the order. Fujimura argues, 'I believe that the rational flows out of the intuitive and the active should be led by the contemplative.'*

Fujimura's perspective and interpretation of the story is interesting. Others might argue that in sitting at Jesus' feet, Mary is adopting the position of a disciple – that is, she is asking to be a disciple; asking to learn. This would suggest she was pursing the rational, learning the Scriptures, rather than simply performing a devotional act of worship. If that is the case, Mary in herself is making the same point – practically positioning yourself before Jesus to learn and grow is an essential part of the worshipful devotional life.

Understanding the complementary nature of Mary's and Martha's gifts and personalities when it came to ministering to Jesus helps us emphasise a key point as we approach the final chapter of this book: while first love is our primary concern, keeping first love alive does not just happen. We must learn the art of abiding in Christ in the midst of everyday life and ministry. Keeping first love alive requires us to get practical. Remember grace is opposed to earning but not opposed to effort. We need to integrate elements of Martha's life, the sister who very practically 'opened her home' to Jesus, if we want to occupy the same place that Mary found at Jesus' feet. Martha helps us understand the 'means', Mary points us towards 'the end'.

Returning to the Apostle Paul, we can assume he, too, knew the challenges of keeping the spiritual temperature of his own heart hot, never mind that of his churches. Timothy could not just presume the fire of God in his heart would keep burning without any of his own effort. Timothy must guard what had been entrusted to him (1 Timothy 6:20). The flame in his heart had been ignited by the grace of God but Paul wanted Timothy to realise that this flame needed constant fanning, and this would take an act of his personal volition.

* Makoto Fujimura, *Art and Faith*, p110.

For this reason I remind you to fan into flame the gift of God, which is in you through the laying on of my hands. For the Spirit God gave us does not make us timid, but gives us power, love and self-discipline.

2 TIMOTHY 1:6–7

Paul knew Timothy was like the rest of us – capable of completely destroying our witness for the gospel in an act of self-centred ambition. Another biblical writer many years before Paul wisely warned, 'Like a city that is broken into and without walls So is a person who has no self-control over his spirit' (Proverbs 25:28, NASB). The credibility of a leader which is built up over decades of faithful leadership can be lost in a moment. In fact, the greater the profile of a leader the more intentional they need to be about guarding their heart. The width of our influence must always be surpassed by the depth of our intimacy with Jesus.

Timothy, however, is not simply being encouraged to pull himself up by his bootstraps, so to speak. Rather, Timothy is being reminded of his ultimate source of strength and motivation – the person of the Holy Spirit – the one who specialises in 'power, love and self-discipline'. The cruciform leader is one who is called to a Spirit-empowered life of mastery; not another self-help program, or the motivation of a high-performance podcast or the repeated attempts to climb up Maslow's hierarchy of needs. Rather than merely hope he can muster up enough willpower every day to 'do better', Timothy is encouraged to continually surrender to the power of the Holy Spirit. In doing so, Timothy will daily receive unlimited mercy to experience the grace-fuelled joy of internal transformation into Christlikeness. I imagine the words of Jesus ringing in Paul's ears as he encouraged his young protégé:

Are you tired? Worn out? Burned out on religion? Come to me. Get away with me and you'll recover your life. I'll show you how to take a real rest. Walk with me and work with me – watch how I do it.

Learn the unforced rhythms of grace. I won't lay anything heavy or ill-fitting on you. Keep company with me and you'll learn to live freely and lightly.

MATTHEW 11:28–30 (MSG)

These words of Jesus are ones I have returned to many times over the years. They have both challenged and encouraged me to return to my first love. They have helped me dismantle my messiah-complex. They have brought freedom where I have assumed false responsibility. They have helped me silence the voice of the enemy. But the point I want to stress as we prepare for the final chapter of this book is that I have had to work hard to put myself in a place to actually hear these words and feel the full force of them in my soul. To become like Mary, I have had to learn how to be like Martha. I have needed to intentionally choreograph a path that allows me to reach a place of stillness where I can know God. I have had to get incredibly practical to untether myself from the demands of ministry and sit at the feet of Jesus. I have had to learn that if I want to be a leader who abides in Christ, I need a way of life that allows me to do that. I need a formation framework.

PRACTISING THE CRUCIFORM WAY

Consider the questions and readings below in discussion, reflection, journalling and prayer.

ONE:

... in order that Satan might not outwit us. For we are not unaware of his schemes.

2 CORINTHIANS 2:11

Therefore put on the full armour of God, so that when the day of evil comes, you may be able to stand your ground, and after you have done everything, to stand. Stand firm then, with the belt of truth buckled round your waist, with the breastplate of righteousness in place, and with your feet fitted with the readiness that comes from the gospel of peace. In addition to all this, take up the shield of faith, with which you can extinguish all the flaming arrows of the evil one. Take the helmet of salvation and the sword of the Spirit, which is the word of God.

EPHESIANS 6:13–17

Reflect on these words written to the churches at Corinth and Ephesus.

- In what ways might you need to 'be aware' of the enemy's schemes in this season of your church leadership?
- In what ways might you need to 'take up' and 'put on' the armour of God also?
- Discuss or reflect on what you are contending for (or against) together, right now.

TWO:

The sober reality every leader called to serve God's church must face is that if you want to lead like Jesus you need to know there is a target on your back! Remember, Paul did not ask his young apprentice Timothy to join him on the bright lights of the platform but in suffering for the gospel. I am convinced many of you reading this book are currently underestimating the degree of spiritual warfare surrounding your lives and your churches. One of the main reasons we must become focused followers of Jesus is because Satan systematically targets those called to lead God's people. We dare not become naïve to this fact.

Reflect on these words from Chapter 8.

- Share or write in your journal the ways you have experienced spiritual warfare as you have responded to God's call to lead the church.
- Pray for those you lead alongside and for their families.

THREE:

Guard the good deposit that was entrusted to you – guard it with the help of the Holy Spirit who lives in us.

2 TIMOTHY 1:14

Reflect on Paul's exhortation to Timothy, his apprentice.

- Discuss or reflect on the significance of this process of 'guarding' what has been entrusted to you.
- In what ways do you feel the Spirit challenging you to guard your heart and life in this season? How can you do this for one another?

CHAPTER 9

A FOCUSED FOLLOWER:
A FORMATION FRAMEWORK

I am the vine; you are the branches. If you remain in me and I in you, you will bear much fruit; apart from me you can do nothing.

JOHN 15:5

At the turn of the twenty-first century, the esteemed theologian and philosopher, Rabbi Jonathan Sacks, wrote about the vital role faith and religion can play in society. Reflecting on the similarities in the world between the seventeenth and twenty-first centuries, Sacks urged people of faith to do better than our seventeenth-century counterparts had done. Secularism, he argued, grew out of religion's inability to meet the challenge of change. He writes:

> As one who deeply believes in the humanising power of faith, and the stark urgency of co-existence at a time when weapons of mass destruction are accessible to extremist groups, I do not think we can afford to fail again. Time and again in recent years we have been reminded that religion is not what the European Enlightenment thought it would become: mute, marginal and mild. It is fire – and like fire, it warms but it also burns. And we are the guardians of the flame.*

* Jonathan Sacks, *The Dignity of Difference: How to Avoid the Clash of Civilizations* (Continuum, 2003), p11.

Sacks reminds us of the powerful and undeniable impact religion plays in the world and of the sober responsibility that comes with it. 'We are the guardians of the flame', Sacks powerfully concludes. Think about this line for a few minutes. The appeal at the heart of this book is that the church in the West needs to heed the warnings of sages like Rabbi Sacks, whose words evoke the teachings of the Apostles John and Paul that we have outlined in the previous chapter: 'return to your first love'; 'fan into the flame the gift of God'; 'guard what has been entrusted to you'. Too many leaders have been burnt by their 'strange fire' offerings. And too many of their followers have been badly scorched in the process.

But the questions remain. How can we ensure the fire of love for Jesus in our hearts burns white with purity and hot with love? Practically speaking, how do we guard this flame?

As I mentioned at the opening of this book, it has been a regular practice for me for over a decade now to take some time in those lazy days between Christmas Day and New Year's Day to prayerfully scope out the rhythms, commitments and ambitions for my life as a new year approaches. There are many practical ways people can engage in such a process. Synthesising some of the best learning I have found over the years from other experienced leaders in this area, leaders like Rich Villodas, John Mark Comer, Glen Packiam and Dallas Willard, I narrow my focus down to four main areas of my life.

1. A life of abiding: prayer and Scripture meditation
2. A life of meaningful relationships: community
3. A life of emotional and spiritual health: rest
4. A life of holy ambition: work

Dividing a page in my journal into four quadrants, I list three or four things in each quadrant that I want to commit to. I believe spending time integrating spiritual practices that fall within each of these areas has formed me more fully in the cruciform way and helped me guard the flame of God's love in my life. Following a formation framework like this for one year will bring some significant change. But doing it over decades – that long obedience in the same direction – is where the real transformation comes. I have taken time to unpack these four areas below, describing how Jesus and the Apostles modelled such principles and then detailing how I try to get practical about each of these areas in my life. Each one of these four areas are subjects which deserve chapters (if not books) in their own right, but I hope the broad brushstrokes I have outlined in each will serve as a helpful toolkit to enable you to establish your own formation framework.

A LIFE OF ABIDING: PRAYER AND SCRIPTURE MEDITATION

Cruciform leaders are 'presence' people. They are John 15 people. They have taken the words of Jesus seriously:

> *I am the vine; you are the branches. If you remain in me and I in you, you will bear much fruit; apart from me you can do nothing ... If you remain in me and my words remain in you, ask whatever you wish, and it will be done for you.*

JOHN 15:5–8

Cruciform leaders build patterns into their lives which help them remain in Jesus. They are people of prayer who are anchored in the knowledge of the Scriptures. Jesus, who identified with our humanity in every way, modelled for us a life of prayer and a clear mastery of the Scriptures which not only sustained his own soul but empowered him to stay true to the mission the Father had assigned to him, and to do so with incredible focus. Luke, who gives us a little more insight into Jesus' development as a young boy than the other gospel writers do, implies this was something Jesus intentionally cultivated in his life. Take, for example, the episode after Passover when Jesus, as a twelve-year-old boy, was mistakenly left behind by his parents in Jerusalem and then eventually found sitting with the teachers in the temple courts, listening to them and asking them questions. 'Everyone who heard him was amazed at his understanding and his answers' (Luke 2:47). Luke goes on to describe how from this point 'Jesus grew in wisdom and stature, and in favour with God and man' (Luke 2:52). I can imagine Jesus cultivating a life of prayer and regular study of Scripture through these years and that this preparation was foundational for three years of intense ministry. It is clear Jesus' mission was sustained by devotion and that he knew this intimacy was his source of strength and power for all the battles he would face. Pete Greig uses the term 'mystical militancy'* to describe Jesus' prayer life and how the accounts of Jesus wrestling with the enemy in the wilderness, shouting rebukes at the storm and casting demons out of people, all flowed from the close communion Jesus enjoyed with his Father.

It's no wonder that Paul, following in the footsteps of Jesus when shaping his young apprentice in the cruciform way, called Timothy to a life of disciplined prayer and immersion in the Scriptures:

> *First of all, then, I urge that supplications, prayers, intercessions, and thanksgivings be made for all people, for kings and all who are in high positions, that we may lead a peaceful and quiet life, godly and dignified in every way.*

1 TIMOTHY 2:1–3 (ESV)

First of all comes prayer. In one sense prayer is the work. Like all the heroes of the faith in the Bible, cruciform leaders know that in some mysterious way God is impacted by the prayers of his people. Yet all of them also remind us that the most effective intercession flows from sweet-spirited intimacy. We will simply not be effective Christian leaders without a well-ordered prayer life. As Eugene Peterson summarises:

---

* Pete Greig, *Dirty Glory: Go Where Your Best Prayers Take You* (Hodder & Stoughton, 2018), p110.

For the majority of the Christian centuries most pastors have been convinced that prayer is the central and essential act for maintaining the essential shape of the ministry to which they were ordained.[*]

Alongside this life of prayer, Paul encouraged Timothy towards a mastery of the Scriptures.

Do your best to present yourself to God as one approved, a worker who does not need to be ashamed and who correctly handles the word of truth.

2 TIMOTHY 2:15

Until I come, devote yourself to the public reading of Scripture, to preaching and to teaching.

1 TIMOTHY 4:13

Watch your life and doctrine closely. Persevere in them, because if you do, you will save both yourself and your hearers.

1 TIMOTHY 4:16

Paul knew that the threads of different ideas and teaching blowing all around the wider culture were infecting the church. As one entrusted with the gift to lead, Timothy must guard against the enemy's tactics to dilute the gospel. To do this Timothy must become a master craftsman of the Scriptures. My friend, theologian Lucy Peppiatt, once pointed out to me that Paul never divorces the Christian life from good doctrine. Too many leaders today want the limelight of the platform without a willingness to commit to robust training and study. And as HB Charles, Jr has said, 'a passion to preach without a commitment to study is just a desire to perform.'[**]

* Eugene Peterson, *Working the Angles: The Shape of Pastoral Integrity* (Eerdmans, 1987), p26.
**HB Charles, Jr, 'Preaching Truth in a Culture of Lies', *Truth in Love Conference*, 27 January 2024, youtube.com/@FoundersBaptist (accessed 8 April 2025).

Each year I prayerfully plan this 'abiding' area of my life, building in practices which include: quiet moments of worship in the morning; a Bible reading plan for the year; quarterly days of retreat; times of fasting; a regular rhythm of praying the Psalms; a weekly commitment to an hour of prayer in our 24-7 prayer room; and the discipline of journalling. All together these things lead me to the presence of God, anchoring me in the Father's love, encouraging me to remain in Christ as a beloved son.

This is my greatest act of warfare.

A LIFE OF MEANINGFUL RELATIONSHIPS: COMMUNITY

The second area of a cruciform leader's life which requires intentional focus is their circle of primary relationships. We've already spoken at length about how the church is a family and we have explained the emphasis the New Testament gives to team-based leadership. But it is important for leaders to get practical about their commitment to friendships and key relationships because, often in the pressures and the busyness of ministry, quality time with these 'significant others' gets squeezed out. Furthermore, while the technology of the twenty-first century has offered us the hope of being better connected, the statistics reveal that most leaders are lonelier and more anxious than ever before. There is a tendency for leaders to view significant moments of connection with friends and mentors as less of a priority than the demands and expectations of pastoral ministry and church administration. Conversations with these significant others in our lives can simply become another tick-box duty in our busy schedules rather than the joy-filled heart connection and empowerment that comes through unhurried time together.

Committing ourselves to deep and authentic friendships with those we lead alongside is not easy. In fact, as we've already identified, most of the spiritual warfare we will experience in leadership is around these relationships. But persevering through these times in prayer, speaking the truth in love, and not giving up on one another is a price worth paying many times over because the alternative is even more tragic: isolation, a key tactic the enemy uses to take leaders out.

Jesus lived a life of intentional proximity to his family and friends. Yes, we read of Jesus often removing himself from the crowds to spend quality time with his Father, but this certainly does not mean Jesus was someone who would constantly 'go into his shell'. On the contrary, Jesus shared his whole life with those in his primary circle of relationship. Even in the most distressing moments of his life, when leaders often find it most difficult to bare their souls to others, Jesus displayed breathtaking vulnerability. In the Garden of Gethsemane, as Jesus contemplated his final hours on earth, listen to his heart cry for the company of his friends, 'My soul is overwhelmed with sorrow to the point of death. Stay here and keep watch with me' (Matthew 26:38). In the previous chapter we also noted this disarming sense of vulnerability in the life of the Apostle Paul. When we take time to read the more anecdotal parts of Paul's letters, where he names his friends, records details of his special times of fellowship with them and outlines his personal needs and desires, we see a man who both recognised and prioritised the company of his friends.

Cruciform leaders are those who have humbled themselves enough to recognise they cannot do life, never mind ministry, on their own. Moreover, they have realised that God has given them friendships, not just to bear one another's burdens but also to sharpen each other's focus. As we have come to learn in the 24-7 Prayer movement, God anoints friendships and partnerships as much as he does individuals. This is biblical. Moses and Aaron. David and Jonathan. Esther and Mordecai. Ruth and Naomi. Paul and Barnabas. All of these provide examples of individuals whose relational alignment was central to their divine assignment. Their partnership attracted the favour of God and somehow provided the relational infrastructure that would carry the dreams of God in the world. Cruciform leaders realise the covenantal nature of these relationships and the significance they have for the advancement of the kingdom in the world. They are therefore prepared to make intentional choices and sacrifices to protect these friendships through scary levels of accountability, confession and vulnerability.

My practice at the beginning of each year is to ask the Lord who my 'significant others' are in the year ahead and what my commitment to them should look like that year. First of all, I begin with my own family. This is a critical priority for a leader. Paul's language to Timothy on this area of a believer's life was forthright, to say the least.

> *Anyone who does not provide for their relatives, and especially for their own household, has denied the faith and is worse than an unbeliever.*

1 TIMOTHY 5:8

The relationships with my wife, my children and wider family circle are my primary area of responsibility. How can one be a leader in God's house, Paul says to Timothy, if one cannot manage one's own household? This requires time. Intentional time. The people closest to us should not be squeezed out to the margins of our life but should be prioritised above all others. Cruciform leaders recognise they are called to be priests in their own homes first and foremost, serving their families in the fear of the Lord, refusing to outsource the discipleship of their kids to others but committing themselves to parenting their spiritual development. Cruciform leaders should model this type of priestly role in their home, but it is also imperative that they encourage and enable their teams – those they appoint as leaders – to do the same. Unfortunately, there are too many stories of leaders these days acting more like CEOs than shepherds, who have driven those they lead, often tacitly, so strongly that they have neglected their own families. Rather, cruciform leaders disciple their emerging leaders and those serving alongside them in the cruciform way and this process starts with teaching them how to lead their own families, not proving their loyalty to the mission of the church or her senior leader.

Secondly, I think about the people who have journeyed with me for years, lifelong friends. I am from Ireland so I can't not speak of the *cymbrogi* – an ancient Celtic term stemming from my apostolic Celtic forefathers and mothers. *Cymbrogi* literally means 'companions of the heart' or what the sagacious spiritual director David Benner has called 'sacred companions'.* *Cymbrogi* are more than acquaintances – they are covenant companions, soul friends, brothers and sisters in arms.** There is an old Celtic saying, 'A person without a soul friend is like a person without a head.'*** At the risk of repeating myself, leaders need friends. Soul friends. I want my *cymbrogi* to have my time. I am blessed to work alongside a few of them in my local context, but I also aim to build space outside of working hours to simply hang out and share life – the good, the bad and the ugly – with them.

Thirdly, I ensure I have time each year with those who have been on the road longer than me. Wise sages, spiritual mothers and fathers whose input I want in my life. Each year I make time to sit at the feet of these trusted mentors, spiritual directors and therapists who speak wisdom and correction into my life.

Finally, there are those coming behind me who I want to commit myself to; emerging leaders for whom God has placed a special affection in my heart. I want to diary time with them so I can be in their lives, listen to their questions, their struggles and the ambition of their hearts. I want to share not just the stuff of ministry with them but invite them into other areas of my life, humbling myself to receive as much from them as I can give to them.

* David Benner, *Sacred Companions* (InterVarsity Press, 2004) is an excellent book on this topic.
** The Order of the Mustard Seed uses this term to describe and foster relationships among its adherents. See orderofthemustardseed.com (accessed 7 March 2025).
*** Ray Simpson, *Hilda of Whitby: A spirituality for now* (BRF, 2016), p46.

Over the years I have found forging these authentic relationships and intentionally integrating them into my life has been crucial for the sustenance of my own soul and the sharpening of my focus as a leader.

A LIFE OF EMOTIONAL AND SPIRITUAL HEALTH: REST

The third area of the formation framework that every cruciform leader should integrate into their life is that of rest and emotional health. In this hyper-distracted, overstimulated world, we have to work hard to rest well. Thankfully, in recent years there has been a corrective to the overworking, performance-based striving many church leaders have allowed their messiah-complexes to be seduced by. The language of emotional health and wellbeing is becoming more commonly accepted in the church and this is an important development. Too many leaders have learned the hard way that they are not invincible.

The incarnation speaks directly to the heart of this issue – Jesus, the Son of God, who is limitless in power and capacity, chose to limit himself to our humanity, modelling for us what an emotionally secure, spiritually attuned, relationally healthy image-bearer should look like. Paul would refer to Jesus as 'the firstborn of creation' and therefore declared, 'we see the original and intended shape of our lives there in him' (Romans 8:29, MSG). It is extraordinary to think that Jesus, in whom 'all the fullness of the Deity lives in bodily form' (Colossians 2:9), was more aware of the finiteness of the human form than we are. In embodying the limitations of humanity, Jesus displayed how an individual human life, empowered by the Holy Spirit, can yet advance the kingdom of God in supernatural ways. Jesus showed us that the triune God is wildly in love with his creation and fiercely passionate about the advancement of his kingdom, yet he is not a workaholic. In tune with the sacred rhythm of sabbath, Jesus trained his disciples how to intentionally build time into their lives away from ministry:

Then, because so many people were coming and going that they did not even have a chance to eat, he said to them, 'Come with me by yourselves to a quiet place and get some rest.'

MARK 6:31

In practising sabbath, the cruciform leader is submitting himself or herself to the ongoing process of recreation in their own bodies and re-storying themselves in the bigger story of the kingdom of God. When leaders do not learn to practise the principles of sabbath rest we begin to believe the lie prevalent in the world which tells us we are less finite than we really are. This is where all manner of dysfunction sets in, because we begin living out of sync with the heavenly rhythm we were created to stay in step with. Ironically, at this point, a leader can become deceived, telling themselves that their coffee-induced, sleep-deprived adrenaline is the power of the Holy Spirit. We can often justify this as simply a 'busy season' but in reality, all sorts of fault lines exist under the surface of this busyness, as we have likely begun to lose godly focus weeks before. I know this because I have been there.

Cruciform leaders, on the other hand, have learned to understand sabbath as a type of 'resistance', a phrase coined by the seminal Old Testament theologian Walter Brueggemann. These leaders realise that, in an anxious and frenzied culture, the best thing they can offer their churches and the world around them is a life of inner harmony embodying the calmness of the God who rests.

We should never understand sabbath merely as a bolt-on recovery day at the end of a turbulent week, but rather the anchoring practice of *shalom* from which all of our life, not just our leadership, flows. Sabbath, Brueggemann argues, 'is not simply the pause that refreshes. It is the pause that transforms.'*

---

* Walter Brueggemann, *Sabbath as Resistance: Saying No to the Culture of Now* (Westminster John Knox Press, 2014), p45.

Coming to understand sabbath as a beginning – a prequel – to the incoming week rather than an end – a sequel – to the week that has just been, has been life-changing for me. I have slowly learned to live from rest and not simply towards recovery. Now, as I set my formation framework at the beginning of each year, integrating a weekly cycle with a 24-hour circuit-breaker, I also get intentional about my day-to-day sleeping patterns and physical exercise, my annual holidays and longer-term sabbaticals. The Apostles, immersed as they were in the ancient wisdom of the Hebrew Scriptures and the example of Jesus, would have practised many of the elements of this approach and so remained spiritually healthy. Listen to the holistic description of emotionally healthy spirituality that flowed from the Apostle John:

> *Dear friend, I pray that you may enjoy good health and that all may go well with you, just as you are progressing spiritually.*

3 JOHN 2

A LIFE OF HOLY AMBITION: WORK

The fourth and final quadrant of my formation framework is entitled 'holy ambition'. This is the area of my life where I seek to understand the unique assignments God is calling me to give myself to for the next twelve months. It is the process of coming into alignment with the Spirit regarding my contribution to the advancement of the kingdom of God in any given year. Reflecting on this area of my life in the context of the other four quadrants is critical, though – if I do not discern my missional objectives in line with a life of abiding, meaningful relationships and rest, I will end up appearing to be doing great things 'in the name of the Lord' while in reality I am completely out of step with what God actually wants me to do. Furthermore, if I don't pay attention to these other areas of my life, discerning wisely the capacity I have to fulfil what God might be calling me to, I will neglect my family, my friends and my church, damaging them and myself in the process. When this happens, my ambition is no longer holy. It is selfish. And selfish ambition with a veneer of 'holiness' is arguably the worst and most destructive type of ambition.

I like the ESV translation of Proverbs 29:18, 'Where there is no prophetic vision the people cast off restraint.' Notice the words 'prophetic vision'. Prophetic vision highlights *the source* of that vision. If vision is to be truly prophetic then it should be divinely inspired wisdom rooted in the 'otherness' of God. If the vision we carry as leaders for our lives and for our churches is not sourced in the presence of God and forged in the crucible of surrender, it is not prophetic vision. Rather, at best it is a version of our own best intentions which are never enough to bring true kingdom breakthrough. At worst it is a projection of our own egos. The exposure of recent years provides all the warning we need; namely, when those who were called to shepherd God's people with the peace-loving rule of Christ sell out for the quick wins of self-promoting success, the results are catastrophic.

Once again Jesus is our model. He, the Word made flesh, lived a life of holy ambition which was life-giving to everyone around him. There are numerous verses from the Gospels we could choose but here are a few verses I have picked as examples of how Jesus embodied a focused life of holy ambition.

For I have come down from heaven not to do my will but to do the will of him who sent me.

JOHN 6:38

For the Son of Man came to seek and to save the lost.

LUKE 19:10

I have not come to call the righteous, but sinners to repentance.

LUKE 5:32

It is clear Jesus lived his life with intent, motivated by holy ambition. Jesus did not come to win a popularity contest. Jesus came 'to do the will of him who sent me' (John 6:38). Jesus came to do the Father's will. Yes, Jesus was warm and friendly, invitational and hospitable because this is who the Father is. But this does not mean Jesus lived to fulfil the expectations of people. On one occasion, Jesus goes off on his own to pray, and the disciples, clearly aware of the demands of the crowds, go and look for him.

> *… and when they found him, they exclaimed: 'Everyone is looking for you!'*
>
> *Jesus replied, 'Let us go somewhere else – to the nearby villages – so that I can preach there also. That is why I have come.'*

MARK 1:37–38

Jesus is not demonstrating classic pastoral care here – he refuses to be driven by the needs, wishes or hopes of the disciples or the crowds. Instead, he is demonstrating resolute obedience to the Father. He is showing us that holy ambition means being obedient to the Father whatever that means for each of our lives. This will not always satisfy the expectations of others. Ultimately, Jesus' life defines the essence of holy ambition as sacrifice. 'I have come down from heaven not to do my will' (John 6:38) is the supreme example of the holy ambition Jesus would declare, and ultimately fulfil, on the cross of Calvary.

Cruciform leaders are those who embody 'the same mindset as Christ Jesus' (Philippians 2:5). They have spent time discerning and refining their unique God-given gifts, passions and burdens so they can live their lives in service to others. Like Jesus, their lives are defined by a kind of missional magnetism because the love of Christ pulsing through their surrendered souls draws others into the blessing of the triune God. Every time I approach a new year, I will spend time asking God the following questions:

- How can I give my life away to others in the year ahead?
- What is my unique contribution to the kingdom of God this year?

I start by acknowledging that I can't do everything I want to or everything others expect of me. This is hard! Then I ask the Father to show me the things which require my focus in the months ahead. This may vary from leading a new church building project to spending time with some young leaders in my church, from writing a book to engaging more deliberately with the parents in my son's football team, from leading a mission team to Uganda to seeking ways to build deeper relationship with my neighbours. The point is, I want to be about the Father's business, not my own good ideas. If I can come out of this discernment process with a strong sense of what God is asking me to say 'yes' to it becomes easier to know what I can say 'no' to, no matter how worthy these things may appear to be on the surface.

A NON-ANXIOUS PRESENCE

These four quadrants do not constitute an exhaustive list of spiritual disciplines but rather provide an example of some of the intentional practices I believe any leader needs to integrate into their life if they want to embody the cruciform way for the long haul. My hope is that this type of formation framework simply provokes you to think practically about the ways you can become a more focused follower of Jesus, enabling you to keep the flame of first love burning bright and equipping you toward increasing Christlikeness.

The reason we need such an intentional formation track is not to prove our piety to others but to help us withstand the inevitable attacks of the enemy that will come. In that sense these spiritual practices are, to an extent, preventative. They will help stop us from falling into temptation or allowing the disease of sin to work its way through our lives. Such an ordered life will help us 'keep our head' in all the stormy trials and tribulations that we face in life and in ministry.

But that is by no means the only reason for them. The fruit of a well-ordered life is far more than that. In some senses we are coming full circle, back round to where we started in our introduction, the picture of that tree in Psalm 1, planted by streams of living water. If the cruciform leader is one who intentionally 'plants' himself or herself beside streams of living water, drawing life from the presence of God, then he or she will not only be able to keep standing through times of suffering and the attacks of the enemy, but will also bear much fruit. Fruit that will last. Fruit that exhibits Christ's nature to the world.

> *I am the vine; you are the branches. If you remain in me and I in you, you will bear much fruit; apart from me you can do nothing.*
>
> JOHN 15:5

The priority is always, always the presence of God. Jesus wanted the disciples to always remember that if they concentrated on learning how to remain in him, they would become agents of healing in the environments they inhabited. The focus is less about techniques, models of ministry and acquiring leadership skills (while all have their place) and more about learning how to remain in him. The benefit of such is not just an integrated and harmonious inner life for the disciple of Jesus but an overflow of the *shalom* of the triune God from their lives into the world around them.

Being formed in the loving presence of the Father into increasing Christlikeness means we get to show up in a frantic and fragmented world as a 'non-anxious presence', a phrase which has become popular with many Christian leaders in the West thanks to the writings and teachings of Mark Sayers. Sayers has drawn on the work of Edwin Friedman, an ordained rabbi, leadership consultant and family therapist who explored the concept of what it meant to be a non-anxious presence.[*] Friedman's research defined non-anxious people as those who are able to maintain a clear sense of

---

[*] Edwin Friedman, *A Failure of Nerve: Leadership in the Age of the Quick Fix* (Church Publishing, 2017).

their own identity, values and goals without being overwhelmed by the anxiety, emotions or reactivity of others. Friedman argued that the real leaders in today's world are those who remain self-differentiated in the midst of all the swirling dynamics at play within their environments. They are individuals able to extract the emotional toxicity out of an environment and instead release renewal and health into the system or team of which they are part.

Sayers applied Friedman's findings to the vocation of the church in this current cultural moment and encourages us to think of God's 'non-anxious presence' as a powerful prophetic antidote to one of the primary ailments of the Western world today – chronic anxiety. Sayers wants the church to restore her confidence in the truth that the ultimate solution for our scared and anxious world actually dwells within us. 'Christ in you, the hope of glory' (Colossians 1:27), the Apostle Paul reminded the first believers in Colossae.

If a spirit of anxiety can spread pervasively through a family, a team, or a church then how much more powerfully can the 'peace of God, which transcends all understanding' (Philippians 4:7) do the same? What if the unprecedented levels of anxiety the West has experienced in the first quarter of the twenty-first century could be reduced through a new breed of leaders who establish churches – centres of *shalom* – characterised by the non-anxious presence of God? In the first part of the twentieth century, AW Tozer is attributed with saying, 'A scared world needs a fearless church.' These inspiring words reverberate ever more loudly today as creation groans for fearless, confident sons and daughters of God to heal our broken culture and lead us into a new creation. The biblical story reveals this is the type of leader the world *has always been crying out for*. Approximately 4,000 years ago, in his final words, King David put it like this:

> *Whoever governs fairly and well,*
> *who rules in the Fear-of-God,*
> *Is like first light at daybreak*

> *without a cloud in the sky,*
> *Like green grass carpeting earth,*
> *glistening under fresh rain.*

2 SAMUEL 23:3–4 (MSG)

David's reflections on godly leadership all those years ago chime well with Sayers' reflections on Friedman's understanding of non-anxious leaders. 'For Friedman, the non-anxious leader played the role within an emotionally unhealthy social system akin to the role that white blood cells play in the human body, fighting infection and bringing the system back to health.'* This type of leader, 'acts like an antibody or a white blood cell, bringing health into the system.'**

The result of a leader's life ordered in and around the presence of God is an overflowing spring of *shalom* – the peace and wholeness of God – cascading through the different teams and systems that leaders find themselves responsible for. Again, we return to Jesus for the ultimate example. Anchored in the Father's love, he released redemptive healing wherever he went, overflowing with the wholeness of heaven. But think about how Jesus dispensed health into his team. When the disciples became competitive, Jesus encouraged them to adopt an attitude of humility (Luke 22:24–26). When they became overbearing and bossy, he encouraged them to become childlike (Mark 10:13–16). When they were overworked, he encouraged them to rest (Mark 6:31). When they became afraid, he encouraged them to receive peace (John 14:27).

The Gospels relate how, when left to their own devices, the disciples would find themselves overreacting, manifesting insecurities, leaking woundedness and being drawn into the dramas that stem from inflamed egos. Yet, when Jesus re-enters the dialogue, it seems his very presence de-escalates the tension, and

* Mark Sayers, *A Non-Anxious Presence: How a Changing and Complex World will Create a Remnant of Renewed Christian Leaders* (Moody Publishers, 2022), p101.
** *Ibid.*

the words he offers – laced with grace and wisdom – help the group find a new, more mature equilibrium. Jesus is the exemplar par excellence of such a self-differentiated leader. In human form, he showed all of us how to be a tree planted by the rivers of his Father's love and bear fruit that brings healing to many.

HEALTH BEFORE GROWTH

I recently took a three-month sabbatical from work. After silencing the dysfunctional narratives of a) guilt for taking time off and b) self-justification for why I deserved to take time off, I finally settled into a place of rest. And it proved to be one of the best things I have ever done. The time to spoil my family on a once-in-a-lifetime holiday, undertake a number of pilgrimages in the footsteps of my Celtic ancestors, play board games with my kids, sit by the fire for hours writing in my journal and feasting on some good books was the purest joy and the richest kind of nourishment my body needed. I tried to resist the pressure (mostly self-inflicted) to return to ministry with an impressive vision of the future, a compelling heavenly download which would reignite the churches and communities I lead. Rather, I worked hard to focus on a complete rest. I knew some of the feedback loops in my mind needed to be broken. Certain neural pathways needed to be rewired. I knew my body was tired and my sleep patterns were out of sync. And I was aware my soul was snacking rather than feasting on the presence of God to get me through the intense nature of ministry I was experiencing before sabbatical. By the grace of God I was getting through. But only just. And I knew if I didn't take myself out of the firing line the enemy would. Moreover, I wanted to give the people I love and serve the best of me, and I knew I wasn't able to. So I tried to trust the Spirit to lead me where the Spirit wanted to take me over those months. I found the Shepherd of my soul, and he led me back to the lush green pastures at the banks of that river flowing with living water. Here, the soil of my heart was tenderly turned over again. The hard crustiness which had set in on my soul's surface over the previous years was gently shaken off and the roots of my inner life began winding their way towards that river, straining for a fresh connection with the water of God's presence.

Three months later, as I stepped back into the frontlines of ministry, I came to realise that allowing myself a renewal in health – physically, spiritually, mentally and emotionally – was the best gift I could ever give those I lead.

Yes, the gifts and personality God has shaped in me will mean my core contribution to the body of Christ will always lean towards vision, movement and ultimately, growth. My natural impulse is to see the bigger picture, the great mission the church is called to and to articulate a strategy to fulfil this. But the Spirit has been whispering to me as I return to ministry in this season:

'Focus on dispensing health, Alain, in all the teams you lead, and I will take care of the growth.'

By the grace of God I am trying to obey. Now I find myself taking more time to centre myself in the presence of God before I lead any meeting. I endeavour to listen to others better than I have in the past, discerning the wisdom in the room rather than feeling I need to have the best solution all the time. I ask the Spirit to help me pay attention to 'the little foxes' (Song of Songs 2:15) that are trying to sabotage relationships in my teams, and I ask him to inspire me to know how to sweeten up the spaces that exist between us. Yes, there will be times I still need to be clear and even forthright with those I lead, but I want to be kinder, more tender in how I communicate – full of grace and truth. I still want to inspire people towards goals which help fulfil the dreams of heaven, but guiding them like a shepherd, and not in a way that is overbearing or drives people into a place of false responsibility. I still want to make sure my teams finish tasks that will make a quantifiable difference in our city and nation but not in a way that compromises our friendship in the process. Some will think I am being overly idealistic, but my deep desire is to 'get the job done' in a way where all those I lead will become like Jesus in the process.

Ultimately, my holy ambition is to finish like Moses – a man whose life and leadership shone luminously in history as a type and shadow of Christ thousands of years before the Son of God enfleshed himself on the earth.

Despite all the tumultuous events of the first half of Moses' life and the intense spiritual highs and lows of the second half of it, it was said of him, as he neared the end of his 120 years on earth, 'His eye was undimmed, and his vigour unabated' (Deuteronomy 34:7, ESV). This is the way I want to go out. Moses, it appears, had found a way to stay rooted in the presence of God, to remain a focused follower, renewing himself in the health and wholeness of the source of his life – the presence of God – right until the very end. Moses proved the wisdom of the proverb, 'The root of the righteous endures' (Proverbs 12:12). His life serves as 'a type and shadow' of the cruciform way, many centuries before Jesus 'the better Moses', fulfilled it. The words of St Gregory of Nyssa, describing Moses' legacy, touch something deep inside of me:

> Time had not harmed his beauty, neither dimmed his brightness of eye nor diminished the graciousness of his appearance. Always remaining the same, he preserved in changeableness of nature an unchangeable beauty.*

'Time had not harmed his beauty.' This is my prayer for my life and yours.

As the saying goes, 'the joy will be in the journey'. The transformation of our lives and our leadership does not happen overnight and the Bible tells the tragic tales of many leaders who

---

* St Gregory of Nyssa, *Life of Moses*, p29.

failed miserably, their legacies left in tatters, much like our current predicament, but it does offer us hope. There are numerous shining lights, stories of lives of faithful focus and leaders who in the end 'fix the character of their times'.* My prayer is that as we have highlighted the lives of the first Apostles, ordinary men and women who followed in the footsteps of the greatest leader who ever lived, Jesus our Servant King, we have provided such inspiration.

PRACTISING THE CRUCIFORM WAY

Consider the questions and readings below in discussion, reflection, journalling and prayer.

ONE:

I am the vine; you are the branches. If you remain in me and I in you, you will bear much fruit; apart from me you can do nothing.

JOHN 15:5

Meditate together on the words of Jesus, spoken to his disciples.

- Discuss or reflect on any impressions, insights or whispers from the Spirit you sense as you do so.
- What might this choice to remain in the vine look like for you and for your church community in this particular season?

TWO:

To become like Mary, I have had to learn how to be like Martha.

* This was part of the epitaph written on William Wilberforce's gravestone, Britain's great abolitionist, and can be found at Westminster Abbey, 'William Wilberforce & family', westminster-abbey.org (accessed 23 April 2025).

I have needed to intentionally choreograph a path that allows me to reach a place of stillness where I can know God. I have had to get incredibly practical to untether myself from the demands of ministry and sit at the feet of Jesus. I have had to learn that if I want to be a leader who abides in Christ, I need a way of life that allows me to do that. I need a formation framework.

Reflect on these words from Chapter 8.

- Take time to make and complete your own Formation Framework, filling in each of the four quadrants and then share this with one another on your leadership team.
- What things are particularly important to you in this season? What aspects do you want your team to help you remain accountable to?

THREE:

...think about how Jesus dispensed health into his team. When the disciples became competitive, Jesus encouraged them to adopt an attitude of humility. When they became overbearing and bossy, he encouraged them to become childlike. When they were overworked, he encouraged them to rest. When they became afraid, he encouraged them to receive peace.

Reflect on these words from Chapter 9 and look up the following Bible passages: Luke 22:24–26; Mark 10:13–16; Mark 6:31; John 14:27. Consider the ways that Jesus promoted the health of his team.

- In what ways can you ensure that you prioritise health over growth in your own life?
- And in the life of your church?

CALLING FORTH THE HUNGRY, THE HOLY AND THE HUMBLE

The good news is that in many parts of the world the church is growing and flourishing. In parts of South America, Asia and Africa the church is experiencing genuine revival and where it is suffering severe persecution the church is growing exponentially. The church in Iran, for example, is now reported to be the fastest-growing in the world.* Even in Europe and the USA many people still identify themselves as 'Christian'. In certain pockets of these nations, I think we are seeing the first fruits of a fresh move of the Spirit. In particular the hunger and devotion we are witnessing among the Gen Z and Alpha generations is cause for great optimism.

The bad news, however, is many of those who identify as Christians, particularly in the Western world, are not walking in the radical ways of the One whose name they bear. Our relative security, greed and comfort has led many Christians into insipid forms of spiritual complacency and what is currently now known as cultural Christianity. Frankly, many have fallen out of love with Jesus and in doing so have compromised the gospel. The latest research from the respected charity Barna has concluded the problem is not so much with non-Christians' lack of interest in Jesus – on the contrary, in America 71% of people view Jesus positively. The problem they say, 'appears to lie in the dichotomy between how people perceive Jesus versus how they view his followers and the

---

* Shay Khatiri, in Daniel Pipes' 'Iran's Christian Boom', *Jewish Press*, 29 June 2021, jewishpress.com (accessed 12 March 2025), wrote last year that 'Islam is the fastest shrinking religion there, while Christianity is growing the fastest'. The evangelical church in Iran has been named by Operation World as one of the fastest-growing in the world. See elam.com (accessed 12 March 2025).

institutional Church.'* The lack of spiritual passion among many believers in the Western church, not unlike the lukewarm nature of the Church in Laodicea, to whom Jesus brought a stern rebuke in the book of Revelation, is the main reason I believe the church is now managing decline at an unprecedented level. Despite the 'excellence' reflected in the buildings, style and staffing structures of many contemporary churches over the past fifty years, something is still badly missing. To make matters worse, an astonishing number of church leaders are leaving the pastoral vocation at a level unlike anything witnessed during my lifetime.

And yet I remain hopeful. For two main reasons.

Firstly, the character and purposes of God are unchanging. The psalmist declared, 'the plans of the LORD stand firm forever, the purposes of his heart through all generations' (Psalm 33:11). In God's long-suffering love and kindness, Jesus will not give up on his church. She may be sick, but God has not finished with her. There is a line in the story of Lazarus's resurrection which I continually return to when I think about the Western church these days. John describes in his Gospel what Jesus said when it was reported to him that his friend Lazarus had died:

> *When he heard this, Jesus said, 'This illness will not end in death. No, it is for God's glory so that God's Son may be glorified through it.'*
>
> JOHN 11:4

We have talked enough about the sickness the church in the West is beset with. But I can hear the word of the Lord whisper words of hope-filled assurance, *'this illness will not end in death'*. Hope is still alive, not because of human ingenuity but because Jesus shows up at the tombs of dead men like Lazarus, saying, 'I am the resurrection and the life' (John 11:25). Of course, God will judge the sin of the

---

* Barna Group, 'Openness to Jesus Isn't the Problem – The Church Is', *Barna*, 17 May 2023, barna.com (accessed 7 March 2025).

church. The Bible, backed up by church history, reveals how God will allow institutions and structures that have become such an abhorrent reflection of his character and nature to die. Yet the Bible also confirms there will always be a remnant of faithful ones to whom God's heart will always be drawn and it is in and through these saints that he will breathe his resurrection life. As Lesslie Newbigin concludes:

> The real triumphs of the gospel have not been won when the church is strong in a worldly sense; they have been won when the church is faithful in the midst of weakness, contempt, and rejection.[*]

This leads me to my second reason for hopefulness. Today, within this remnant of faithful ones, a wave of emerging leaders, men and women I referred to in the introduction as the hungry, the holy and the humble, are rising up out of hidden places of obscurity. These are the new breed of cruciform leaders who have been marked by the presence of God in the secret spaces – from prayer rooms to soup kitchens, a far distance from platforms and media.

The biblical story reminds us of this pattern throughout history. When it appears that the story of God is hanging by a thread, God gets hold of a heart. When God's people have stopped seeking God, God will seek out a person. David, Samuel, Esther and Mary were all seen by God before they were known by humankind. They had no public profile when God recognised the private beauty of their souls.

Today, despite the current leadership crisis we have been experiencing, God's eyes have continued to 'range throughout the earth to strengthen those whose hearts are fully committed to him' (2 Chronicles 16:9). God is raising up a vibrant sub-culture of Christlike shepherds who will pulse with the character of Jesus and carry his vision for the nations. These are men and women who,

---

[*] Lesslie Newbigin, *The Open Secret: An Introduction to the Theology of Mission* (Eerdmans, 1995), p62.

like the Apostle Paul, will pour their lives out like a drink offering to see the bride of Christ moving once again in the power of the Spirit, for the sake of God's fame and renown in the nations.

My prayer is this book will be a rallying cry to those God has been preparing for this hour. The church desperately needs courageous and capable leaders with a vision to see the kingdom advance and a steely-eyed determination to see healthy, flourishing churches planted and established. The crucial caveat to the truth that the church desperately needs visionary-type leaders in this particular cultural moment, is that it needs hungry, holy and humble servants even more.

I started this book describing how God spoke to me at the beginning of 2020 in what at the time I felt was a particularly underwhelming way. God's encouragement to me as I stepped into a new decade was – *be like a tree*! I also quoted Martin Luther, who, when asked what he would do if he knew the world was ending, answered, 'I would plant a tree'.

It only struck me halfway through writing this book that when I was in primary school, no more than six years old, my mum allowed me to buy a fledgling (and flimsy) little oak tree. She planted it in her garden and has tended to that tree carefully ever since, using it symbolically as a reminder to pray for me every day.

Maybe the whisper of the Lord in 2020, *'be like a tree, son'*, was the fruit of almost forty years of prayer from my mum. Maybe this desire to become an oak of righteousness had been internalised within me before I was even able to recognise it myself. Maybe it took these forty years for me to begin to accept that the way of a tree – steady, resilient, faithful, fruitful and growing steadily in season and out of season – was more in line with the cruciform way of Jesus than the worldly ways of leadership which have sought to seduce me over the years.

Maybe I have a chance now of being one of the hungry, holy and humble ones.

PRACTISING THE CRUCIFORM WAY

Consider the questions and readings below in discussion, reflection, journalling and prayer.

ONE:

> Today, despite the current leadership crisis we have been experiencing, God's eyes have continued to 'range throughout the earth to strengthen those whose hearts are fully committed to him' (2 Chronicles 16:9). God is raising up a vibrant sub-culture of Christlike shepherds who will pulse with the character of Jesus and carry his vision for the nations. These are men and women who, like the Apostle Paul, will pour their lives out like a drink offering to see the bride of Christ moving once again in the power of the Spirit, for the sake of God's fame and renown in the nations.

Reflect again on these words from the last chapter.

- What does it mean for you to be a part of 'the hungry, the holy and the humble'?
- What are some of the ways you personally sense the Holy Spirit leading you deeper in the cruciform way?

TWO:

> The church desperately needs courageous and capable leaders with a vision to see the kingdom advance and a steely-eyed determination to see healthy, flourishing churches planted and established. The crucial caveat to the truth that the church desperately needs visionary-type leaders in this particular cultural moment, is that it needs hungry, holy and humble servants even more.

Consider these words drawn from the last chapter.

- What are some meaningful action steps you can implement in the life of your local church leadership team to ensure you continue to stay true to the cruciform way?

THREE:

That person is like a tree planted by
streams of water,
which yields its fruit in season
and whose leaf does not wither –
whatever they do prospers.

PSALM 1:3

Revisit Psalm 1 and reflect, specifically, on these words.

- In what ways can you and your leadership team become more like 'a tree planted by streams of living water?'

In the kingdom of God, if servanthood is beneath you, leadership is beyond you.

The church in the Western world is facing a leadership crisis. Tragic stories of scandal, abuse and decline, arguably stemming from the adoption of secular leadership values, have had a devastating impact on the witness of local churches to their communities.

And yet there is hope. For across the world, a new breed of leaders is rising up. These are the hungry, holy and humble ones, shaped and formed in the hidden places, finding their voices and leading the church into a fresh move of the Holy Spirit. These leaders have heard the cry at the heart of this book – to return to the cruciform way. Inspired by the first apostles who embodied the cross-shaped, sacrificial ministry of Jesus, the true model of perfect leadership, they too believe the power of such radical obedience will literally change the world.

From the author of the raw and profound *Luminous Dark* comes this heartfelt call to churches to return to biblical leadership. With unapologetic sincerity, Alain lays bare the failings at the heart of the church and points to the solution – cruciform leadership.

Alain Emerson is husband to Rachel and dad to Annie, Erin and Finn. He is lead pastor of Emmanuel Church in Northern Ireland, director of the 24-7 Prayer Communities Network, author of *Luminous Dark* and co-author of *The God Story*. Alain oversees the Tobar church network and is excited about seeing a 'new thing' happening in Ireland. He is also passionate about reading, sports, hanging out with friends and Liverpool F.C.